"This book highlights the expertise too often missing from discussions around education – the expertise of professionals working in child development and psychology, the expertise of parents, and the expertise of children themselves. I do believe that these are frequently the missing pieces of the puzzle."

– **Rebecca Brooks**, Education Policy Advisor at Adoption UK

"It's groundbreaking! Most books focus around CBT and other behaviourist techniques. This explores a range of different ideas centred around child development, trauma informed and relational practice. It's also the only book I am aware of that uses such a range of different ' experts by lived experience' in the form of children, parents and professionals. It's really going to stand out as something new and different and, most importantly, it contains techniques that really work."

– **Catrina Lowri**, Neurodiversity Trainer and Consultant, Neuroteachers

"A complete departure from most of what is available in this subject area. I love it."

– **Dr Lisa Cherry**, Director, Trauma Informed Consultancy Services Ltd

"By now even the staunchest proponent of the 'tough love' approach to school refusal must have an inclination that sanctions are not solving the problem: the children are not coming back to school. This book explains why and offers alternative ways of identifying and tackling the difficulties experienced by all."

– **Jo Grace**, Education Consultant, Researcher and Founder of The Sensory Projects

"*What Can We Do When School's Not Working?* is a fantastic resource and an absolute must read for parents of children struggling with school as well as all professionals and policy makers working in Education and anyone working with children. Bringing together the different perspectives on the purpose of school, on behaviour and attendance and why school isn't working for so many, this much-needed book explains why behaviour and attendance are signs of an underlying, systemic problem, rather than the problem being located in children or their r easy-to-read, insightful way and brought to life by lived experiences, this book explains school trauma and burnout and how to support children with these experiences as well as drawing upon psychological research in order to consider how to produce psychologically healthy schools, where children are more likely to enjoy learning and thrive. It also offers alternative ways to support young people when they decide not to return to school and examples of those who have engaged young people with learning in different and more psychologically healthy ways."

– **Dr Hayley Smith**, Clinical Psychologist and Systemic Family Psychotherapist

"This is a fantastic book that challenges key theories of education and highlights the fact that we have slipped into a rut of a system which is clearly not meeting so many children's needs. This book also challenges the status quo of the education system but in a sensible and non-emotional way. It is not a negative, scaremongering or combative read, and offers sensible alternative approaches to education. Filled with lovely illustrations and honest and enlightening quotes from young people and teens, this book will be highly relatable to parents, and I hope show educators that there is another way for young people to thrive."

– **Laura Kerbey**, Founder of PAST – Positive Assessments Education Support and Training

What Can We Do When School's Not Working?

An increasing number of children are struggling to attend school. The conventional approach prioritises a rapid return to their setting. For some children, this simply doesn't work. They are stuck, not attending school but not learning out of school either. What happens then – and what can we do about it?

This illustrated guide lifts the lid on the experiences of children and families who are struggling within the school system and explores how we can work with these young people to maximise their chances of a positive and fulfilled life.

The book encourages professionals to take a new perspective and to consider what can be done differently. It explores the ways in which difficulties with school are understood by children, parents and professionals, and shows how things can go wrong (and right), using real-life examples from a range of settings. Chapters delve into common interventions and the impact these can have in practice, before introducing alternative approaches which have the child at the centre. The voices of young people are foregrounded throughout, shedding light on their struggles with attendance – including when placements have completely broken down – and, importantly, showing how they have gone onto succeed. Original illustrations are included throughout to bring these ideas to life.

Placing authentic experiences at the core, this book offers a valuable insight into the lives of children and families when school has gone wrong and will leave you with new ideas as to how to turn things around. *What Can We Do When School's Not Working?* is essential reading for professionals working with children who are struggling with school attendance, from SENCOs and educational support workers to educational psychologists, senior leadership teams, and local authorities.

Abigail Fisher is a qualified teacher and educational psychologist. She has worked with schools and local authorities supporting staff and children with a wide range of issues, including children struggling to attend school. Abigail taught in primary schools across London before training as an educational psychologist.

Naomi Fisher is a clinical psychologist and author. She has a PhD in Developmental Psychology (Autism) in addition to her doctorate in clinical psychology, and she specialises in trauma and autism. She runs popular webinars for parents on school distress and works clinically with families whose children are not fine at school. She is recognised as an expert in neurodiversity and alternatives to school.

Eliza Fricker is an author and illustrator. She is the mother of a child who experienced barriers to school attendance and gives talks to local authorities about the experience. Eliza also runs a blog focused on anxiety and school attendance issues.

What Can We Do When School's Not Working?

An Illustrated Handbook for Professionals

Abigail Fisher and Naomi Fisher
Illustrated by Eliza Fricker

LONDON AND NEW YORK

Designed cover image: Eliza Fricker

First published 2025
by Routledge
4 Park Square, Milton Park, Abingdon, Oxon OX14 4RN

and by Routledge
605 Third Avenue, New York, NY 10158

Routledge is an imprint of the Taylor & Francis Group, an informa business

© 2025 Abigail Fisher, Naomi Fisher and Eliza Fricker

The right of Abigail Fisher and Naomi Fisher to be identified as authors and Eliza Fricker as illustrator of this work has been asserted in accordance with sections 77 and 78 of the Copyright, Designs and Patents Act 1988.

All rights reserved. No part of this book may be reprinted or reproduced or utilised in any form or by any electronic, mechanical, or other means, now known or hereafter invented, including photocopying and recording, or in any information storage or retrieval system, without permission in writing from the publishers.

Trademark notice: Product or corporate names may be trademarks or registered trademarks, and are used only for identification and explanation without intent to infringe.

British Library Cataloguing-in-Publication Data
A catalogue record for this book is available from the British Library

ISBN: 978-1-032-57115-7 (hbk)
ISBN: 978-1-032-57114-0 (pbk)
ISBN: 978-1-003-43787-1 (ebk)

DOI: 10.4324/9781003437871

Typeset in Optima
by Apex CoVantage, LLC

 Printed and bound in Great Britain by
TJ Books, Padstow, Cornwall

Contents

1	Not Fine at School	1
2	When School Meets Child	33
3	Creating Psychologically Healthy School Environments	71
3A	Three School Stories	93
4	When Things Go Wrong	106
5	What Can We Do Instead?	145
6	Deciding Not to Go Back to School	171
7	School Trauma and Burnout	192
8	Working with Children Who Are Not Attending School	225
9	One Step Removed: Indirect Work with Those Not Attending School	253
10	Stories of Hope after School Attendance Difficulties	271
	Index	287

1

Not Fine at School

What you'll find in this chapter:

1. Perspectives on School Attendance
2. Behaviour and Attendance
3. What Is the Problem?
4. The Language of School Attendance
5. EBSA, School Refusal or Just Behaviour?
6. One Size Does Not Fit All

Introduction

My daughter did quite well in primary school. She got into it. She had very nice teachers.

Then she went up to secondary school, and she struggled straight away. She found the whole environment hard and the attitude of teachers to be really different.

She said, "At primary school, everyone knew me and they knew my parents." Going to secondary school was different. As a parent, I didn't know any of the teachers.

The first person I got to know at secondary school was the Attendance Officer because I'd have to ring up and tell them why my child wasn't coming in. She had a very stern manner and she was very procedural. These are people that see my child more than I do, and suddenly I don't know any of them, they don't know me. It's a very odd experience.

My daughter would have stomach aches a lot. I would drive her into school most days and we'd take half an hour or more getting in, and that went on for two years really.

What Can We Do When School's Not Working?

Then at age 13, the school was like, "Right, you've got to make your choices now about your thing." They said to her, "This is when you start thinking about your future and your job. This is when you've got to knuckle down." It's weird. I think her school was really trying to be tough for the kids that need a tough approach. But the kids who don't need the tough approach, they were destroying them. It's like a really broad mallet, it just hit them all on the head. "Right, so you've got to knuckle down."

My daughter was someone who works really hard all the time. She really cares about her work. She goes, "I don't know. I am 13. I don't know what I want to do."

I think she felt this pressure. I think the teachers were feeling a lot of pressure as well to achieve things. She was missing more and more days. There's a hub at her school she'd go to. But that was only about two or three weeks where she could go to this hub and then after a week, she had to go back to normal.

By this point I was walking her up to school. I'm someone who's worked with people with differences a lot in my life, and I was using all my tactics I could think of to help my daughter. I was trying to engage and distract her and work through things. After about six months of it, I was just like, "It's not working. That really isn't working. The school system isn't working. I just have to take her out."

I think the hard thing is you feel a lot of guilt as a parent as well. We're tribal creatures. We usually all do what other people do. When your child is failing in the system everyone seems to be thriving in... Even though when you take your kid out, everyone else goes, "Yeah, my kids hate it. They're not having a great time."

We took her out of school, and then suddenly we could actually deal with what the situations were and understand her anxiety and look into her just finding out who she is. She's now 16, and she's doing media studies and she wants to be a director. She's got ambition. She understands her anxiety more. She still gets anxious, but she understands it more.

(Tom, parent of two, June 2023)

The "unwritten agreement" between parents and schools in England has broken since the Covid-19 crisis, according to Ofsted's chief inspector Amanda Spielman, with pupil absences remaining stubbornly high and disruptive behaviour now more common.

Delivering her final annual report in the role, Spielman said she had noticed a disturbing "shift in attitudes" among pupils and parents.

"This breakdown is feeding into a troubling shift in attendance, in attitudes, in behaviour since the pandemic. Absenteeism has become a stubborn problem. Some of that is down to illness, including mental health problems, but nevertheless disruptive behaviour has become more common.

It's a problem in colleges as well. And it's clear that there's more friction between schools and parents, who are increasingly willing to challenge school rules."

Spielman, who steps down as chief inspector next month after seven years, said parents were partly to blame for the disruption because of growing hostility towards school rules over discipline or uniform requirements.

> Parents were "a little bit less willing to support schools, and a bit more willing to find fault", she said, with Ofsted recording increased numbers of complaints from parents but no increase in complaints that required action.
>
> (The Guardian, Adams, 2023)

School Attendance

You've just read two perspectives on the same problem. One from the parent of a teenager who struggled with attending school, and the other from a former chief Ofsted inspector. Reading them next to each other, the tension between their views is apparent. Tom, the parent, sees his child breaking down in a system which isn't working despite his best efforts. He feels he had no choice except to remove her from school. Spielman sees attendance and behaviour in school deteriorating – and puts it down to a problem in attitude among pupils and parents.

This difference is the starting point for this book. Among the three of us, we hold and hear many perspectives. We are a clinical psychologist (Naomi) who works with parents and young people who are struggling with school. An educational psychologist and former teacher (Abigail) who knows the system from the inside, and has worked for local authorities. And the parent of a young person who was deeply distressed by school, and who ultimately was unable to attend (Eliza), and who has written and drawn about their experiences. All of us also bring our own experiences of school, of success, failures, and attendance difficulties, and Naomi has lived experience of school-related distress (and attendance problems) at ages six and 14.

No one comes afresh to the subject of school. We are all informed by our own experience of being at school ourselves and then perhaps working within the education system or being the parent or carer of children within the education system. We all have our own prejudices and assumptions. The word "school" will bring up different associations for each person.

When writing this book, we talked to professionals, parents and young people. The professionals in particular talked about how their previous assumptions about learning and education had been challenged by seeing how much some children struggled with school. They told us how flexible they had become in order to help those children access education.

In this book we are foregrounding the experiences of parents and young people, because it is our experience that while many schools feel they are listening (and may be trying very hard to do so), many parents and young people do not feel listened to. It can seem like professionals and parents are in different worlds. Parents complain that professionals do not hear their concerns about their children, and professionals complain that parents are unsupportive of school policies and discipline. Teachers feel under siege and criticised from all angles. Everyone is defensive and the situation can easily become combative, with both sides feeling attacked and undermined. And caught in the middle are the young people. Young people who are struggling within the school system and who may not be getting much of an education.

For that is something on which parents and professionals can generally agree. Young people are struggling, more than before. More of them are not attending school regularly, and for those who do attend, reports are that their behaviour has become increasingly disruptive. This has got to the point where, as we write, there are reports that at a Kent school teachers are striking over pupil behaviour. Teachers are leaving the profession in higher numbers than ever before, and one of the reasons they give is poor pupil behaviour.

How do we make sense of what is happening – and what can we do about it? That is the core of this book. We'll start by talking about the different ways in which difficulties with school are understood and the implications of that. We'll then move on to talking about the school system, particularly examining the assumptions on which it is built and asking what impact those assumptions have on our young people. We'll talk about the interaction between children and school, and how things can go wrong (and right), using real-life examples.

Next, we'll move on to talking about what happens when children are struggling with school. We'll discuss common interventions and how they work in practice. We'll talk about the different ways in which school attendance difficulties are understood by the different groups involved, and how that affects what happens next.

Finally, we'll move on to talking about a group of children who have always existed, but which has become larger since the pandemic. Those who have completely stopped going to school, and who have often withdrawn from life as well. Those who may not even be leaving their bedrooms. We'll talk about what happens to them, and how we can work with these young people to maximise their chances of a positive and fulfilled life.

What This Book Is Not

This book does not attempt to review the research literature about young people with school attendance difficulties, nor will it provide a comprehensive overview of the way in which this is addressed in different contexts and countries. These reviews have been done elsewhere (see Finning, Ford and Moore 2022 and Thambirajah, Grandison and De-Hayes 2008) and we would urge readers to consult these books if they wish to inform themselves about the research.

This book is first and foremost a practical book for practitioners who work in education, and it is informed by research, clinical practice and lived experience. It aims to bring together diverse perspectives on school attendance and to offer different ways to approach this difficult and complex area with young people and their families. It aims to give professionals insight into the experience of families and young people who struggle with school attendance.

This book focuses on school, what happens there and how this affects children. We know that for many children home is a difficult place and that they show the impact of this at school. We do not dismiss or discount the importance of this. However, when defining the scope of this book, we have decided to focus on education and school and how things could be different there rather than on things which may be going on at home and within the family.

To start with, we will talk about the difficulties which young people have with school and how adults usually understand those problems.

Behaviour and Attendance

Whenever school comes up, there are two things we hear about more than anything else. Behaviour and attendance. How do we make young people behave, and how can we ensure that they attend school? There's sometimes a decrying in the media that this generation are *the worst*, they have the highest levels of persistent absenteeism from school, their behaviour is the most unacceptable – and their parents aren't backing up the schools in the way that schools would like. Parents are challenging school policies and rules – as one headteacher says in *The Guardian*, *"They question more than they support"*. He doesn't mean that as a positive.

Behind the headlines are stories like Tom's. Stories of families who are trying to support their children to attend school, but who are faced with overwhelming distress, expressed both physically and emotionally. Families whose experience is that the focus on behaviour and attendance is seriously missing the mark when it comes to their children's needs. Those families say that they are being met with sanctions when they need support, and that the advice they are given makes things worse rather than better for their children.

How do we make sense of all of these stories, and what we can we do to help these young people?

Distressed by School

Since the start of mass schooling at the end of the 1890s in the UK, the expectation has been that children from aged five upwards should be at school. This has become part of the culture, and school is generally seen as an unequivocally good thing for all children. There is an (often unspoken) social contract, where parents get their children to school, and support them through reading, or homework, and the school, for its part, provides an education in the form of lessons, as well as oversight and safeguarding of the children during school hours. It's a contract which few question until something goes wrong.

When a child is distressed by school, or refuses to go, they challenge this social contract, and it often seems to catch both parents and schools by surprise. Parents describe the child's distress manifesting itself in a number of ways; some children refuse to go entirely, while others go reluctantly, and complain of stomach ache or headaches. Parents talk about children "losing their spark" or "having checked out". Some young people are disruptive while at school or try to abscond. As they get older, some of them will absent themselves from school without their parents' knowledge. Others behave perfectly while at school but are extremely difficult to manage at home.

Many parents tell us that they are told that their school has never experienced this situation before, and that their child's behaviour is unique. Many families will have other children who have no problems with school or may even be thriving there. Some parents are themselves teachers and are highly invested in the school system, and having a child who isn't thriving at school challenges their whole belief system. One of the things we learnt while writing this book was that school-related distress can affect families from all walks of life, including those who least expect it and who are highly invested in the education system.

Unhappiness at school is unfortunately not rare at all. Disillusionment with school affects a lot of young people, particularly as they get older. A recent research study by the Edge Foundation found that nearly half of 15–16-year-olds described school as something they just had to get through and that many of them found the teaching methods in their English secondary school alienating and stressful (McPherson et al. 2023). This problem isn't unique to the United Kingdom: a recent large-scale, nationwide study in the United States found that 75% of the feelings that students reported about school were negative (Moeller et al. 2020). The study was carried out by researchers at Yale university. "Overall," said study author Marc Brackett on their website, "students see school as a place where they experience negative emotions."

In this context, one way to see those who stop attending school or who have great difficulty attending is as the tip of the iceberg. These are the young people who are demonstrating the most obvious distress, but it would be

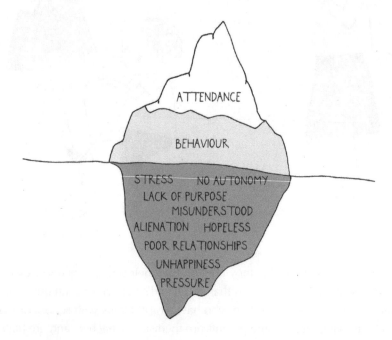

wrong to assume that they are the only ones for whom school is an unhappy place and that everyone else is fine. It may be more accurate to see them as the visible manifestation of a wider problem of school-related distress, or the canaries in the mine. Many young people are unhappy and feel negative about school, even those who do not have visible problems with attendance or behaviour.

Much of what is written about school attendance problems and behaviour does not make this connection. There is a consistent assumption that school is the best place to be for all children. This bias may well be partly down to the fact that professionals tend to be those who have done well at school, since achieving at school enables people to access professional qualifications and careers. Education professionals in particular have made the choice as adults to spend their careers working in and around schools. Even if they themselves had bad experiences at school, their faith in the school system as a force for good was enough to lead them back. This may mean that they find it hard to consider the possibility that school itself is not a positive or beneficial experience for a child.

What Is the Problem?

What actually is the problem that we're talking about here? You may think it's obvious, just as Amanda Spielman says in the article we quoted at the start. Persistent absenteeism and poor behaviour. Children not attending school and behaving badly when they are there. This is certainly the priority of many government campaigns and something which Ofsted are preoccupied by. If only children would just go to school without a fuss and behave themselves while there then the problem would be solved. If only their parents would just insist and be firmer.

Well, yes and no. Poor school attendance and behaviour is what we see, but that doesn't necessarily mean that those things in themselves are the root of the problem. Poor attendance and behaviour could instead be a sign that there is a problem elsewhere. Behaviour is one way in which children express themselves and show us how they are feeling. Attendance and behaviour are feedback on what is working (or not) in a child's life.

Defining what the problem actually is matters because it affects the solutions we use. If a child is deeply unhappy at school, for example, and is not attending as a result, then insisting that they attend will not solve the real issue. It could in fact make their unhappiness worse. An unhappy child attending school because they are forced to isn't a positive outcome.

Just as in the two accounts at the start of this chapter, there is often a clear divide in how people understand school attendance difficulties. From one perspective, the child's behaviour *is* the problem, while from another perspective the child's behaviour or distress is a signal, *alerting us* to the existence of a problem.

Tom, the parent, thinks that his daughter's behaviour is alerting him to a problem in the way that secondary school affects her emotional wellbeing. He thinks that any intervention would have to start with his daughter's wellbeing at school, and when none of this helps, his intervention was to remove her from school. Amanda Spielman, Chief Ofsted Inspector, thinks that behaviour and attendance *are* the problem, and that there has been a "shift in attitudes" within children and their parents. From this perspective, the interventions include fines and sanctions, anything which will bring the children back to school. In this perspective, it doesn't matter if they are distressed or not by attending school, nor whether they are learning or happy when they get there. What matters is that they attend (and behave themselves).

This clash in perspectives means that many parents feel that the support they need is very different to what they get. Many feel that their child needs help and that they are working hard to get them into school, but they say they are met with punitive measures which aim to compel them to force their children to attend. Tom told me about the experience of being fined for their daughter's low school attendance.

> When you get fined, both parents get fined. We got fined £100 each just before Christmas. It felt like they were saying "The parents don't care. The money will make the parents care."
>
> I care. I deeply care about my child. To fine me just makes me go: "You don't care about my child." It pushed me to a point of going: "Well, this system is really stupid."
>
> I think it's the County Council that fines you. They go: "The attendance has gone too low, this is triggering a response by our computer to send this thing out." It feels very inhuman. "You fall below this threshold, therefore you will be fined now."
>
> It's horrible when you're trying to explain: "My kid's really struggling with this and that." She'd start off with a stomach ache when she started going to secondary school. That would become worse and worse. I would be spending an hour in the car trying to get her through the door with her crying.
>
> That was my life for two or three years. Get up, drive my daughter to school, try and cajole her and use all the tricks I have from working with autistic kids and kids with challenging behaviour to get them into school.
>
> After a while, you go: "If the school is really damaging my kid, why am I doing this?" But then again, what else is there to do really? I've got to pay the rent. It's a big thing to take your kid's education into your hands.
>
> Especially when you find out there's no support at all, and instead you'll be questioned and doubted. Sometimes I think people think that I'm just doing this for fun.

The intervention which Tom's family experienced – fines – is punitive. He picks up on this when he says it felt like they were saying that he as a parent just didn't care and should be made to care. Lack of care was not the reason why his daughter was struggling to attend, and fines just pushed them further down the road towards removing their daughter from school entirely.

Below is a simple flow chart showing how attendance and behaviour exist as part of a system.

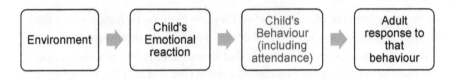

Different perspectives put a different emphasis on the different parts of this flow chart – which leads them to different ideas as to how this should be approached.

If we emphasise the influence of the environment, we might focus our efforts on changes schools can make in their environment. If we focus on the child's emotional reaction, we might focus on trying to reduce their anxiety, using anxiety strategies. If we focus on their behaviour as the problem, we might introduce an attendance goal, or put pressure on the child's parents to get them to attend.

The Language of School Attendance

Over the last 40 years, school attendance difficulties have variously been described in different contexts as school refusal, school phobia, truancy, skiving, mitching, absenteeism, dropping out, barriers to school attendance and emotionally based school avoidance or non-attendance. The language we use shapes how we think about what is going on, sometimes without our even being aware of it. In interactions with parents and families, the language we use can make the difference between a successful interaction or one which becomes combative. In the next few pages, we're going to unpack the assumptions behind some of these descriptions.

Can't or Won't?

One issue which runs through any discussion about attendance and behaviour is that of intentionality. Essentially, the point of contention is this: are young people *choosing* not to attend school or is this something about which they have little choice? Is it a "wilful decision" or something beyond their control? The implication is that if this is a choice, then families and children deserve no sympathy, but if it is because they are incapable of attending, then that should be treated differently (and with more compassion).

Many of the most heated debates between parents and schools are about this issue. Parents feel that their children cannot attend school, while schools (often) feel that they could, if only they were more motivated. In Australia, the parent support organisation for those with children who are struggling with school attendance is called *School Can't* which makes it very clear where they stand.

Discussions are typically highly polarised as a result, something which we aim to step away from in this book. Many struggles between parents and schools focus on this issue, and it is often not helpful for the children involved. Both sides can become entrenched. Those who think it is intentional put in place harsher consequences and bemoan modern parenting. Those who think the problems are due to a lack of capacity, arguing that poor school attendance is not a "choice" but what happens when schools do not meet a child's needs. Both positions have drawbacks and lack nuance.

The drawbacks to the "won't" narrative are easy to see. By framing poor attendance as a choice, the problem is located directly in the young people and their parents who are seen as lazy, defiant, anti-social – the list goes on. In practice this can mean that the onus is entirely on the young person to "change their attitude" while the adults try to pressure them into doing so. It can also mean that parents are told to force their children into school, or to make them deliberately unhappy at home.

However, we also have reservations about the "can't" narrative, having seen it play out for some young people. The problem is that, while it has the effect of making it clear that problems at school are not a choice, it simultaneously removes agency from young people and frames them as incapable. They hear repeatedly that they can't do things other young people do and they believe it. Sometimes multiple assessments will be done, all documenting the things that this young person cannot do as well as their peers. The focus is on deficit and impairment, because that seems like the only alternative to blame.

It may well be true that at this time they can't do some of the things that other children do. However, one result of the focus on "can't" is that young people tend to think that their difficulties are set in stone and it will always be like this. Childhood is a time of great change, learning and development, and our approach would always be to try and keep opportunities for change open. In some cases, the "can't" narrative closes options down. We meet children who, aged 10 or 11, tell us all the things they can't do (like organise themselves, work towards a goal, concentrate) with, apparently, no expectation that they will be able to learn to do these things as they grow up. They sometimes say things like "my brain doesn't work like that", which precludes the possibility of change.

In reality, of course, the can't/won't dichotomy is much less clear than it first appears. Naomi has resigned from jobs which she strongly disliked, and which made her ill – she physically *could* have continued to go but chose not to when she saw the effect on her. We all make life choices based on a range of factors, and it's worth thinking about why we think this agency shouldn't apply to children, that the only option open to them other than "won't" is "can't". We want to empower children to make choices, even if those aren't the choices adults would choose for them. Otherwise, they may grow up to see themselves as incapable.

We think the question "Is this a choice?" is unhelpful when it comes to school attendance. It's always possible to argue that people have choices. We can choose to do things which make us feel extremely ill or unhappy. Instead, we see choices as something which are made in reaction to circumstances and context. They are the best option that the child can come up with right now.

As a final drawback, both "won't" and "can't" narratives locate the problem in the individual child or family. As an alternative, we prefer Dr Ross Greene's philosophy which he sums up as "kids do well if they can" (Greene 2014). The follow-up to this is, if they aren't doing well, what can we change so that they can?

We raise this issue here because it runs through the language that is used. School attendance difficulties have been described and categorised in many ways over the years. None of these terms are neutral. Some people dislike every single one of them. None of these descriptions are official diagnoses. They are not included in the diagnostic manuals of mental health problems used by clinicians. However, they are often used in the same way as a diagnosis, with families being told that a child "has emotionally based school avoidance (EBSA)" in the same way as they might be told their child "has chicken pox". However, unlike "chicken pox" (which is an illness caused by the varicella-zoster virus), the terms below have no explanatory power. They are just labels that describe the situation. In physical health terms, it's like saying a child has a rash. It describes the problem, but doesn't explain why.

The reason why language is important is because it's the argument of this book that the way we understand a problem informs what then happens. If we think a child is wilfully refusing to do something, then an intervention might focus on trying to change their mind (or force them to accept what we say). If we think that they aren't capable of doing something, then there is no point in trying to change their mind. We'd have to change the task or help them learn the skills that they need.

This difference underlies many of the most fierce arguments about school attendance and behaviour. People come from very diverse perspectives, often without realising how different things look from the other side of the room.

School Refusal/Avoidance

School refusal is perhaps the mostly widely used term describing those with difficulties attending school. Many parents dislike it, because they feel it assumes that this is a wilful refusal by the child. It's right there in the name – the problem is defined as refusal, which leads us to interventions that focus on changing refusal to compliance.

There are many books written about school refusal and how to overcome it, both for parents and professionals. The motivation for school refusal is assumed to be either behavioural or anxiety. The literature on school refusal generally conceptualises it as irrational behaviour on the part of the child, who either needs to learn that school isn't as bad as they think it is, or that their life will become increasingly unpleasant if they don't attend school. This will motivate them to behave differently. Interventions for school refusal are largely focused on the child and parent (who is often assumed not to be insisting hard enough and not parenting well enough).

Christopher Kearney, a clinical psychologist who has written many books with "School Refusal" in the title, takes what he calls a "functional approach" to school refusal. This means that he looks at what function the school refusal apparently has and what the child achieves through that behaviour. He then plans interventions to change that. His research identifies four main types of "school refusers".

1. Those who refuse school in order to avoid general school-related distress (for reasons either known or unknown).
2. Those who want to escape the social or academic pressures of school.
3. Those who refuse to go to school in order to get more attention from their parents.
4. Those who have things which they would prefer to do at home and who refuse to go to school in order to do those things.

Kearney is clear about what he thinks a successful outcome is – one of his most popular books is called *Getting Your Child Back to School* and to this end he advises parents to stop reacting to what their child is doing and instead to take control of the situation. He recommends setting up a system of consequences for not attending school, saying: "Your child should dance to your tune . . . You are the boss!"

School Phobia/Anxiety

Phobias are irrational fears. A phobia is an anxiety disorder, where there is a persistent and excessive fear generated by a specific object or situation. Labelling anxious feelings as a phobia implies that the fear is out of proportion to the harm caused by the object. Common phobias are spiders, driving and snakes. People with a spider phobia will go out of their way to avoid spiders at all costs, even choosing their holiday destinations or housing in order to minimise their chances of meeting a spider.

Not Fine at School

The term "school phobia" implies an irrational and specific fear of school which prevents the child from attending. Interventions for phobias are generally cognitive-behavioural and involve a graded exposure to the feared situation. The idea is that the person will learn over time that their fears are unjustified, and that the feared situation is not as bad as they think it is. When applied to school, this can mean a reintegration programme which starts with getting to the school gate and then gradually increases the amount of time that the child spends at school.

The term school phobia both situates the problem in the child (who is assumed to have an irrational fear) and also contains the assumption that school is less aversive than they think it is. Interventions are therefore exposure based, with the idea that more exposure to school will show the child that it's not as bad as they fear.

School Distress or School-Related Distress

We are choosing to use the term school distress in this book, because it widens the discussion to include all children who are distressed at school, whether they are attending or not. It shifts the focus from the child's non-attendance (terms such as truancy and school refusal focus on this) to their emotional response. It also includes behaviour, since behaviour is one way in which children express distress. This term has been used by some researchers (Connolly, Constable and Mullally 2022).

We know that children often struggle with school for a long time before their attendance is affected (although there are also others for whom something changes and they quickly start having difficulties having been fine before). Research into school distress emphasises the long-standing nature of such distress. Parents describe distress which often started years before the child starts to demonstrate any difficulties with attendance. This means that when a child starts to not attend school and interventions are put in place to "nip it in the bud" then parents will often feel that this is years too late.

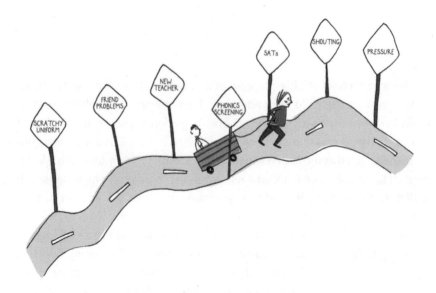

Truancy

Much of the literature on school attendance difficulties is explicit that their theories do not apply to truancy. Truants are defined as young people who do not attend school without the knowledge of their parents. They may leave house in the mornings dressed for school and then go into town or to a friend's house. This leaves them without adult oversight, as no one knows where they are, and they are vulnerable to exploitation.

Truants are typically seen in an entirely negative light. This extract from a handbook for professionals on school refusal is a good example of how truancy is often conceptualised and how both groups are stereotyped.

> It is important to differentiate between SR (school refusal) and truancy. The child with SR is invariably a good student; the truant is a poor student. Truants openly acknowledge their dislike of schools; school refusers wish they could attend. The truant usually avoids both home and school, whereas the school refuser stays at home. Moreover, truants fabricate excuses to cover up their absence; the child with SR draws attention to their inability to leave home or stay in school.
>
> (Thambirajah, Grandison and De-Hayes 2008)

This passage makes it clear that the authors' sympathies are firmly with the "school refusers", while they see truants as beyond the pale. Many parents are keen to maintain this distinction, as they (understandably) do not want their children to be seen as truants. However, when it comes to interventions, the approaches that the professionals we talked to described were very similar.

The distinction between "truancy" and other forms of school attendance barriers highlights something important in how these children are managed. This is the question of choice and blame. We are often asked whether children aren't "just choosing" not to attend school, and therefore need to be given harsh consequences for non-attendance which will persuade them to choose to attend instead. Those who have been identified as truants are particularly likely to be seen as at fault, or their school absence as anti-social behaviour.

Skiving/Mitching/Wagging

There are many regional terms used for those who do not attend school, all of which have negative connotations.

These terms imply truancy but are sometimes used – particularly in the press – to describe all young people who are not attending school, no matter what the reason. This frustrates parents of young people who are not attending school for reasons of health or distress.

Politicians use this rhetoric, with Sky News reporting on 28 February 2023 that "Michael Gove suggests parents of skivers should have child benefit stripped" (Browne 2023). The term "skiving" is invariably used in a context which suggests that more discipline and less leniency is needed.

Terms which are used to denigrate young people with school attendance difficulties include dropouts, malingers, bunking off or wagging school. All of these are typically used to imply that these are young people making bad choices, or whose parents are not supervising them enough. They are never neutral terms although young people sometimes use them about themselves or others.

Emotionally Based School Avoidance (EBSA) or Non-attendance (EBSNA)

Emotionally based school avoidance is now the preferred term used by many local authorities in the UK, in place of the earlier terms "school refusal" or "school phobia". It is a descriptive term which appears to have been coined by educational psychologists in the UK and which is extensively used by local authorities. It is not well known as a term outside the UK, nor is it well understood outside educational settings. Tina Rae, an educational and child psychologist who writes extensively on EBSA, defines it as such.

> EBSA is not in itself a mental health disorder, but rather is a combination of symptoms that indicate that a young person is experiencing emotional distress relating to school attendance. This typically includes high levels of anxiety. Pupils may exhibit one or more of the following associated behaviours:
>
> - Crying
> - Pleading
> - Refusal to get ready for school or leave the house
> - Rumination and worry around school-related issues
> - Sleep problems
> - Psychosomatic illness.
>
> (Rae 2020)

EBSA describes the emotional distress experienced by the child and links that to the avoidance. In plain English, EBSA really means "this child is distressed by school and therefore does not want to go". It does not identify why this might be happening, nor whether their distress is a reasonable response to their experiences.

The problem is still frequently conceptualised as an anxiety disorder about something (school) which is essentially benign, similarly to school phobia. If young people identified as having EBSA are referred to mental health services, they will usually be offered cognitive behaviour therapy which will be focused on reducing their anxiety response and challenging their negative thoughts about school. EBSA as a term is usually confined to the education system, and it is our experience that those in the mental health system have rarely heard the term.

Barriers to School Attendance

In the last ten years there has been a burgeoning number of parent advocacy groups for families of children with school attendance difficulties in the UK. These include *Square Peg, Define Fine* and *Not Fine in School*. In a short video for educational psychologists available on YouTube, Fran Morgan, founder of Square Peg, explains why Square Peg and other parent advocacy groups prefer and use the term "barriers to school attendance" rather than any of the terms discussed above (Morgan 2021).

Morgan explains that in the view of the parents in her organisation, terms such as "school refusal" or "EBSA" focus attention on the child and the child's behaviour. They feel that the focus should rather be on the barriers which exist in the school system which prevent children from attending and from thriving once they do get to school. Square Peg would like to shift the focus from the child's behaviour and emotions to the barriers which they see as the cause of those behaviours and emotional responses. They see school exclusion and school refusal as two manifestations of the same problem – unmet needs at school. They therefore reject the division often used by professionals where young people are divided into those with problematic behaviour (described as truants or those who are excluded from school) and those in psychological distress (described as school refusers or as having EBSA).

Exclusion is often the end result of persistent disruptive behaviour, and so Square Peg and other parent organisations see both behaviour and attendance as signs of the failings of the school system. From their perspective, children are pointing out a problem. They aren't the problem.

EBSA, School Refusal or Just Behaviour?

Naomi: It has never made sense to me that difficulties with school attendance (whatever we term it) are said to be caused by anxiety. For I remember vividly my own period of teenage "school refusal". It started when we moved country and I started at a large comprehensive school. I was 13. I had excelled at my previous school, had had friends and had been liked by teachers. I had never had any problems with attendance because I enjoyed being there.

This new school was different. There were nine forms in each year – over 250 pupils in each year group. Even recognising all the others in your year group wasn't possible. From the start I thought that a lot of what we did was a waste of time. The work was significantly easier than in my previous school and we had much less independence. I was used to open-ended projects and teachers who would get inspired by helping us write plays or make huge artistic presentations. At the new school we did tasks like filling in the blanks or reading passages and answering comprehension questions for a significant proportion of the day. There was a lot of memorising and not much thinking. I thought it was pointless.

I stood out. My accent was different, I used different words. The rest of my class had been together for years. They noticed that I was different, and they mocked me for it. School felt like a hostile environment. Just things like where to sit at lunchtime could be stressful. I could sit down and the people I had sat next to would get up and move away. I wouldn't want to eat alone because it felt like I had a target on my back. People would "accidentally" knock into me or spill drinks on me. They called me names, just whispered as they walked past.

The school was so large that I did not recognise most of the teachers, and they did not recognise me. My days passed surrounded with other teenagers who mostly ignored me, or ridiculed me. The lessons were boring and uninspiring. I was spending my life in a place which I hated.

I started to feel ill when I was at school. My muscles ached. I had no energy. My throat swelled up. I felt worst on Sunday evenings. I was anxious about the week ahead, but the symptoms weren't the cause of my difficulties. It seemed clear to me that the cause was this school, and how unpleasant I found it.

The school did try to help, but I couldn't explain what the problems were. It was everything. And because it was everything, it was nothing that they could do anything about. They made some changes which made things worse. They changed my class, but now the old class wanted to know why I'd left them. They'd shout out when they saw me around the school. They arranged for me to do more challenging maths, but now my class wanted to know why I thought I was too clever for the maths they were all doing. They disliked me even more.

I couldn't keep on complaining, I was meant to be grateful for the efforts they had made and they were running out of patience. *Why can't you just fit in?* They might not have said it, but I definitely felt it.

When I stayed at home it was boring. I watched daytime TV and lay around on my own. I didn't want to be at home alone, but I didn't want to be at school either. I was bored wherever I was. I started to feel very low. My symptoms were defined as glandular fever (although the blood test was clear) by a doctor which gave me a ticket to a part-time timetable. I never stopped going entirely, but I went less and less. I took the work home and did it there. It wasn't hard and not attending the lessons didn't seem to make much difference. I didn't feel I was missing out on any learning by not being at school.

How should my difficulties have been understood? Was this school refusal – and my parents just needed to show me that they were in charge? Was the problem my attitude to school, or my parents' attitude, as Spielman might say? Did they need to be fined? Or was it anxiety-based, as Rae might say, and did I need to be gradually exposed to school so I could learn that it wasn't so bad after all? I am sure I would have met criteria for anxiety and depression at the time, had anyone tried to diagnose me. I think I could probably have become a truant, had my parents not allowed me to stay home. I could have got on that bus and then just sat in the local park, waiting for the hours to tick by, although my intense fear of getting into trouble might have kept me going through the school gates.

I didn't have any sort of special educational need, unless an intense dislike of school and a failure to thrive there is a special need in itself. My unmet needs were for community and purpose. I needed to be doing things I found meaningful, and instead I was offered boredom. I found the whole school environment aversive and unpleasant – and spending your days in a place that you find aversive and unpleasant eventually has an impact on your health. I don't think that any barriers could have been lowered which would have made that school the right place. The way that things improved for me is that my parents moved cities and I started at a smaller school where I no longer felt like one in an anonymous crowd and there was more space to be an individual. I didn't love it, but it wasn't anything like as bad. I went to school and passed my exams. I went onto university and ultimately got two doctoral degrees.

Yet many parents are advised against changing their child's school, with books telling parents confidently: "Don't change school. It is usually unhelpful because the problems tend to recur in the new setting" (Thambirajah, Grandison and De-Hayes 2008, p. 149). This can make families feel even more trapped – not only is the problem bad now, but they are being told that it will happen anywhere they go.

One Size Does Not Fit All

In childhood and adolescence, it is assumed that the school environment is the right place for all children, no matter how much distress they report or how challenging they find it. We don't make this assumption for people when they are older, or at a different stage of development.

For adults, we acknowledge that different people thrive in different ways, and that meaningful work could involve doing very different things. Some adults choose to spend all their time outside and work with their hands, while others spend their lives sitting at a computer and immerse themselves in programming code. Most of us know from experience that the wrong job can make us unhappy and anxious and that changing our job can often help – but we don't allow this for children.

We know from research that a high proportion of children with school distress are suspected to be autistic, to have ADHD, dyslexia, dyspraxia or dyscalculia, something which is now often described as "neurodivergence". We'll discuss neurodiversity more in Chapter 2, but essentially it is a term used to describe those who differ significantly from the average in a way that makes their life more challenging. However, school distress isn't a problem only experienced by neurodivergent children. Parents have told us of their frustration when professionals assume that a child who is distressed by school must be neurodivergent, and how those whose children did not meet criteria for a diagnosis felt that the only alternative was for it to be their fault.

Identifying children who struggle at school as neurodivergent can be a way of deflecting any analysis of what is going on in our schools to cause so many children distress. It locates the problem in particular children, for whom individual accommodations are considered to be the answer. School is assumed to be working fine for everyone else. Sometimes this is an explicit part of the neurodivergence lens, with children and families sometimes told that the world isn't designed for them, with the implication that it *is* designed for everyone else. This narrative causes a lot of frustration for families whose children don't meet diagnostic criteria but who are still very much struggling with school. They feel that it reinforces the idea that they must be to blame for their problems.

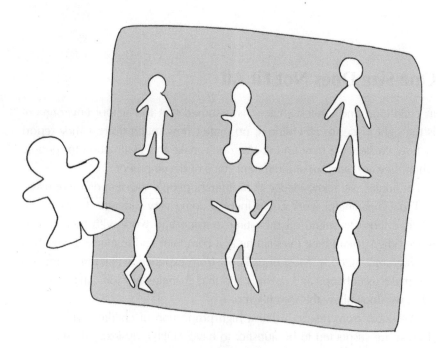

Many of the parents we interviewed for this book told us how stepping away from the assumption that school was the only place for their child made all the difference for them. They told us that once they started seeing school as one way to learn, rather than the only way, then they could look for other opportunities for their children. In some cases, this led to their child returning to school and in other cases it didn't.

In this book, we conceptualise poor attendance and behaviour as the most obvious manifestations of school-related distress, something which is far more widespread than "school refusal". Therefore any intervention which increases distress is likely to exacerbate the problem, and this is the pattern which parents describe to us. We do not see this as a problem which should be located in children and parents, but rather something that is a challenge for the school system. We see it as a problem that happens in the interaction between young people and the system they are in.

The question we pose for this book is, why are so many children distressed by school, and what can be done to help those children learn?

Summary

- Parents and professionals generally have very different perspectives on problems with school behaviour and attendance.
- These different perspectives affect how young people are perceived and what interventions are offered.
- The language used around school attendance often comes with assumptions and tends to locate the problem in the child and their family.
- The biggest difference in perspectives is whether behaviour and attendance are seen as the problem themselves, or whether they are seen as the way that a child is signalling a problem.
- This book will take the perspective that behaviour and attendance are signs of an underlying, systemic problem, rather than the problem in themselves.

References and Further Reading

Adams, R. (2023). School leaders in England feel lockdown "broke spell" of bond with parents. London: *The Guardian*.

Browne, F. (2023). Michael Gove suggests parents of skivers should have child benefit stripped. https://news.sky.com/story/michael-gove-suggests-parents-of-skivers-should-have-child-benefit-stripped-12822206

Connolly, S. E., Constable, H. L. and Mullally, S. L. (2022). School distress and the school attendance crisis: A story dominated by neurodivergence and unmet need. *Front Psychiatry* 14: 1237052. doi: 10.3389/fpsyt.2023.1237052.

Finning, K., Ford, T. and Moore., D (2022). *Mental Health and Attendance at School*. Cambridge: Cambridge University Press.

Greene, R. (2014). *Lost At School: Why Our Kids with Behavioural Challenges Are Falling Through the Cracks and How We Can Help Them.* New York: Scribner.

McPherson, C., Baytakdar, S., Gewirtz, S., Laczik, A., Maguire, M., Newton, O., O'Brien, S., Weavers, Winch, C. and Wolf, A. (2023). *Schools for All? Young People's Experiences of Alienation in the English Secondary School System.* London: Edge Foundation.

Moeller, J., Brackett, M., Ivcevic, Z. and White, A. (2020). High school students' feelings: Discoveries from a large national survey and an experience sampling study. *Learning and Instruction* 66: 101301.

Morgan, F. (2021). Let's not talk about school refusal, let's talk about barriers to school attendance. *Educational Psychology Reach-Out,* YouTube. www.youtube.com/watch?v=gKMhaFKBvqg

Rae, T. (2020). *Understanding and Supporting Children and Young People with Emotionally Based School Avoidance (EBSA).* Northampton: Hinton House Publishers Ltd.

Thambirajah, M., Grandison, K. and De-Hayes, L. (2008). *Understanding School Refusal: A Handbook for Professionals in Education, Health and Social Care.* London: Jessica Kingsley Publishers.

2

When School Meets Child

In this chapter you will find:

1. Child Development
2. The Science of Learning
3. What's This Got to Do with Attendance and Behaviour?
4. Difference and Diversity
5. Neurodiversity
6. Special Educational Needs

Introduction

In Chapter 1 we talked about how we understand school related distress and the different ways in which people talk about children who aren't fine at school. We've outlined how attendance and behaviour can either be defined as the problem or as signals of an underlying problem. We've argued that many schools (and government policy) see attendance and behaviour as the problem, while parents and young people are often more likely to see attendance and behaviour as signals of an underlying problem.

In this chapter we are going to look at child and adolescent development, how children learn at different stages (in very broad terms) and how this interacts with school expectations and requirements. We will discuss special educational needs and neurodiversity and ask what this means in the context of the school system.

Why are we doing this, when the focus of this book is on school attendance difficulties? We have noticed that an unspoken assumption underpinning almost every book on attendance difficulties is that schools are *by definition* beneficial places for children to be. Many teachers and education professionals understandably are highly committed to this belief and often become defensive at the very idea that any school might be harmful for some young people.

Alongside this assumption that there are no problems with schools themselves comes the conclusion that children who are distressed by school must be the problem. The way that this problem is conceptualised varies, depending on both the child and the adults around them. Some children will be seen as badly behaved (and if they are not attending school they are likely to be called truants). Others are seen as having special or additional needs, and they are more likely to be described as having EBSA or anxiety. Others don't seem to fit into either of these groups but are still distressed by school, and they confuse everyone.

This book takes a different stance. We are going to ask you to think critically about some of the things you may never have questioned about how schools work – and think about how schools interact with the developing brains of children. To do that, we will start with a whistle-stop tour of child brain development.

Child Development

Human beings change dramatically between birth and age 18, when most people finish school. Much of that is visible, as they learn to walk and talk, and grow from tiny babies into adult-sized humans. And more of it is invisible, as their brains change in ways which we are only just starting to understand.

The neurological changes which children go through as they grow up mean that young children are different to adolescents and adults in ways which go beyond their lack of experience and knowledge. Young children approach the world in a qualitatively different way to adults. They find different things hard and they also find some things easier than adults. A 4-year-old brain works in a different way to a 14-year-old and both are different to a 24-year-old. That difference is about more than experience and knowledge. There are big structural changes to their brains as children grow up.

Developmental psychologists divide child development into three main stages (excluding infancy, which is outside the scope of this book). Early childhood, which is usually defined as up to about seven. At this stage children are in a period of intense exploration and discovery. What this looks like is play. They play everywhere and with everything and it requires a significant effort on the part of adults to stop them. As developmental psychologists such as Alison Gopnik argue, they are constructing hypotheses about the world around them and testing those out constantly (Gopnik 2016). What this usually looks like is getting into everything and making a lot of mess. They are often divergent and creative thinkers, resisting any efforts to get them to do things the "correct" way, and instead insisting on mixing all the playdough colours together or putting the sand in the water play. The way that they learn at this stage is called "discovery learning". It is wide-ranging and often involves exploring through different senses.

What Can We Do When School's Not Working?

Most attempts to get children of this age to sit down and focus are doomed to failure and they do not deliberately apply themselves to learning a particular skill. They learn through play, but they do not typically set out with the intention of learning. They play because it is fun for them, and they learn as they do so. There is evidence that children of this age pay attention in a different way to older people – their attention is wider and they are more prone to distraction. This means they may observe and notice things which adults don't. What they aren't generally good at is paying attention to one thing while ignoring other things. Adults will describe them as "flitting" from one thing to another, and this often causes frustration and worry for adults who are (usually needlessly) concerned that they will never start to be more focused.

As children get towards the age of seven, there is a qualitative shift in their behaviour. This is often perceived by adults as them becoming "more sensible". They start to be able to ignore distractions slightly more, and therefore their attention span expands. They become capable of more complex thinking – they can hold two concepts in mind at the same time, for example being able to understand that different people can hold different opinions about the same thing. They are still discovery learners, exploring ideas and the world around them – but they are also starting to make the shift into being capable of mastery learning.

Mastery learning is the type of learning which enables us to develop expertise and automaticity. Mastery learning is when we become highly skilled in something, and that is achieved through practice. This is made possible by the maturation of the brain's pre-frontal cortex. This part of our brain is responsible for executive functioning – which means control over the rest of the brain. Executive functioning is what makes it possible to think about our thinking. This makes it possible to set a goal and work towards it – something which psychologists sometimes call "holding the goal in mind". That means that a child is able to decide that they want to learn to do something – and also hold the knowledge that in order to do that, they will have to keep trying when it's hard. When a child decides that they want to learn to ride a bicycle and practices for hours, despite falling off, until they can, that's mastery learning in action. They are able to hold the future goal (of being able to ride the bike) in mind for long enough to continue to motivate themselves through the not-so-fun process of falling off many times. At this stage, they learn well through watching adults, imitating what they do and having a go themselves. An apprenticeship model of learning, as Gopnik calls it.

There's a loss to this shift from discovery to mastery learning. When Naomi was at school in the 1980s, she was taught how to touch-type. She practiced for hours and it became automatic. She can now type without thinking. Unfortunately, part of what she was taught was to press the spacebar twice after every full stop. Over 30 years later, she is still automatically pressing that spacebar twice after every full stop, even though the rules were changed at some point and it is no longer thought of as best practice. It is very hard for her to change this. Automaticity and mastery come at a cost and that cost is a loss of flexibility.

Discovery learning is not inferior to mastery learning. It is different and fulfils a different function. The brains of young children are not inferior versions of adults. Their brains are highly flexible and adaptable to circumstances. They learn from anything and everything. They are learning broad concepts about the world. As brains become more capable of mastery learning, they also become more rigid and more specialised. This change is gradual.

The next big shift in brain development happens around puberty. This is when it can seem like life is getting messy again. The previously "sensible" nine- and ten-year-olds are transformed into teenagers who relate to the world in a very different way. Adolescence is a time of change, flexibility and innovation, rather like the early years – and rather like young children, adolescents can be hard to live with. The current understanding of this stage by neuroscientists is sometimes called the "two-system" theory of adolescence. This suggests that there are two different systems in the brain which are going through rapid change at this time – both of which are necessary in order to turn children into adults (Blakemore 2019).

The first system is to do with social rewards and motivation. Teenagers become highly sensitive to the judgement and perception of their peers. Their emotional reactions to the approval or disapproval of their peers are more intense than those of adults – which can drive risk-taking behaviour, particularly when they are in groups. This system motivates teenagers to turn outwards from their families, towards the world outside, something which they will need to do in order to leave the comfort of their home to venture out into the world as independent adults.

The second system is the self-management system. This is the part of the brain which makes it possible to reflect on and control your behaviour and thinking. It allows people to inhibit impulses and to engage in long-term planning. It makes it possible to evaluate risk, weigh up consequences and make

decisions. This system is slower to mature than the social rewards system and it is experience-dependent. The way in which it develops is through practice. Practice in making real decisions, seeing the results and then changing your mind. Practice in setting goals and accomplishing them (or failing to accomplish them).

Adults often confuse young people accepting being controlled with them practicing self-control – but from a psychological perspective the two are different. Self-control is about setting your own goals and being able to control your impulses and make decisions so that you can work towards them. Being controlled is about complying with what someone else wants you to do, often working towards goals they have set for you. A young person who does what they are told in school may be praised for their self-discipline, but actually what they are doing is submitting to external discipline. They have not had the space to set their own goals. Young people may comply with adult control, but this is not the same as developing the ability to make good decisions for themselves. Many of our young people get very few chances to develop real self-discipline until they leave school, and at that point, some find that they have no idea how to plan their own time and set their own goals. They haven't had any practice.

These changes in how children learn do not have to be imposed upon them. The changes are not dependent on formal education or training. Adults are often afraid that if they don't make young children practice writing and reading through enforced repetition, for example, they'll never become

Table 2.1 Changes in How Children Learn as They Grow

Stage of development	Approx. ages	What makes this period distinctive?
Early childhood	2–7	Children of this age are active explorers of the world. They are usually highly energetic and have a short attention span. They move quickly from one thing to another. They are motivated by what is fun and interesting for them. They acquire skills but they typically do not set out to deliberately acquire or practice skills. Their skills develop through play. They learn through activity and experimentation. This stage of learning is called discovery learning. It is wide-ranging and very different to the way in which most adults interact with the world.
Middle childhood	7–11	Children are still exploring the world but they are also starting to develop some more complex cognitive abilities. They are still discovery learners, but they are starting to become capable of some mastery learning as well. Mastery learning comes at a cost, as brains specialise they also become more rigid and less flexible. Children in this stage learn well through apprenticeship – doing something alongside a competent adult.
Early to mid-Adolescence	11–18	Two brain systems are maturing and this is a time of high innovation and flexibility, as well as vulnerability. The social rewards system means that teenagers are highly motivated by the perceptions of their peers, and this can mean that they take more risks, particularly when with their peers. The self-management system is the system of executive control. This system is slower to develop than the social rewards system and is experience-dependent. It makes it possible for young people to set goals, inhibit their impulses, plan for the future and to become better mastery learners.

(Continued)

Table 2.1 (Continued)

Stage of development	Approx. ages	What makes this period distinctive?
Late Adolescence	18–25	Neuroscientists tell us that in neurological terms, the period of very active adolescent brain development continues until at least the age of 25 and that for many people, the self-management system is still in development (and out of balance with the social reward system) until their early 20s. Some young people do not develop the necessary self-control skills for successful mastery learning until this stage, and those who were not academically successful as younger adolescents may become capable of much more in their 20s if they are given second and third chances.

mastery learners. They think that they must teach young children to stick at things by refusing to let them give up when they've had enough.

The research does not back this up. The cross-cultural research of scientists such as Barbara Rogoff (2003) shows that young people who grow up in countries where they do not attend school do not stay as perpetual discovery learners. They grow into adults who are capable of mastery learning and acquiring complex skills, just as humans did for the whole of human history until school because the accepted way to educate children. Young people do not need to be pushed through these stages, but they do need opportunities to explore the world and practice emerging skills, particularly the skills of self-management and self-control.

The Science of Learning

There's been a battle raging over learning and education in the last decade or so, and a lot of it revolves around how learning is defined. To developmental psychologists such as Gopnik, children's learning is the process of coming to understand the world, something which human beings have evolved to do. She says: "All children are naturally driven to create an accurate picture of the world, and to use that picture to make predictions, formulate explanations, imagine alternatives and design plans. They all want, even need, to understand the world" (Gopnik 2016, p. 180). In developmental psychology, everything that children do is seen through this lens, it's the reason why young children are so motivated to explore and to discover basic principles about the world (such as, if you knock a cup over, the water falls out and if that water falls on you, you get wet). Then as children get older, they start to practice the skills of their own particular culture which will enable them to become competent and independent adults. The child's drive to learn and to participate in the world is an essential part of this process.

But this isn't how learning is being talked about in schools across the UK. Here, a different type of learning theory currently holds sway. These are theories which don't come from developmental psychology at all.

Instead there has been a shift in the last ten years towards "cognitive science". Cognitive science as it is defined in education is quite different to cognitive developmental psychology which I have described above. In cognitive science, learning is thought of as information processing. Children are essentially seen as data processors. Information goes in one end, and is retained (or not) before being retrieved and evaluated at the other end. Learning, seen through this lens, is defined as a change in long-term memory. The studies on which these theories are based were not done with children at school. They are usually done with undergraduate students learning lists of words in a lab.

Much of the science around this is based on John Sweller's cognitive load theory (Sweller 1988), and increasingly teachers are being told they must understand this as it is a key part of understanding how learning happens. I'd recommend Oliver Lovell's "Cognitive Load Theory in Action" (Lovell 2020) for a thorough but succinct introduction to this theory if you are interested.

When School Meets Child

Cognitive load theory is sometimes referred to as the "science of learning" and it is implied that this is well understood. This is misleading. The real science of learning is complex and not at all well understood, particularly when it comes to children. Learning is about a lot more than remembering information that you are told.

A narrow focus on this type of cognitive science has led some (including the UK Department for Education) to advocate direct instruction as the most efficient way for children to be educated. Direct instruction means formal, traditional teaching, where an expert teacher delivers information to children whose job is to retain it and show that they have learnt it at a later date. Proponents vary on how they define "direct instruction" but in some cases teachers are exhorted simply to tell children the information that they want them to learn, and to dissuade them from trying to work things out for themselves or from asking them to form their own guesses (or hypotheses).

Or as the then UK Education Secretary put it in March 2021 in a speech to the Foundation for Education Development (FED): "We know much more now about what works best: evidence-backed, traditional teacher-led lessons with children seated facing the expert at the front of the class are powerful tools for enabling a structured learning environment where everyone flourishes" (Williamson 2021).

Teachers are told that in order to ensure that children learn the information they want them to learn, they must minimise the amount of time taken on activities which are not directly related to learning outcomes. Practical applications of cognitive load theory are about how to do this effectively – by breaking information down into small pieces, for example, and by getting students to regularly answer questions and self-quiz in order to promote retention of the information. Part of the model suggests that thinking skills – including creativity and problem solving – are only possible with a good store of background knowledge, which has to be taught first by direct instruction.

There are many flaws in the model from a developmental psychology perspective – not least the reality that small children lack extensive background knowledge and yet are highly creative problem solvers – but also the way in which the meaning and purpose of what children are learning is not part of the model. From the point of view of these models, it doesn't matter what information the children are learning. Content is irrelevant. Learning can be loaded into children, rather like a memory card. But from the point of view of the child, what information they are learning matters a great deal. The topic they are learning about makes the difference between a day spent bored and a day spent engaged and stimulated. It can be this difference which determines whether they are happy to come into school the next day. There is no space in the cognitive science models for the child's personality and cultural context. They simply weren't designed to address those factors.

Creativity

Creativity is an area where the clash between how children naturally learn and what the cognitive models say they should be doing comes into sharp relief. There is mismatch between what many claim is "evidence based" – that background knowledge is necessary before creative thinking can take place – and what all teachers and parents of young children observe, which is that highly creative thinking is possible without much background knowledge at all.

How come? It comes down to what we mean by "creativity". The research that shows that background knowledge is necessary for creativity are referring to a particular sort of creativity– sometimes called "big C creativity". This means ground-breaking creativity, where you are coming up with original ideas or works of art which no one has had before and which are recognised by others as exceptional. A new mathematical theorem, for example, or Beethoven's 5th Symphony. It's true that to engage in "big C creativity" you need a high level of expert knowledge in a subject. It's unlikely that a novice will come up with a new theory in maths or physics or a truly innovative work of art.

However, most of us (and particularly most children) engage in "little C creativity" which is when you might be making creative and novel discoveries for yourself, but they are not original or ground-breaking for the rest of the world. When children discover through creative exploration that blue and yellow paint mixed together make green and then if you add red you get brown, the discovery is new for them but not for other people. For this type of creativity, extensive background knowledge is not necessary and may in fact inhibit exploration (if you think you know all the colours you can make with paint, you're not going to try new mixtures just to see). Little C creativity is how children learn. They try things out in novel ways and explore their options. They spell things creatively, using what they know of the world. They put things together in ways which are new for them, and in the process they learn and make connections. When we restrict children from little C creativity in the belief that they are not capable of creativity until they become experts, we limit their capacity for learning. Creativity exists on a spectrum, and the skills that children are developing through mixing those paints may help them to become adults who are creative on a different scale. Those who become original innovators did not start their creative careers with "big C creativity" and writing world-class symphonies. They spend years honing their craft first, with little C creativity.

Motivation

There's another problem with applying cognitive science models in schools from a psychological perspective. It is an unavoidable truth that many children do not choose to be at school and they are therefore significantly different to adult learners in terms of their motivation. Adult learners typically choose to be in a class because they want to learn whatever is being taught, and therefore the most important question could be said to be "how can I learn as efficiently as possible?" (to which the answer might be, by using strategies derived from cognitive load theory).

The same cannot be assumed of children at school. The aim of most children at school is not to process information as effectively as possible. Many of them would prefer to be doing something else. The information they are being taught does not necessarily have meaning for them and they have no choice about learning it. They find a lot of school boring and they show this through their behaviour. This means how children feel about their learning is an essential part of a successful model of education. If they don't want to be there, it doesn't matter how well informed about cognitive science the teachers are. Motivation isn't part of cognitive load theory. It is assumed that those who are learning want to do so and therefore the main problem is how to do that learning. This cannot be assumed at school.

Consequently, many schools find that in order to persuade young people to conform, they must control their behaviour to a high degree. There are an increasing number of schools that expect young people to behave in a highly regimented way and punish them with immediate detention escalating to isolation for minor transgressions such as forgetting a pen or the wrong colour socks. They may describe themselves as "no excuses" or "warm-strict" and use scripts for teacher-pupil interactions. Michaela School in West London is an example of a school which has put both cognitive science and high control behaviour policies in practice, you can read their books for detailed descriptions of how it works (Birbalsingh 2016). They get excellent exam results. Joanne Golann's (2021) research provides an balance to the Michaela books. She is an ethnographer who embedded herself in a "no excuses" school in the USA, where she observed many lessons as well as interviewing parents, teachers and young people. She also gives a detailed description of how it works, and of the unintended effects on many of the young people, who she argues are not learning how to work flexibly and be at ease with authority, but instead are learning to follow rigid rules for fear of consequences. She calls the process she observed "hyper regulation of vulnerable students in the name of success".

You might have noticed that cognitive load theory and cognitive developmental psychology conceptualise children and learning very differently. For cognitive psychologists, the drive to learn is an evolutionary necessity and children are always active participants in the process. Learning is driven by children's need to learn about the world and to participate in it. Process is as important as outcome, particularly for younger children. For the cognitive science enthusiasts, learning is a matter of retaining information, and it makes no difference how old a person is. Nor does it matter what they are learning or if that information has meaning or significance for them. The process is the same. The learner is essentially a black box whose interests and desires do not matter.

What's This Got to Do with Attendance and Behaviour?

Enough about child development and different ways to think about learning. What's the point? Why is this relevant to school attendance and behaviour?

It's relevant because it is our argument that most schools were not designed with child development and recent neuroscientific research in mind. As a result, there is a mismatch between what many schools are providing and what many children need in order to flourish, and they communicate this through their behaviour. For some of those children whose psychological needs are not being met in school, this will then show up as attendance difficulties or not attending school at all.

Schools take a particular model of learning – that of acquiring information which is later tested – and design education around that. A "good school" is defined as one where the children get higher test results, and "good teaching" means helping children to retain more information. Over the last 40 years, the amount of testing in English schools has increased significantly, particularly through primary school. Each time a new test is introduced, the pressure for children to do particular things by a certain age increases. The introduction of the "Multiplication table check" in Year 4 (age 8–9), in which children have only six seconds to answer each question, has led to children spending many hours at home practicing doing their times tables at speed, and apps such as *Times Tables Rock Stars* which are specifically designed to train them on this skill. They are ranked against each other, classes are ranked against other classes and even schools can be compared. The pressure not to let your class down can be intense, and some children will feel this pressure more than others, while some, inevitably, will find performing times tables at speed significantly hard than others. This difference is made extremely clear to everyone when children are publicly ranked against each other, with the result that some children learn to think of themselves as less competent due to their performance on a specific measure. We know from research that thinking about themselves as less capable affects children's later academic performance.

One unfortunate result of the increase in testing in primary school is that mastery learning is valued over discovery learning. It is far easier to test. Many educators believe that children must be made to go through the motions of mastery learning when they are young in order to learn how to do it later despite the research not backing this up. The result of this can be six-year-olds spending hours doing mundane tasks, and they start to dislike school. Discovery learning isn't valued as the important developmental stage that it is.

Some educators have noticed this discrepancy between how children learn naturally, and how schools try to teach them, and this has led to the development of what is often called "inquiry learning". This type of education tries to put curiosity and the child's own drive to learn at the centre of their education. However, developing these ideas is hampered by the persistent focus on test results as the most important outcome of education. If the most important outcome is accepted to be test results, then it's unsurprising that educational strategies which prioritise remembering and retaining relevant information for tests are going to come out top.

Children spend a lot of their childhoods in school. Schools focus on academics, and that is what they assess. However, children are learning many things at school apart from academic subjects. They are learning how to think about themselves and how to interact with the world. They are learning where they fit in the social hierarchy and what they can expect from adults.

They learn these things through the way that they are treated in school, not through what they are told in class. The more rigid the system becomes, the larger the number of children who don't fit – and some of those will show us that they are struggling through their behaviour and attendance.

Alison Gopnik, Professor of psychology and philosophy, is blunt about the short-comings of school from a developmental perspective: "in most schools, outside of the gym children not only have limited opportunity for discovery, they also don't get a chance to attain real mastery. Schools aren't institutions that promote discovery, and they aren't centres of apprenticeship, either" (Gopnik 2016, p. 116).

Abigail: It's so common that it's almost a cliché amongst educational psychologists, to be asked to become involved with a six-year-old, summer-born boy, who is causing a great deal of concern. They are often disruptive in class because they talk and move too much, perhaps they are struggling to read or write. Questions are asked about special educational needs. School staff are concerned because at the back of their minds are upcoming national tests, on which they are judged. They are concerned because all six-year-olds are expected to reach the same level. This raises teachers' anxiety levels. They often put more pressure on their class, and they expect them to sit still more. Some children are not ready for this, and they show it in their behaviour. The advice, from a developmental perspective, is always to let them move more, and to let them learn in a multi-sensory way, let them play, explore and discover. But that can be very difficult for schools to implement, as most primary schools don't have the facilities for discovery learning above the early years.

When you think about it like this, then problems with behaviour and attendance in our schools take on a different significance. For if schools are in fact not designed with child development in mind and are in some ways preventing children from learning in the ways that they learn best, then those who have difficulties with school may not be the problem themselves. Perhaps many anxiety and behavioural challenges aren't due to poor parental discipline or a shift in attitudes. Perhaps instead we should see them as the cries of children who know that this is not how they want to spend their childhood, but who have been told that there is no other option. Perhaps difficulties in attendance and behaviour are feedback on the system.

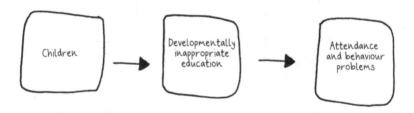

Difference and Diversity

So far we have been talking about child development in broad sweeping terms. We've defined developmental stages by age, and grouped children accordingly. There's a danger in that, and it is that this can lead to the assumption that all children develop in the same way, on the same time scale, and require the same things. Advocates for the "cognitive science" approach will sometimes say that all children learn in the same way, the model applies to everyone and therefore different approaches are not necessary.

In fact, human children are extraordinarily variable. Right from birth, they have very different temperaments and interests, even when born into the same family. Not only are they different, but they develop at different rates. We can see that even in infancy, when some are quickly walking and climbing while others may shuffle on their bottoms for months before taking their first steps. Some talk before they are even one and start with single words, while others wait until they are two or nearly three and go straight to sentences.

These differences are a strength of the human species. Differences within a community mean that that community can adapt to changing circumstances and that different people can specialise in diverse ways. For ourselves, our skills are useful when writing and illustrating a book, but if we had to produce our own food we'd quickly starve. Luckily for us, other people are better at producing food and are willing to sell it to us (or to supermarkets, who will sell it to us). Diversification helps the human race to survive even when some of us do activities like writing books which don't put food on the table.

School, however, has a single, narrow goal for all young people. Good exam results in tests taken at the same age as everyone else. It's the same for everyone, and what this does is turn variability into a problem rather than a strength.

For if schooling isn't well adapted to typical child development, it is even less well adapted to those who are significantly different to the average. Schooling expects children to become capable of particular things when they turn a certain age, and if that doesn't happen, it's a problem. In the UK, five-year-olds are meant to start learning to read, and by the age of seven or eight most are expected to be fluent readers. Eleven-year-olds are meant to be able to organise themselves in a large school environment, moving from classroom to classroom and remembering which books to bring each day. If they can't, then it's a problem.

Many children whose development differs significantly in some way from the average describe becoming acutely aware of this at school, and of feeling that the problem is them. They say that they feel that there is something wrong with them, and that this feeling stays with them into adult life. Hope told me about her own experience of that.

Hope (who prefers the pronouns she/they) is dyslexic and has other additional needs. She was ten when I talked to her and was home educated after becoming increasingly distressed by school. Her parents had found a new school but it didn't help. She told me about how hard she had found school.

> I needed head space and school always felt rushed. I think school is like a theme park, where there's one big long queue for one ride through school. And I think: "Why can't we have loads of different rides at the theme park?" And then everybody gets a shorter queue.

In my school we were learning French. I don't remember any French from school. None of it. So literally, I felt like I wasn't even learning French. We were just doing activity stuff with not really French stuff, but a little bit of French stuff. Like, learn one or two French words, and then next week, the next day, we're on something different. [and I] Hadn't even learnt it yet. I don't even know what it means. I can't even remember what it means.

I need to focus on one word for a month and then I might learn it. Then we can work on another word for the next month, then another word for the next month and carry on, but in months, not in days.

School progressed too fast for Hope. She struggled academically and the result was that she was increasingly unhappy.

When I would wake up, I didn't really want to get dressed. Then after school, I would just get off the bus and I'll just be grumpy because it was like I put all my energy into school, and then when I get home, it's like I'm all cranky and grumpy and I don't want to socialise.

I'll just get in and be too tired and too grumpy and not sociable. I would just go in the front room and just sit on the sofa and watch telly for the rest of the day.

There is no law which says that five-year-olds must be ready to start reading (or spend all day away from their families), nor that nine-year-olds should be able do timed multiplication tests. These requirements have been imposed by the school system. Some children can and do meet them, but a significant proportion can't. And when they can't, then this quickly becomes a problem for them and those around them. Natural variation becomes a matter of shame and anxiety – and once shame and anxiety are introduced into learning, it becomes more difficult. Something which might have simply been a matter of developmental difference – perhaps the child might have been ready to learn to read at eight rather than five – becomes a serious problem, and sometimes turns into something that affects the way that child feels about themselves and their learning in the long term.

What this means is that the more rigid a school system is about what it expects of young people, the more young people will fail to meet the grade, which may have long-term consequences for them.

Life Experience

Children arrive at school with very different experiences behind them. By age five, some children will already have experience of being in care or being fostered, while others will have rarely left their parents. Some will have had had to leave their country of origin due to conflict or hardship and others will have lost a parent or even both. Some will have been removed from parents due to abuse or neglect and some of those will live with kinship carers. Some will have experienced poverty, while it will never have occurred to others that there might not be enough food to eat. Some will be living in unstable housing, or camping out on the floor of a relative or friend while waiting for housing.

These differences are not always obvious, but they make a profound difference to how children are able to engage with what is offered at school. That's not just because of what children have learnt up to this point (life skills or academics), but it's also about what they arrive at school expecting. Research shows that children whose backgrounds have been unstable and unpredictable may learn not to trust adults. They may not be able to wait when an adult tells them to, because they do not believe that adults are reliable.

They may find it hard to form relationships. They will find it difficult to know how to behave appropriately, because stability and consistency has not been part of their experience. They come into the school environment carrying the expectations that they have formed in their life so far, and they approach the world accordingly. This means that their behaviour is often challenging, particularly when managing a large group of children.

These children arrive at school, and they are compared against each other on measures of "school-readiness". Many of them are immediately found wanting. The risk is that these children will be treated as "badly behaved" or "poor attendees" and so their early experience of school confirms what they have learnt so far. They can end up being punished by teachers and ostracised by the other children.

As they progress through their school years, these differences in life experience will only increase. In the UK we dress children up in school uniform in an effort to make economic disparities less visible – and perhaps one side effect of that is that we can forget just how different children's lives are.

These children need reparative experiences of positive relationships with adults, and some schools (some of whom we hear from in Chapter 3A) make a monumental effort to provide this. However, teachers tell us that this can feel at odds with a focus on academic achievement and behaviour. They say that they feel they are swimming against the tide by prioritising emotional safety for those who are not experiencing that at home. They also say that it can be hard to get support for these children in the current system, because they may not fit the boxes for "special educational needs" or fulfil criteria for a diagnosis, and their needs are therefore not well recognised.

Neurodiversity

In the last 20 years, there has been a move towards describing the variation in human development through the lens of neurodiversity. Neurodiversity is a term used to describe the fact that human beings think and learn in different ways, and suggests that this variability does not have to be seen as due to disorder or disease. The term was originally coined in reference to autism, but it has since expanded to include a wide range of differences including ADHD, dyslexia, dyscalculia and dyspraxia.

Neurodiversity is often defined in contrast to the medical model, which does see difference as being due to disorder or disease. The medical model categorises children's behaviour in terms of areas where they are doing significantly less well than others of their age and gives a diagnosis (such as autism or ADHD). The diagnosis gives the impression that we now have a reason for this child's behaviour. In fact, neurodevelopmental diagnoses are descriptions, not explanations. Getting a diagnosis of autism is not the same as getting a diagnosis of Covid-19. With Covid-19, a test has identified that it's the virus which is causing the symptoms. With autism or ADHD, we've simply given a name to a group of behaviours. In particular, the diagnoses of autism and ADHD do not identify neurological differences, despite the term "neuro". Researchers are not able to predict what diagnosis a person has by looking at their brain scan.

For many families, receiving a diagnosis comes as a huge relief. It feels to them like this means that a reason has been found, and that it is clear now that it is not their fault or their child's fault.

Luke (15) told Naomi what that was like for him:

> *The [autism] diagnosis was a relief, really. Some people don't feel good about being autistic, but actually, I felt like it's just a part of me that was there all along. I just instantly accepted it. It's different with other people. It's sometimes different because sometimes they start to think there's something wrong with them when they get the diagnosis.*
>
> *Sometimes when I was being more depressed, when I feel a bit more depressed, I sometimes feel like, "Why can't I be like people who just go to school, normal people?" That's sometimes a thought, but it passes, really.*

Neurodiversity is dimensional – it refers to everyone. We all vary from each other in thousands of different ways and many of these differences are small. If a person is far from the average in ways which makes their life more difficult, then they are sometimes called "neurodivergent". With children, in particular, someone might be far from the average at one point in their life, but then as they grow up this changes. A child who struggles to learn to read can become a teenager who can't stop reading – and an adult who writes a book. Great change can happen long as they get the opportunity to learn and they don't start to think about themselves as someone who can't (and never will) read.

Many neurodivergent children have what is called a "spiky cognitive profile" which originally meant that when tested on a set of tests, the results of the different tests were not consistently on the same percentile. They might have a very high score on expressive language, but be below average in language comprehension, for example. They might be exceptional when it comes to problem solving, but have very slow processing times. The concept of a spiky profile has been extended beyond cognitive testing to refer more generally to children who may be above average at some things while being significantly below average on other things.

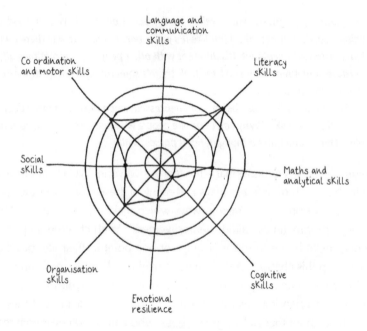

When someone has a spiky cognitive profile, then school can be particularly difficult for them. They may appear to understand more than they really do, and it might be assumed that they are just not trying hard enough. This can particularly be a problem when it's non-academic skills which are lagging behind. A child may be capable academically, but have the emotion regulation or self-management skills of a much younger child. This can mean that their school work is fine, but they are struggling with the non-academic aspects of school such as the playground, managing their emotions or getting from class to class. These children are often those who schools will say are fine, but who are highly distressed and angry outside school. This can be frustrating for parents who feel blamed for their child's behaviour.

Table 2.2 Some Ways in Which Children Can Differ

Sensory	Some children experience the information from their senses in a different way. They may find noises too loud, lights too bright, textures too rough, tastes and smells too intense and try to avoid them. Alternatively, they may experience sensory information as not stimulating enough and will seek more sensory stimulation. Children with these differences may put their hands over their ears or may complain that the dining hall smells disgusting. They may avoid the school toilets altogether which can cause problems. They may find wearing school uniform distressing as the texture hurts their skin.
Social	Some children's social interactions are different to the average for their peer group. They may dislike large groups, or they may find reciprocal relationships challenging. They may still prefer to play like a younger child or have interests which are typically associated with younger children. They may be picked out or bullied by their peers. Social cognition is highly complex and can include things like - The understanding that other people have thoughts and feelings. - Understanding of intentionality (whether something was done on purpose or is an accident). - Being able to take the perspective of others who are not like yourself. Social differences can particularly be difficult in unstructured situations such as the playground. These children can sometimes be ostracised by their class and are vulnerable to bullying.
Executive Functioning	Some children's self-management skills are significantly different to the average for their age group. This can include: - Setting goals - Planning - Sequencing - Managing transitions - Controlling impulses (e.g. to hit someone else if you are angry) - Paying attention and ignoring distractions - Working memory

(Continued)

Table 2.2 (Continued)

	Executive functioning differences can particularly cause a problem in the transition to secondary school, where the executive function demands increase significantly, or at other points in the school system when more is demanded of children.
Communication	Some children have differences in spoken language which can be both receptive (understanding) and expressive (producing language and communication). Some children will communicate in non-verbal ways. Some will appear to understand what is being said to them but will have differences in comprehension. These children may take things literally and find metaphor confusing.
Academic	Some children find acquiring reading and writing significantly more difficult than other children while others acquire these skills exceptionally early. Others find maths particularly difficult and struggle with basic number concept for longer than others. The English school system is particularly inflexible when it comes to age of acquiring reading, despite this being something that different countries have different expectations for. Reading problems will often be identified early on, but some children continue to struggle into secondary school.
Emotional Regulation	The ability to regulate your emotions effectively is one that all children are in the process of acquiring and which is highly variable throughout development. Those who have differences in emotional regulation may get easily distressed or angry and will struggle to bring themselves back to equilibrium when unexpected challenges occur. Emotional regulation differences can manifest themselves in disruptive behaviour, meltdowns or responding to teachers and peers in an angry or aggressive way. This can go rapidly wrong if the response of adults is to be harsh or punitive, as this makes it even harder for the child to regulate their emotions.
Demand Avoidance	Some children find the demands of daily life anxiety-provoking and they respond to this by avoidance. This can particularly be a problem in school when children find instructions and commands anxiety-provoking. Demand avoidance can vary across settings and over time. Demand avoidance can look like disruptive behaviour, distraction, trying to escape from school, going into role play (sometimes seen as "being silly" by adults), complete withdrawal and lack of responsiveness.

When School Meets Child

There are many ways in which a child's development can vary in a way which makes school more challenging for them. Table 2.2 lists some of the ways in which children can invisibly differ from the average in a way which may cause problems. It is not comprehensive.

Neurodiversity is not the same as either distress or disability. It simply describes variation. However, when a child meets an environment with expectations that they can't meet – and particularly when they are blamed for that – then differences can become disabilities, and cause distress. Imagine a six-year-old child who can't yet read. If they are in a setting where reading is not yet expected (for example, a school in Denmark or Finland, or a Steiner Kindergarten), then they will not be considered to be behind and will not see themselves in that way. Nor will the adults around them. If, however, they are in an English primary school, they will be expected to take the Phonics Screening Check and if they fail, this will be flagged up as a problem. This will affect the way that they learn to think about themselves and the way that others think about them. Their parents will worry that perhaps they are behind or they might have a serious problem with reading.

Naomi has even met English parents whose children are at primary school in another country (where reading isn't taught so young) who have expressed concern that they know that their children would fail the Phonics Screening Check. There's no intrinsic reason why six-year-olds should be able to do phonics, particularly if they haven't been taught them, but by introducing the screening check, it has become a focus of anxiety for parents.

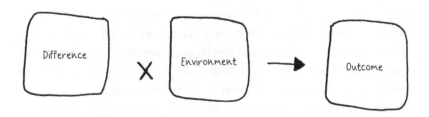

Diagnoses and Neuro-affirmative Practice

In recent years there has been a rapid change in how we talk about neurodevelopmental differences. This shift away from deficit and impairment-laden language is a welcome one. Many professionals now describe themselves as "neuro-affirmative". This is a term that means different things to different people. For some, it simply means using language which avoids terms like "deficit" and "impairment" and not defining some children as "disordered" because they differ significantly from the average. For others, it means something far wider which includes accepting self-diagnosis as equal status to a formal diagnosis (e.g., if they think they are autistic, then they are, or if their parent think they are autistic, then they are), privileging lived experience over other forms of knowledge and seeing all of a person's differences (sometimes including mental health problems such as bipolar depression or obsessive compulsive disorder) as caused by innate brain differences, rather than as something which might change or the person might want to change.

For others, neuro-affirmation is a world view which positions those with neurodevelopmental differences as oppressed, while those who are closer to the average are the oppressors. This often goes along with seeing "autistic" or "neurodivergent" as an identity and culture rather than as a descriptive term. When you use the term "neuro-affirmative", you can't tell how it will be understood by others.

Neuro-affirmative practice starts with great intentions. People wanted to move away from defining the world in terms of the "disordered" and the "normal", and to stop pathologising people because of their differences.

However, as this develops there are some concerns about the effect that too much focus on being "neuro-affirmative" can have. Part of this is that it can inadvertently be used to locate the problems in the child rather than the environment. The term "neuro" is now widely used when describing differences, in terms such as "neurotype", "neurodivergent" and "neurotypical". The prefix "neuro" is understood by the general public to mean that something has been identified as different in the way that a person's brain works, whereas in fact a neurodevelopmental assessment is entirely behavioural and there are no biological tests for neurodevelopmental conditions. There are many reasons why a person might behave in the way that they do, and focusing in on the brain can lead us away from looking at the environmental reasons.

The problem with this narrative is that many parents think that a neurodevelopmental diagnosis means that a child's difficulties are immutable, as they think that the differences being located in their brain means that it is "hard-wired". This closes off the possibility of change. Naomi has been told by parents that since their child has "a nervous system disability" (by which they meant autism) they do not expect that their anxiety will reduce and that it's just part of who they are. Autism as currently diagnosed is not a nervous system disability. There are no tests of the nervous system in the diagnostic process and no reliable differences have been found between the nervous systems of those who are autistic and those who are not. Autism is a diagnosis based on behaviours that do not map well onto specific neurology or nervous system differences.

The other problem with professionals declaring themselves to be neuro-affirmative is that a significant number of young people who have school distress do not meet criteria for a neurodevelopmental diagnosis. They tell us that they feel excluded by the focus on those who do. In the last ten years it has become increasingly common for the parents of a young person who is having trouble at school to either be referred or to self-refer for a neurodevelopmental diagnosis, usually either autism or ADHD, and this diagnosis is often used as a gateway to decide who gets extra support in schools and who doesn't. It also often means that these families are able to access disability benefits. This creates extremely high anxiety about diagnosis, with many parents and young people expressing great relief when they do get one (and high levels of distress when they don't).

In this context, it's unsurprising that numbers of people seeking diagnosis have soared, with research suggesting that there was an increase in autism diagnosis in the UK of 787% between 1998–2018 (Russell 2021). For many, a neurodevelopmental diagnosis has become the only way to get access to support services.

This has gone along with great positivity about neurodevelopmental diagnoses, which is a welcome change, but also has a flipside. Some diagnostic clinics now send very positive letters and offer post-diagnostic support to those who reach diagnostic criteria, congratulating them on being part of the neurodivergent community – but there is no equivalent for those who do not meet the threshold. They are still struggling, but they are not welcomed into a community, will not be able to access support and are not offered any sort of explanation for their difficulties. This can be particularly difficult for those whose children have developmental trauma, are adopted or fostered or have foetal alcohol spectrum disorder (FASD). They tell us that they feel their challenges are not recognised or supported unless they get a neurodevelopmental diagnosis.

Much of this change has been driven by late-diagnosed adults, and their experience is different to children and families. Many of those who were diagnosed as adults found receiving their diagnoses to be a positive moment in their lives. They often feel that if only they had been diagnosed as children, their whole lives would have been different. However, this isn't the story we hear from those who are diagnosed as children. They rarely say that their life improved from that point. Their relationship with their diagnosis

When School Meets Child

is different. It was usually something which was sought by their parents or school, rather than by they themselves, and they sometimes say that it separated them from their peers and made them a target. For some, it made them feel more different, rather than being a relief. It may have led to their being excluded or subject to interventions which they did not want. Naomi has worked with teenagers who want to get their autism diagnosis removed from their medical record, and who find that it is impossible to do so. It is a lifelong diagnosis.

A final concern about the term "neuro-affirming" (and "neurodiversity") is that it excludes some families. Some parents feel very strongly that their children's difficulties are a disorder, not a difference or an identity, and some autistic adults feel the same about themselves. This is particularly likely to be the case for those who have significant learning disabilities as well as being autistic. These people feel that their voices are not being heard by the neurodiversity movement, and that the needs of their children are being overlooked in the desire to focus on strengths. They, for example, say that they need functioning labels (something which many advocates for neurodiversity eschew), because otherwise it is obscured that the majority of autistic spokespeople are relatively capable and independent, while the voices of those with severe learning disabilities and their families are less commonly heard.

These families will self-exclude from a service which is explicit about taking a neuro-affirmative or neurodiversity informed approach. They will assume it's not for them. In order to be truly inclusive, we need to welcome all these perspectives and not have preset ideas about how a person should relate to their diagnosis.

For all of these reasons, we think it is more important to be needs-based and child-centred rather than diagnosis based, and to remain curious about the reasons for behaviour. Even when a child does have a diagnosis, we need to bear in mind that this is a description rather than an explanation and make it clear to families that a diagnosis does not mean they can't learn new skills and that they won't change as they grow up.

Each person will relate to a diagnosis (or lack of diagnosis) in their own way, and professionals need to hold the space for that to be both positive and negative. Not everyone sees their diagnosis is an important part of their identity and if professionals insist that they should, then that is not a person-centred approach.

Special Educational Needs and Disability (SEND) or Additional Support Needs (ASN)

A growing number of children in the UK are being identified with special educational needs and disability (SEND), additional support needs (ASN, the term used in Scotland) or additional learning needs (ALN, the term used in Wales). These are umbrella terms which essentially say that mainstream school is not working well for this child. Many children identified with SEND will have a diagnosis, but others will not. Some will have physical disabilities while others may have been identified as anxious or having other mental health problems. Some will have genetic differences such as Down Syndrome which will be identified early on, while others will have difficulties that do not emerge until they are much older.

The most recent statistics from England show that over 1.5 million children in England have been identified as having some sort of SEN in the academic year 2022/2023, and that there has been an increase of 87,000 on the year before: 17.3 % of English children were identified as having some sort of SEN, and 4.3% got an EHCP. In a group of 30 children, this represents about six children identified with SEN, 1–2 of whom will have EHCPs. Numbers in Wales are similar. In Scotland the numbers are higher, with the Scottish government reporting that 34% of Scottish children were recorded as having a ASN in 2022.

There has been a general trend of increase since 2016 (Statistics 2023). When they looked at those who got an Education and Health Care Plan (EHCP) in England, there has been an increase of 64% since 2016, from 2.8% to 4.3% of pupils.

This represents a significant proportion of the school-aged population. Why are more children being identified with SEND? Can it really be the case that so many more children have special needs in Scotland than in England and Wales? The SEND classification system is example of locating problems in children – children are often described as "having SEND" as if this represents something immutable about them.

This will be the case for some, but there are reasons to think that this cannot account for the whole picture. Researchers at the London School of Economics (LSE) have looked at who is identified as "having SEND" and they have found that there are certain immutable factors which raise a child's chances of being identified and these aren't necessarily what you would expect. Being a summer-born boy, for example, means that a child has a 40% chance of being identified as having SEND by their primary school, and only 39% of those summer-born boys were said to have a "good level of development" at the end of reception, as compared to 80% of autumn-born girls (Campbell 2022). English schools test children at the end of Year 1 with a Phonics Screening Check, and only 64% of summer-born boys met the expected standard, while 84% of summer-born girls reached the same level. In England, the year you go into at school is determined by your birthday, with a year group being defined as those born between 1 September–31 August. The summer-born children are therefore the youngest in their year. They are starting school earlier, and they are being tested when they are younger.

It's not really plausible that being a summer-born male means you are more likely to have immutable difficulties in learning. It's more likely that this is a result of young children who are being subjected to a system filled with expectations which they are not yet ready to meet. Dr Campbell, a professor at LSE's Centre for Analysis of Social Exclusion, argues that an inflexible and developmentally inappropriate system sorts children into "good" and "deficient" very early on, and children then carry this with them through school.

How can this be? SEND is often defined as not meeting expectations at school. If those expectations are developmentally inappropriate, then an increasing number of children will fail to meet them, and will be identified as "having SEND". Imagine if we decided that all two-year-olds should

What Can We Do When School's Not Working?

learn to read and then tested them on phonics. We could then decide that any two-year-old who hadn't learnt had SEND. We would very quickly identify lots of two-year-olds "with SEND". That situation would have been entirely created by the unrealistic expectations that they should learn to read.

It's easy to see how inappropriate that is for two-year-olds, but the situation is similar when we expect immature four- and five-year-olds to enter school and to follow a formal curriculum when they are still discovery learners. They lack the basic skills necessary, and that isn't because they needed to be prepared for school better by their parents. It's because they are young and they learn through play rather than formal learning. They are not deficient adults; their brains work in a different way and have different strengths and weaknesses. If the system doesn't accommodate this, then it's no surprise when many of them struggle and become distressed.

It's our argument in this book that when a rigid system meets variable children, distress – shown by problems in behaviour and attendance – can be the result. The system isn't meeting their needs. Their distress can be seen as feedback on the system – and in order to address what they are telling us, we need to think about how to organise education so that school meets their psychological and developmental, as well as their academic needs. How do we do that? That's where the next chapter starts.

Summary

- Children's brains change dramatically as they grow from early childhood to adolescence.
- These brain differences affect how they learn, with younger children being discovery learnings and the skills needed for mastery learning only maturing later.
- Child development is highly variable and problems can result when a rigid education system is not able to adapt to this.
- Neurodiversity and neuro-affirming practice are terms which are being increasingly used by services but they may exclude some who do not agree with these perspectives.
- The number of children diagnosed with special educational needs is increasing year on year in the UK, and there are reasons to believe that this is not simply due to better identification.
- Behaviour and attendance problems can be seen as the result of an interaction between a child and a system which cannot adapt to their needs and developmental stage.

References and Further Reading

Birbalsingh, K. (2016). *The Battle Hymn of the Tiger Teachers: The Michaela Way*. London: John Catt Educational Ltd.

Blakemore, S.-J. (2019). *Inventing Ourselves: The Secret Life of the Teenage Brain*. London: Transworld Publishers.

Campbell, T. (2022). Relative age and the Early Years Foundation Stage Profile: How do birth month and peer group age composition determine attribution of a "Good Level of Development" – and what does this tell us about how "good"the Early Years Foundation Stage Profile is? *British Educational Research Journal* 48(2): 371–401.

Golann, J. W. (2021). *Scripting the Moves: Culture and Control in a "No Excuses" Charter School*. Princeton: Princeton University Press

Gopnik, A. (2016). *The Gardener and the Carpenter: What the New Science of Child Development Tells Us about the Relationship Between Parents and Children*. London: Bodley Head.

Lovell, O. (2020). *Sweller's Cognitive Load Theory in Action*. London: John Catt Educational Ltd.

Rogoff, B. (2003). *The Cultural Nature of Human Development*. Oxford: Oxford University Press.

Russell, G. (2021). T*he Rise of Autism: Risk and Resistance in the Age of Diagnosis*. Oxford: Routledge.

Statistics, O. f. N. (2023). *Special Educational Needs in England*. England, UK.

Sweller, J. (1988), Cognitive Load During Problem Solving: Effects on Learning. *Cognitive Science*, 12: 257–285. https://doi.org/10.1207/s15516709cog1202_4

Williamson, G., Department For Education (2021). Education Secretary speech to FED National Education Summit.

3

Creating Psychologically Healthy School Environments

> In this chapter you will find:
>
> 1. We Just Want to Teach
> 2. What Works in Education
> 3. Psychological Needs
> 4. Prioritising Psychological Health in School
> 5. What Can You Do, Right Now?

Introduction

This chapter sets out some of the key principles of this book. It will discuss the purpose of schools and education and will suggest that young people are learning very important things while they are growing up which are not well captured by the school curriculum and can't be measured by exams. These things can influence the whole path of their future lives. They are learning how to think and reflect on themselves and the world – metacognition. And how to manage their emotions and behaviour – self-regulation.

These things are not learnt through being told about them. We cannot instruct young people in metacognition and self-regulation and expect them to change. They are learnt through experience and practice. Young people learn about themselves and the world around them by the way in which they are treated and how their schools operate, and they learn self-regulation through seeing how other people do it, and through practice. Not practise of being controlled, but practise of making choices and decisions for themselves. Even if those decisions aren't what adults would have chosen for them.

This is what we mean by a "psychologically healthy" school. These are places where educators are thinking about what children are learning about themselves and their place in the world, through the way in which the school environment functions. They are intentionally designing the environment so that children feel safe and valued. The things which children learn implicitly at school are sometimes called the "hidden curriculum" (Gatto 1992). When that "hidden curriculum" leads to young people learning negative things about themselves, or not having the space to develop as individuals, then our argument is that this shows up in problems with attendance and behaviour.

In this chapter, we'll show you through the voices of young people how they felt about the way in which they were treated at school and we'll ask what school is really for. We'll then show you some of the ways in which schools have tried to meet the psychological needs of their pupils, and give you some ideas which could be implemented in a classroom at no cost.

This chapter has an annexe – Chapter 3A. In it you'll find three case studies. These are of schools – infant, primary and secondary – who have set out to change the "hidden curriculum" and to focus on relationships and inclusion. They are written by teachers and head teachers, and they explain the often difficult and bumpy process of change.

We Just Want to Teach

What is school and education actually for? Is it for children to acquire the knowledge that they will need to pass tests, with teachers' role being the expert holders of specialist knowledge to be passed on? Or is it childcare, in place so that parents can work knowing that their children are safe? Should school aim to be engaging and interesting, or does that not matter? Why do we require children to attend school for so many hours, and does every minute really count?

Many teachers will say that school is for learning the curriculum, and will sometimes say that they "just want to teach". They are deeply frustrated by the amount of time that isn't spent doing that, particularly the amount of time they have to spend on behaviour management. Some schools believe that "real learning" is only happening where there is a formal transfer of information going on, and so structure their timetables to maximise instructional time and minimise anything else. Time in front of a teacher (and listening to that teacher) is valued over anything else that a child might do.

Children and young people spend the majority of their waking time in school for their entire childhoods. In that time, they grow from four-year-olds, learning basic living skills, to near adults, leaving for the world of work or further study. They go through huge developmental changes. It's a period when they are learning how to be in the world. They are learning how to interact with others, how to think about themselves and are acquiring expectations about how other people will react to them. They are always learning much more than the content of the formal curriculum, and part of how they are learning that is through the way that teachers interact with and respond to them.

The hidden curriculum isn't written down. Children learn it through the way that the school operates and how they are treated. The hidden curriculum includes things like learning that your role is to keep quiet and listen, or that the teacher holds the ultimate power to judge your work (and therefore that you are dependent on their approval). The hidden curriculum is what children learn about learning and about their own capabilities and place in the world. When someone says "I'm no good at learning" they've usually learnt that at school even though no one intended to teach it to them. When a child learns that there's no point in speaking up about bullying or injustice because what they think it doesn't matter, that's the hidden curriculum.

The hidden curriculum is learnt through relationships, both between pupils and teachers and between pupils themselves. There is no way to avoid this. Young people are always learning about themselves through their school experiences, even if their teachers only intend to teach them History or French. And because school takes up so many hours and is so culturally significant, school is a crucial influence in young people's psychological development. Do well at school and feel liked by your teachers, and you learn to think about yourself as a worthwhile person. Do badly and feel disliked, and you may think about yourself as a loser for years afterwards.

Joanne Golann's book *Scripting the Moves* documents her research into the hidden curriculum at a "no excuses" school in the United States. She raises concerns about how the structure and systems in the school led to children (the majority of whom were Black or Latino and who came from economically deprived background) implicitly learning that their voices didn't matter, and that they should defer to authority in all cases.

What Works

There's currently a lot of talking about "what works" in education. This usually means "gets the outcomes that we want". Those outcomes are typically defined as good test results, and behaviour which makes the school easier to run (so that the test scores go up). Compliance with the school system, in other words. Educational research often uses these as outcome measures. Test scores go up and it's assumed that this is a "good school". No matter what else is going on.

What is less often discussed are the other effects of "what works". For it's possible for something to have a positive effect in one area, while causing problems elsewhere. Side effects, as Yong Zhao (Professor of education at the universities of both Kansas and Melbourne) calls them (Zhao 2018).

Side effects are a recognised problem in healthcare. Any treatment, no matter how beneficial it might be, can have unwanted and serious side effects, and those side effects can be too severe for the treatment to continue to be used. Side effects are often not obvious and do not apply to everyone. Some only emerge when a drug is being used in the general population. For this reason, there is a Yellow Card system in the UK where doctors can flag up potential problems they are hearing about from their patients. A side effect will frequently not affect everyone.

There is no equivalent Yellow Card system for education. There's rarely any acknowledgement that what happens in schools can, in some situations,

have adverse effects for some young people. There is no formal or informal way for young people, parents or health professionals to flag up side effects when new policies or programmes are introduced in a school.

The accounts from parents and the young people that we work with suggest there are significant side effects to some parts of the education system which are often dismissed. For example, the focus on "what works" to improve test results has led to increasingly controlling approaches to behaviour in many UK schools, with an increasing number of schools using quickly escalating systems of demerits or "behaviour points" for minor transgressions alongside frequent use of detentions and isolation. This approach is sometimes called "no excuses" or "warm-strict", a topic we introduced in Chapter 2. One element of this is immediate and escalating sanctions for minor transgressions, often to do with uniform and equipment. The philosophy is that if schools keep tight control of the small details, then they will be able to spend less time worrying about the bigger things.

The young people that we talk to report that one side effect of these policies is increased levels of distress and anxiety which can then lead to attendance problems. Below, you'll hear from some young people about the impact of these systems.

The Side Effects of School

Emily, who had just had her 15th birthday when Naomi talked to her, told us about the impact of school on her. She was increasingly unhappy at school through Year 7 and 8 (aged 11–13), and started to struggle to attend in Year 9 (age 13–14). When Naomi talked to her, she had recently decided that she would not be returning to school, something her whole family were adjusting to.

> *I was never naughty in school. I never misbehaved. It really mattered to me what everyone thought of me, and that included the teachers. Then, when I went from being this person who was really good and achieved well in lessons and was really well-behaved in school to someone who didn't want to be there at all, everyone was like, "Well, we can get you back to this person that you were." I was like, "No, you can't."*
>
> *I was that person for a very long time, but I wasn't happy. I would go into school, and I'd be scared of, like "Oh, what if I lose my tie?" You get these things in*

school called C-points, which are behaviour points for when you've done something bad. You can get one if you've just forgotten your pencil. So every morning would be like, do I have literally everything that I could possibly need? Do I have five spare pencils?

In Year 7, I went through a whole year of not getting a single behaviour point. We had these clip-on ties. If you don't put it on tight enough, it can just fall off, and you can get a behaviour point for that. I was just so stressed the entire time. Then at the start of year nine, I was like, "Do I really have to do this again?"

Year 7 and Year 8, I was really worried about getting a C-point. I tried really hard in lessons because I wanted to be good at my work. I wanted to be at the top of the class.

Halfway through Year 8, I got a C-point because my biro had broken, and I didn't bring a spare one in. You get a C-point for that.

So I got it. At the end of the day, it was such a relief. All it does is you get a little red circle with a one in it next to your picture on the whiteboard. You don't get any other consequences. You stay in the lesson. It was actually such a relief when I finally got one because I've been so worried about it.

It was at the start of the lesson when they did the register, they would have all the names up on the board, and it would tell you how many R-points, which are the good points, and how many C-points you had. Then everyone would be able to see that and that bothered me as well. They were trying to scare us with it.

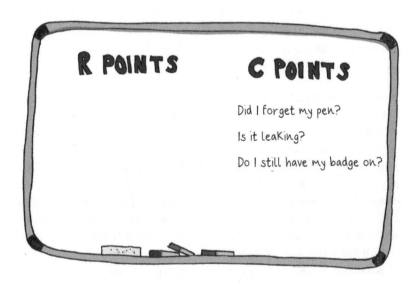

If you got two C-points in one day, you had a detention, and three, you went into isolation. That's in one day. But you got C-points for things that could be accidents.

If your pen broke, and you'd forgotten to pack an extra, or you'd given your spare one to one of your friends and your pen breaks, then you get a C-point, and then later in the day, you lose your tie because it just fell off. Then you would be in detention.

It was like everything you did, you had to be careful about. You'd spend your whole day checking, do I have my tie or do I have my little badge on still? Do I have all my pencils and my pens?

Emily felt that returning to school would not represent healing or moving forwards for her, as she associated the school environment with high anxiety and stress and did not think that this could be mitigated. After a year of efforts at re-integration, she had stopped attending altogether.

These systems aren't just in secondary school. We talk to primary school aged children who also describe systems which created high distress. Rose was eight when Naomi talked to her and her mother Rachel. She had recently moved school. She told me about the behaviour system in her old school.

Although she was only aged seven when she was at that school, she was acutely aware of the way that the system worked and the impact it had.

Her mother told Naomi how preoccupied Rose had become by the house point system. Points were awarded every day, meaning that if she was ill for a day, she would get no house points and would probably not make her target for the week. Her mother saw this system as something which had directly led to Rose's difficulties, which had culminated in her not attending that school at all.

Rose told us how it worked.

> If you did well in a lesson, or you were kind to somebody, then you got a house point. At the end of the week they emptied them out. They put up a tally on the wall. They highlighted where you got and you could see what everyone else got. And they changed the paper every week. You started again on Monday.
>
> It made me feel sad. Really pressured, because if you were ill, then you miss getting house points. The kids who didn't get house points, they didn't get the prize. In assembly, they announced who got them, and they took them out to collect their prize. They'd announce who'd got the 15 house points every week. You would be worried because if you got 15, you would be worried that they wouldn't announce it, or you'd feel sad because you hadn't got your 15.
>
> Sometimes they forgot. Once one of my friends got 25 house points in one of the weeks. They didn't announce it in assembly, and he didn't get his prize or anything.
>
> He was really sad.
>
> When kids didn't behave, sometimes they got sent to the head, and sometimes they had to miss playtime. Sometimes the teachers threatened that they would take away house points.
>
> That was for the whole class not just one person.
>
> They didn't actually do it, but it was scary knowing that they could.

Both Emily and Rose stopped attending their schools, Emily to be home-educated and Rose to go to another school. They (and their parents) make a direct connection between their experiences with school behavioural systems and their struggles with attendance. They were well-behaved children who became highly anxious about making mistakes and the consequences of this.

Psychological Needs

There is a robust body of research accumulated over the last 60 years which shows that when people feel controlled and lacking in meaningful choices about their lives, their internal drive to learn decreases. This is called self-determination theory (Ryan 2000)

Self-determination theory is a theory of motivation – it seeks to explain why humans behave as they do. But it's more than that, because it is also a theory of psychological flourishing. It is a series of conditions which set out what humans need in order to feel psychologically fulfilled and to thrive. Deci and Ryan suggest that there are three basic psychological needs which all humans have, and if these are not fulfilled, then the result will be disengagement, poor motivation and, ultimately, poor quality learning. If you want to understand this theory in detail, I suggest reading *Drive* by Daniel Pink, or *Punished by Rewards* by Alfie Kohn.

Those three psychological needs are autonomy, connection and competence.

Autonomy: the human need to perceive that we have choices and options within boundaries. A sense of control that we are the source of our actions.

Connection (or relatedness): the need to feel a sense of belonging and genuine connection to others and to contribute to something greater than ourselves.

Competence: the need to feel that we can be effective, that we can learn and to feel a sense of possibility and growth.

Some aspects of school environments can work against these principles. Many schools introduce systems where children are rewarded for desired behaviour and sanctioned for undesirable behaviour. Children are given *Star of the Week*

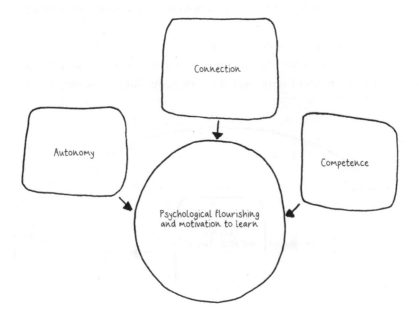

certificates for things like "Being helpful when clearing up". Unfortunately the research shows that these systems change how children feel about their behaviour. Previously, they may have been helpful because they wanted to be involved and that was its own reward. Adding a certificate changes the situation. No longer are they being helpful just because they want to, because now the behaviour is for an extrinsic reason – awards. The adult has taken control and the child has lost some autonomy. Over time, the research shows that adding extrinsic motivation will undermine their intrinsic motivation. They will have less desire to be helpful when the certificates stop coming.

This is the opposite to what most adults think. Most of us think that adding rewards will incentivise children to do better, and don't realise that there is a downside. Children like rewards, and so it can seem like positive reinforcement is a win-win.

With the best possible intentions, many schools remove autonomy from young people. Unfortunately the research indicates that this will lead to poorer quality motivation. We can make children go through the motions of learning and behaving, but we cannot make them want to learn or behave. Short-term improvement in test results may have a long-term impact on motivation to learn.

Self-determination theory predicts that an increased focus on controlling behaviour and learning in schools will lead to young people who are increasingly uninterested in learning and behaving. The way that this would show itself will be in problems with engagement with learning, behaviour and attendance, which will lead to young people being blamed and punished – which will make the problem worse.

This means that while high control techniques may lead to higher scores in exams, they can have negative side effects which can last a lifetime. They prioritise the short term over the long term. And for some children,

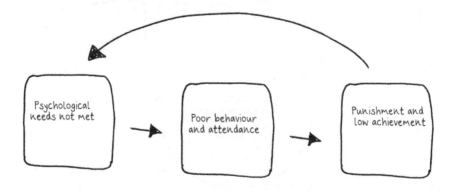

Creating Psychologically Healthy School Environments

they can lead to exactly the behaviour and attendance problems which schools want to avoid.

The good news is that it doesn't have to be this way. Many schools bring in high control strategies without appreciating what the research shows that this will do to their pupils' motivation, but there are schools and individuals who have deliberately chosen to take a different approach. They prioritise psychological flourishing, and see this as central to what a good education should be. Three examples in mainstream schools are given in Chapter 3A.

Prioritising Psychological Needs in School

There are many different ways in which a school can prioritise psychological needs, from a whole-school approach to changes that an individual teacher can make. Here are examples of interventions to prioritise psychological needs in school, and some ideas which might help you to think about what that looks like in a classroom.

Seeing Themselves as Active Decision Makers

Shared decision making with pupils can increase their sense of being part of their school community, and helps them to see themselves as active decision makers. Many teachers do this with their classes.

What Can We Do When School's Not Working?

Dr Geraldine Rowe, educational psychologist, describes some ways in which teachers do this in her book *It's Our School, It's Our Time*. Her research focused on collaborative decision making (CDM) in mainstream schools. She describes CDM as a process when teachers and pupils collaborate on making decisions which affect either their class or the whole school. She describes how CDM positions decision making as part of the curriculum and how decision making becomes a skill to practice.

Her approach can be used by an individual teacher in an otherwise traditional-minded school. Her research found that pupils are very accepting of a "mixed economy", meaning that you don't have to do it all the time. Pupils can be involved with the teacher (and Rowe is clear that collaboration does not means that the teacher has no voice) in making decisions about anything to do with their school, including their curriculum, behaviour, learning and use of time. More than a school council, or one-off consultations, the mechanisms can vary from using class meetings to discuss issues, to using whole class impromptu problem solving, informal plenaries or delegated pupil decision makers.

Rowe argues that children need to have more control over their life in school, and to be given the chance to make decisions, particularly children who are not having those experiences elsewhere. She argues that CDM not only improves learning, behaviour, wellbeing and relationships but that it also teaches pupils how to make decisions with other people. It creates space in the classroom for children's own skills, motivation and knowledge to be used. Working in this way builds trust and relationships in the classroom, both with the teacher but also between pupils. Pupils came up with ideas and solutions the teacher would not have, demonstrating skills and motivation which surprised staff.

The examples in Rowe's research led to visible increases in young people's confidence and show their thoughtful responses to being given more autonomy. Very young children asked to be able to pour their own water at lunch and to serve their friends, and suggested using teapots rather than jugs to do so, as they felt able to pour well with these. Other examples involve pupils coming up with innovative solutions to resolve problems such as muddy changing-room floors and classroom noise levels. Because the class understand the problem and have generated the ideas, they are then more invested in the solution. Rowe doesn't shy away from the challenges of CDM, and also shares stories of staff using CDM which don't go to plan, and discusses how to handle tricky situations.

Rowe describes a secondary school maths teacher with a mixed ability class of 12-year-olds. The teacher established a collaborative class culture where pupils helping each other was encouraged and supported. They began working in groups, writing maths books for each other, explaining key concepts and then they taught the whole class using their material. The teacher was surprised by the pupils' ability to select appropriate tasks for themselves, and she found their attitude and motivation for writing changed – they were writing for themselves and using writing as a tool, rather than writing for the teacher. They also covered the curriculum at the same speed as the other classes who were not using these methods.

Creating Opportunities to Speak and Be Heard

How can schools practically enable their young people to feel that they have a voice? Finding My Voice is a whole school approach to cultural and curricular change grounded in self-determination theory. Using a phased approach, the project starts with a course for senior leaders, followed by wider staff training, and ongoing access to curricular resources. Through a focus on relatedness and oracy (spoken language), the approach supports the integration of academics with personal development work and emphasises the need for staff as well as student development.

Abigail met with Rachel Higginson, a qualified headteacher who has been working in education for 26 years. She explained how it works.

> *Teaching and learning is personal development. Everything we do is shaping young people. What tends to happen, particularly in secondary is that we separate the academics from the pastoral and personal development.*
>
> *Currently in our education system, we need to work on relatedness. In school students get the sense that they're cared for but they don't get a sense of their personal value that they bring to a space. I use the analogy that I take food to the homeless person who sits outside the station. Every day we have a chat, and I give them some food. That's great, but I'm not building that person's sense of value. If I say, things are quite tricky in my life, the way you smile makes a big difference to me, that gives them value in the relationship. It has to be authentic, but you're making a shift from relationship to relatedness.*
>
> *There are two key strands – relatedness and oracy. The key tenets of the project are belonging as who you are, equitable status for all, and a culture of "deep talk" and dialogic approaches which go across all aspects of school life. Research shows that when kids talk more, all of their outcomes improve, academic and life. This isn't a fluffy thing; this is something that has rich research behind it that makes a big difference in life chances.*
>
> *We work on a shift into a relational culture. All primary interactions with young people should be about who they are. Rewarding someone for sitting quietly isn't a*

Creating Psychologically Healthy School Environments

relatedness moment. A certificate for getting the highest mark is different to being noticed for really keeping going when it got tough. We talk about social norms, saying "these are my needs as your teacher, these are your needs as a set of pupils, these are the needs of this subject, what it demands, therefore we can curate together what it demands". For example, in art it might be we don't use rubbers, because mistakes are happy accidents. That's a social norm we've created for that subject. In maths, we always think before we ask a question, because we are learning to think of ourselves as mathematicians. What is it that this subject demands of us, this space demands of us. We also have norms that are more generic, which we might have as a whole school, like "we respect each other's difference" or "we always listen". So it's not to take away from a respectful environment with boundaries, it's a shift of this is what we all need as a collective.

We have a dehumanisation within our system because we're trying to control behaviour, we're trying to control outcomes. Young people are no longer humans with their own stories in the space. Every pupil has a right to have their story heard but unless we're providing space for them to be heard, it isn't necessarily discovered. I know a college which recently got an outstanding Ofsted. They collapse the curriculum for a week every term so each pupil has a progress review with their subject teachers. Those reviews are gathered by their tutors who then put also meet with the pupils to put that in the context of the individual. They are

What Can We Do When School's Not Working?

asking questions like: How's it going in your life? What part time jobs have you got? What's going to happen next? Somebody is saying, I value you, I'm stewarding this story with you.

Finding My Voice has a rich creative team. Christian Foley is a spoken word poet and Emmanuel Awoyelu is the Director of the Reach Out Project in London, and they've created these TikTok style beautiful videos for pupils. We've got life bites, philosophy bites, neuroscience bites, emotion bites, inspiration bites, life bites and responsive bites. They are played in lessons, so we're just doing a daily little munch, three minutes of ideas thrown into a space. Then people do some journaling so they get to reflect for themselves, then we have some dialogue prompts, a discussion. It's light touch, but high impact, by doing it short bursts on a daily basis. That's the personal development curriculum.

The whole school project is based on the concept that we, as adults, are not the complete article. We try very hard to ensure that it has as much positive impact on the staff as it does the young people. Staff meetings model what we want from

Creating Psychologically Healthy School Environments

dialogue, they are not led from the front. We have that deep exploratory talk and that model of self-determination for staff as much as we do for pupils.

I urge colleagues to lean into that which they love about what they teach, and this is the bit where teachers' eyes start to sparkle again. You're teaching history, you're aiming towards this curriculum, but what is that special thing about history that you love? What is it you want your young people to gain personally for their lives through this subject, and how can you use oracy to translate that more deeply? If I'm speaking like a historian, I'm beginning to think like a historian. That then means I can listen when I'm being taught like a historian. There's a whole beautiful shift that happens when you have a speaking classroom.

In P.E., when you're asking pupils at the end of a match and everyone's throwing their kit around because it's gone really badly, you sit down as a group and you're able to step out of it because you've nurtured this and they can have a discussion. You draw some pictures on the wall about what technically went wrong. They're using their knowledge, but they're also learning to collaborate in a difficult time.

I was speaking to an English teacher and she said: my pupils just weren't getting that deeper analysis of poetry. So I took a lesson out and we got a new poem in the room and we just talked about it the entire lesson. And she said: but I felt dreadful afterwards because I hadn't done any recording, I was worried that I was going to be *found out. But then they came in the next lesson and I did a writing task based on that poem and the quality of their writing was phenomenal. The power of talk for deeper thinking.*

We're currently in a teacher-first approach [in the education system], where we're learning lots of models, we're applying them, but we're applying them out of sync to where our learners are. Everyone's exhausted and fed up because there's not a flow. I talk about the learner first approach. You look first at the learners and then you think as a professional, and then decide what to do. There is research showing that when the shift was made to a learner first approach for CPD, it had a profoundly higher effect on the attainment in the class and the quality of teaching and learning.

When we talk about metacognition and self-regulation, we tend to talk about it in the context of cognitive science and learning. I think we can take it much deeper, to ask how can we help them to physiologically and psychologically regulate themselves. We do things like at the beginning of the lesson, take two minutes to transfer ourselves into the space – we're just going to take a moment to arrive, and to settle. We're physically allowing space to regulate, mentally preparing ourselves. We're also learning techniques we can use for the rest of our lives.

Meeting Psychological Needs in the Classroom

Prioritising psychological needs can start small. It does not have to be far-reaching or ambitious. It could be as simple as adjusting your use of language around particular things or asking yourself how you could make more space for autonomy, connection and competence in your classroom. Imagine your classroom and school through a child's eyes – maybe sit at one of their desks. What are they learning about themselves and the world from the way that this environment works?

In this chapter we've suggested that it's not possible for schools to focus only on academic learning. Schools are where young people spend the majority of their time, and it's where they do much of their growing up.

In their time at school young people are learning how to think about themselves, and how to understand the world – often called metacognition. They are learning how to manage their emotions and behaviour – often called self-regulation. They are learning just as much from how they are treated as from what they are being taught in their lessons.

There is no way to stop young people from learning from the way that their school environment functions. If a school shows young people that it does not think they can be trusted, then young people will learn to expect

Creating Psychologically Healthy School Environments

Table 3.1 Strategies for Meeting Psychological Needs

Psychological need	Strategies to meet this need in a classroom
Autonomy	Introducing choices about how a child does a task (e.g., you could write about your pet or you could imagine that you are a pet, or you could write about something else if you have a better idea). Very simple choices – saying that children can choose which side of the page they write on, or whether they start their maths at the beginning or the end of the exercise. Make space in the week for choices within boundaries (e.g. we are going to learn about the Tudors and you can decide how you want to present what you have learnt in small groups. Other groups have made models, written a play or done some art work). Dropping the pressure to perform (e.g. in assembly) and instead making it optional but also open to all. Not using competition between children to motivate. Not using reward systems to try and motivate (particularly not ones which are publicly visible). Not using class behaviour apps (and disabling the feature which projects any scores onto the whiteboard). Changing from general praise based on the child seeking adult approval ("Well done, I'm proud of you") to specific feedback ("I like the way that you've drawn that bird. How did you get the feet so accurate?"). Making sure that everyone gets a turn to do desired tasks or go on trips, and not making this a reward for compliant behaviour. Giving responsibilities in the classroom (e.g. plant watering). Thinking about how to manage things like going to the toilet safely while building autonomy – can they manage this independently (e.g. with photos at the door, so you know who is out of the room)?
Connection	Promoting non-hierarchical relationships between children and staff. Not pitting children against each other. Being consistently warm and welcoming, no matter what the child's behaviour. Stopping public ranking systems which encourage children to see themselves as winners or losers (e.g. charts on the wall showing reading scores). Prioritising staff wellbeing so they can remain calm even when faced with challenging behaviour. Using joint non-competitive activities (e.g. music, drama or art) to bring the class or groups of children together. Dropping whole class rewards and punishments (e.g. a class Attendance Bear or Golden Time for the whole class) as this can lead to one child being blamed or ostracised.

(Continued)

What Can We Do When School's Not Working?

Table 3.1 (Continued)

Psychological need	Strategies to meet this need in a classroom
Competence	This means focusing on the things which a child does well, feels effective and where they feel good about themselves. Noticing a child's interests and strengths and asking them about them, even if they are in areas such as Pokémon cards or video games. Using positive feedback more than negative. Give them opportunities to use their strengths in school – for example, a child who loves video games could write a story based in a game, or design a character for that game. Appreciating and valuing competence which goes beyond academics (e.g. a child who can fix a bicycle, or who knows all the football teams in the league). Creating opportunities for all young people to feel good about their abilities. Pointing out strengths rather than weaknesses. Asking for their advice and ideas when there is a shared problem.

that and will relate to the adults accordingly. If a school shows young people that their voices don't matter – perhaps by accepting "no excuses" for transgressions or by ignoring student requests – then that is what young people will learn. The results of this will be seen in their reactions – behaviour and attendance.

There is a robust field of research which shows that psychologically healthy environments which promote high quality learning and motivation prioritise three distinct areas: autonomy, connection and a sense of competence. When schools focus on controlling behaviour and do not see the behaviour in context, these needs are not always well met. This has unwanted effects for some children which include increased distress which can lead to attendance difficulties.

In this chapter you've heard from young people, talking about the way in which their schools made them feel and the effect that had on their wellbeing. Creating psychologically healthy schools requires deliberate shifts on the part of educators and school leadership teams towards collaboration and relationships. It doesn't just happen.

It takes a brave educator to make that change, because the prevailing culture of education is that the focus should be on improving test scores, with many interventions being judged against this benchmark. The costs of this are often invisible. However, there are many who are working within the mainstream system to increase student voice, improve relationships and take a psychologically-informed approach to behaviour. They want to change the "hidden curriculum" in their school. In the next section, you'll hear from three of these educators about this process of change.

Summary

- Children learn as much from how they are treated as they do from formal lessons.
- In particular children are learning how to think about themselves and others – metacognition – and how to manage their emotions and behaviour – self-regulation.
- The hidden curriculum are the things which young people are learning about themselves and the world through their experience at school, without being explicitly taught.
- Self-determination theory suggests that psychological needs are autonomy, connection and a sense of competence.
- There are individuals and schools who are deliberately working to promoting autonomy, connection and a sense of competence for young people.

References and Further Reading

Gatto, J. T. (1992). *Dumbing Us Down: The Hidden Curriculum of Compulsory Schooling*. Gabriola Island, BC: New Society Publishers.

Golann, J. W. (2015). *Scripting the Moves: Culture and Control in a "No Excuses" Charter School*. Chicago, IL: University of Chicago Press.

Hannam, D. (2020). *There Is Another Way: A Guide to Radical Education*. London: Radical Education Press.

Kohn, A. (1993). *Punished by Rewards: The Trouble with Gold Stars, Incentive Plans, A's, Praise, and Other Bribes*. Boston, MA: Houghton Mifflin.

Pink, D. H. (2009). *Drive: The Surprising Truth About What Motivates Us*. New York: Riverhead Books.

Rowe, G. (2016). *It's Our School, It's Our Time*. San Francisco, CA: Educational Publishing.

Ryan, R. M. and Deci, E. L. (2000). Self-determination theory and the facilitation of intrinsic motivation, social development, and well-being. *American Psychologist* 55(1): 68–78. https://doi.org/10.1037/0003-066X.55.1.68

Zhao, Y. (2018). *What Works May Hurt: The Side Effects of School*. Bloomington, IN: Teachers College Press.

3A

Three School Stories

In this section, you'll hear the stories of three schools. There's an infant school, a primary and a secondary school. All are non-selective, mainstream schools in England. They are working with different ages and in different contexts, but there are striking similarities. They have all focused on how to make their school a welcoming place and showing the children that they are glad that they are there. They prioritise inclusion and keep children in school, and they prioritise looking after their staff. They recognise that staff who are too stressed will not be able to respond calmly when faced with challenging behaviour – and they acknowledge that challenging behaviour will always occur in a school with hundreds of young people.

They talk about the foundation of their school being the relationships between pupils and staff, and they see part of their role as providing a reparative relationship for those young people whose relationships at home may be chaotic or inconsistent. Relationships are the bedrock of their schools, and they see behaviour, attendance and academic achievement as building on that firm foundation.

We'll Still Be Smiling Tomorrow

Sarah is the SENCo at an infant school in the north of England who have moved to an attachment and relationship-aware approach. She explains how her school sets out to provide a safe and secure place to learn, particularly for the children who do not have secure attachments at home.

> Our school is an attachment and relationship-aware school, so it's really trauma-informed practice. It's written in our behaviour and relationships policy that behaviour is communication.
>
> I do a lot of training with my staff about reasonable adjustments. It's something that I really wrestle with because I feel there's a limit to what you can reasonably

adjust at school. School is school, and I can put every adjustment in place, it's still school. There are still hundreds of kids. It still smells funny. The lighting is still weird. The ceilings are still low. There are lots of transition points all the way through the day. We can put all these mitigations in, but that doesn't mean that solves the problem.

Every year, every new school year, we spend half a term where our focus is relationships. With our new class, we focus on relationships. We have lots of key adults that support lots of individuals. Our staff bills are heinous.

A lot of our children don't have secure attachments at home, so we try and prioritise attachments in school before we do any learning. I think lots of schools think, "We've got to hit the ground running in the first week of September. We've got to make progress, and we've got our data point in October or whatever it might be." We don't think that.

We say, for at least the first six, seven weeks, the priority is children and developing relationships. We prioritise getting to know them as individuals, getting to know their families, and understanding what support they need.

Then we have loads of pastoral support that we put in place for our children. Hundreds of things like process art, or sensory circuits, or different things that go on for all those different groups. And we try and keep those adults consistent. If there's a key adult supporting a child, we try and continue that through the year groups, so we don't have so much change.

We plan around those relationships rather than fit the people in afterwards, so our staffing is really important to us. We also recognise that a lot of our parents have traumatic pasts, so we try and prioritise our relationships with our parents as well, so that they can take care of their children better. That comes first and then hopefully learning comes second. That's how we do it.

Derbyshire runs a thing called Attachment Aware Schools. It's run by Virtual Schools Derbyshire. It's something that I've been interested in for a while as SENCo, so I signed up for the programme.

It was started in 2019, so we did it over COVID, which was really interesting. It's a two-year programme. It was really helpful because everyone had a trauma over COVID, so we could use that trauma-informed model when we came back to support the children as they arrived.

We won the Alex Timpson Award for trauma-informed early years practice, which was really good. The reason that we started it essentially is because what we were doing before wasn't working.

I'm not saying that we don't have children with challenging behaviour. We have plenty. We feel like that doesn't go away, but it's how we approach it which changes. You won't hear staff shouting in our school unless there is imminent danger. We don't shout.

We do a lot of emotion coaching, lots of restorative practice, lots of calm. We aim to be the considered voice of reason quietly in a child's ear in the background. We try and make this place a really constant, calming place for our children.

In many ways, it hasn't fixed the problem, because I don't think it's fixable, but I think it makes the time that the children are here with us as good as it can be, as valuable as it can be. Then hopefully if they're calm and regulated, then they can learn. But if they're not in that position first, then they're not going to learn.

We have a lot of the children who don't have positive attachments at home or who have a lot of very inconsistent parenting. We really try and recognise the fact that a trauma isn't necessarily a single incident. It might be, but it might not be, and they're probably still living in the trauma. We have a lot of families who have issues with drug use, with domestic abuse.

Our children are toing and froing between the place of trauma and school all the time, it doesn't go away. There's a lot of low-level neglect. So we do things like provide breakfast. We've changed our school uniform policy. We've made it so children can come in joggers and trainers. We've carpeted the school, so we want to make it really welcoming for them.

In general, most of our children who present with challenging behaviour that we think is because of trauma, they're still in the trauma. It's not done and dusted. They're still living in it.

> We have a lot of the parents who deliver their child in the morning, shove them through the door and say, "Oh, he's been a f-ing nightmare."
>
> So I think the children feel really confused about what the expectations are about how adults behave and about how adults treat them. We try and provide that consistency. I try to show them that I'm really reliable and whatever you do, I'm still going to be talking to you like this, and I'm still going to be smiling when you come in tomorrow.

Toast Every Day

Rachel Tomlinson is Head of Barrowford Primary School in Lancashire. She explains how they changed their behaviour policy for a relationship policy.

> At the beginning, when I became head, the school was quite punitive. We had traffic lights, house points, Golden Time. I went on a course for new heads and in one of the sessions, someone spoke about relational approaches and understanding child development. It was the first time anyone had ever talked to me about child development. I had two children and had been teaching for over a decade. We began to develop our understanding of child development, attachment and trauma, and things which underpin behaviour.
>
> We set up a nurture group, and then we almost immediately had calls, and received several children who had lots of trauma in their history. We had to learn really quickly how to deal with them. There were some really tricky behaviours, and we had to invent lots of things to keep them in school. They had experienced massive amounts of trauma and attachment difficulties. It was like "this is all the stuff, here, at once". Those first experiences blew our minds. We invented a curriculum and a space and it was really rapid learning for all of us. I said no matter what the circumstances, we are not excluding these children, because they've experienced enough rejection, enough trauma, enough separation. Whatever happens, we just need to find solutions. That became the mantra. By the time they left in Year 6, those children were in class with everyone else and they achieved age-related expectations.
>
> What we do is create a context where people feel accepted and valued and safe. We're going to work with you and we're going to work around whatever's going on. Because whatever's going on impacts on your child and we need to know. Parents trust the school, because they know we'll help. We have 315 children, and 42 children with an education, health and care plan. That's three times the national average. About half of our children have a SEND need. We also have two SEMH specialist units on site, which are part of the school.

We used to do Star of the Week, Learning Hero, dinner time awards, all those kinds of things. But we asked the School Council how does it feel when you get Star of the Week or Learning Hero? And there was this discomfort around the table. Eventually one brave little soul went, we know you really like it. They didn't care when they didn't get it either, so we pulled it. We asked them what do you need, if you've done something really well, and they said we want to tell somebody whose opinion means something to us – so we facilitated that. We then asked if Star of the Week feels like that, what does it feel like when you get a sticker, or a wristband and they meant nothing to any of our children. They said we'd rather have a conversation or go and show somebody like the caretaker or the dinner ladies, share it and be proud. We're big on social media, so the children said we'd really like to put it on Facebook so our parents could see it while they're at work.

We became punishment-free and reward-free and it became about intrinsic rather than extrinsic motivation. To be intrinsically motivated, you had to feel safe. You had to feel valued, you had to feel seen, you had to feel like you matter, you had to feel like you belong, all of those things. And if you feel those things, you don't need a sticker or a punishment. The punishment is feeling like you've let people down and the reward is feeling like you fit in, or pleased people.

At that point I decided we're not going to exclude, but also, we're not going to punish. We're going to have a relational approach, because we know our children and our families really well. We were able to have those conversations with parents. As soon as we did that, we had a massive influx of kids.

We moved to a relationship management policy rather than a behaviour management policy. That influenced our staff and our decisions about staffing. We appointed staff with different skill sets than we would normally go for, we appointed a therapist, sent staff on therapy training and counselling training, and we appointed a social worker, to help get the right support in place for our families.

Our children and parents feel seen and feel welcome straight away from the minute they walk into the playground. There's probably six or seven members of staff in the playground in the morning. In the afternoon, we open the gates early and have 15 minutes when we can be there. That stuff builds the foundations.

Registration's really important, it's a proper greeting, you are in, and you're loved and you matter. Some of our children have really soft landings where they're met by a TA and then they go somewhere else. We have lots of quiet spaces, lots of regulation spaces, lots of transitional spaces around school. Reception and year one have key workers, and go straight into key worker groups. The rest of the year groups don't necessarily have key workers, but implicitly we do for individual children.

We're really conscious about groupings. We don't group by ability, we don't even talk about ability. We know that if you call one table "circles" and call the other table "squares", children know which who sits on what, and why.

Our teaching assistants are now called interveners rather than teaching assistants based on Karen Treisman's principle that every interaction is an intervention. We're saying to the staff, you're not an assistant to the teacher, sometimes you might intervene in learning, but actually you're intervening in relationships all of the time.

We have toast every day, so toast goes around all the classrooms every day. All the classrooms are really low stimulus so they're all painted white, they all have hessian backing, nothing hanging from the ceilings, any displays are on the display boards, there's no bright colours, display boards are black lettering, it's all, dyslexia friendly, autism friendly, ADHD friendly. We try and get a baseline that's good for everybody. We don't have any bells, they are really triggering but also really disruptive. Teachers can decide we'll have a playtime, because there's flexibility within the timetable. We eat lunch in class because it's really calm, and there are no new staff [supervising lunch time]. We timetable our staff throughout the day, so you've got those safe relationships right across the day.

We have pupil strategic meetings for each year group, each term. We go through the needs of the class and we create programs for children who need them. We use regulation plans and we do body mapping. I think really importantly our staff feel really safe. If a relationship has broken down into conflict, there's no blame in it.

Three School Stories

We're not blaming anybody. We say that's life, because relationships do falter. We acknowledge that the work is relationships and that it can be exhausting.

Intelligent Inconsistency

Ben Davis is the headteacher of St. Ambrose Barlow RC High School, a non-selective 11–16 secondary school in Swinton, Salford with 1082 pupils on roll. In this piece he writes about how the school has deliberately changed over the last four years in order to put safety and psychological wellbeing at the foundation of their approach. His story shows how even a large secondary school can focus on relationships and safety, alongside academic achievement.

> *It is Wednesday lunch time and, with the deputy head, I am on duty near the canteen. We can hear, and then see, Rose in Year 11 talking animatedly into her phone. Like many schools we have clear and well-established rules prohibiting pupils' use of phones in school, although like most rules staff apply them with intelligent inconsistency: not everyone needs the same rule in the same way all the time. This is one such moment. The deputy head intervenes and ushers Rose, who we all know well, into a meeting room. Rose follows, with a little reluctance. I turn my attention to the Year 8s whose turn it is for the growing queue of those waiting to get fed.*
>
> *A few minutes later the deputy head appears, Rose is with her, beaming. The moment that held potential for conflict, for a tricky stand-off between an individual's choices and a school's rules has not just been defused, it's been understood.*

After several difficult days Rose was phoning home to tell her gran that she had had a brilliant morning: "Look at my report!" She grins, waves and heads off for lunch, "Sorry about the phone thing."

There may be those who think that what was required in this interaction was a firm consequence, that Rose represented a threat to good order, that her actions, unsanctioned, undermine the school. That is not the approach we have chosen to take. We know Rose, she knows us. She doesn't need more shame in her life, she needs more love. Other young people who may have witnessed what occurred will have seen a peer receiving dignity, they will have witnessed (and may have learnt) equity, the prioritising of relationships.

It hasn't always been like this. Over the past three years we have been on what a consultant would term a "journey of improvement" at the heart of which has been the creation of a psychologically healthy school. It has not been straightforward, nor is the work ever finished. We are, to paraphrase the famous prayer, "workers not master-builders... Prophets of a future not our own."

We had attempted similar work in 2017-2019, but I did not implement it well, had not thought through the architecture of execution and the complexity of what we were attempting. It was one of many factors that contributed to our school, over time, declining and became less, not more, healthy and welcoming. I found this extremely difficult, both personally and professionally; I was effectively not delivering on my vision and running a school that was diverging, however accidentally, from my values. COVID brought a time to regroup, a different focus on community, care, welfare and need; from then on we did not look back. Four years later, after a period of very radical and sometimes painful change, we are closer to where we wanted to be. And I think it is important to underscore the importance of this being a collective, communal effort – our staff are very tightly-knit and "bought-in" to what we have done. Explaining what some would call our "ethos" is a big part of the process of induction for staff.

Mission and Vision

We operate our school guided by a very strong mission and vision: "Love, Learn, Lead". This is best described as triangle, reminiscent of Maslow's hierarchy. The foundation is "Love", our short-hand for knowing our pupils and assuming the best of them. This encompasses attendance, behaviour and relationships, the various things often described as "standards" and, crucially, how we care for our most vulnerable pupils. "Love" is the way in which we frame the psychological health and safety we feel is vital for pupils to thrive and learn. For what it's worth (and we do not place great store by it) our most recent Ofsted inspection graded us Good, with Outstanding for Personal Development.

Three School Stories

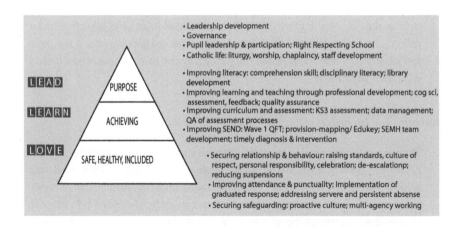

What is good for pupils is good for staff. We have a large and generally happy team – we have worked very hard on building a deeply-felt sense of shared endeavour based, like our work with pupils, on strong, dignifying, relationships.

We are one of those schools who proclaim that everything rests on relationships, but we mean this and when the idea is challenged, we don't find it hard to explain what we mean. While rules and routines are important (we are a large and diverse organisation with many complex functions) they are secondary to the connections between people. In fact, I would contend that our rules and routines depend on the connections between people and that these factors are mutually reinforcing. It would be possible to secure an ostensibly calm and purposeful school environment through rules and routines, but at the expense (or disregard) of relationships.

Keeping Young People in School

As a school we have taken the deliberate decision to keep young people in school – avoiding permanent exclusion, AP and off-site direction as much as possible, but not entirely. The difference, for us, is that we do not view exclusion as an inevitability. This means that there are, on any given day, a "small minority" (Ofsted's words) of pupils who most staff will find difficult (Ofsted mis-represented this as "persist in misbehaving"). These pupils are supported by a very wide range of provisions. We have a great deal of success with them, by any significant metric, although we have yet (our approach is two years young) been able to track academic outcomes. Nevertheless, their presence means that at times other pupils or staff will have difficult encounters with them, interactions that may be a threat to their psychological safety. I share this because it goes to the heart of the difficult trade-off (as some see it) that schools are managing. For us it isn't an either/ or; it's both/ and. Our school is *a richer place for ensuring that all young people attend. It is a fairer place that better reflects the community and the world young people are growing into. It is a more just place: all of these young people are entitled, by law, to access our school and we want them to be there.*

Strategies for Inclusion

There are a number of strategic actions that we undertake to ensure that our school can work in this way, of which strength and depth of vision is the first. The second thing we do is talk about it. A lot. A great deal of inclusion is about maintaining commitment, the same is true with psychological safety: messages matter. Everyone talks about it, so everyone understands it and owns it. We reinforce key messages to all staff twice a week in briefing. We share information endlessly with all staff about the stories and vulnerabilities of our pupils and their families. We interrogate data and information throughout the week to triangulate what we are seeing and hearing. In particular this is done across functions, in a multi-disciplinary way so that professional silos do not mitigate against good and effective care and support. We listen and adjust our actions, particularly in relation to what young people and families tell us – the sense of being listened to and actions flowing from this is vital for creating safety. When things get difficult, as they do and will, we make sure (especially those of us who hold positions of authority) that we return to our principles and our values.

People Make the Difference

Having the right people, in the right roles, doing the right things has been fundamental to our work. This sounds obvious, but it is easily overlooked – it's not just that people need to believe in our work, they need to be ready to do it. This means achieving alignment between staff, their personal values and the school's vision – especially ensuring that leaders are aligned. More than that, there needs to be a strong team ethos and a tendency away from silos of thought, function or action – the work of key groups in the school must be integrated. For example, our leads for Safeguarding, SEND, wellbeing, behaviour and attendance work very closely, meeting once each week. They then approach the leads of (for example) literacy or learning and teaching so that emerging issues are shared and addressed in the round. Their work is solution-focused.

Prioritising Resourcing

A great deal relies on the decisions we have taken regarding resourcing. Our strategic view is that by resourcing the relatively expensive things that foster a culture of inclusion and psychological safety we are able to do the free (or cheaper), but difficult things that make a huge difference, such as sustaining relationships. Consequently, we have skewed resources over a three-year period into strong SEND provision, one of our three ongoing priorities that everyone knows and talks about.

Our SENDCO (special educational needs co-ordinator) is the Senior Mental Health lead. He also leads staff training, along with our assistant head teacher for Learning, Teaching and CPD. This means that across the main remits of the leadership there is a strong network of shared understanding that prioritises safety.

Our efforts to make pupils feel safe sometimes have unexpected consequences. We went through a phase of feeling overwhelmed by the substance abuse issues we were facing, before realising that we were finding them precisely because we were creating safe spaces for pupils to open up about this difficult subject. Our response, although not without its sad and tricky moments, has ensured safety while keeping young people in education. You can find the same signature in our work on attendance, using part-time timetables and, increasingly, flexi-schooling to reduce stress, improve wellbeing and offer hope as well the possibility of academic outcomes.

To reiterate, all of this work is underpinned by our mission as a public service, a place that young people have a right to be and where their families have a right to heard. It is about addressing complexity with a response of equal complexity, rather than reducing the messiness of human experience to simple, inflexible routines and structures.

Relationships and Behaviour

Our Relationships and Behaviour policy looks like thousands of others across the country and early on we state that "all behaviour is communication". Read it carefully (especially the principles, the equality impact information and the research base) and you will see that there is a careful combination of "law" and "spirit" that encourages flex, reasonable adjustment and takes account of the individual. In practice our policy relies heavily on staff applying it with compassion, humour, intelligence, informed by training. It is also predicated on us all remembering that the dignity of relationships come first. This is brilliantly modelled by the assistant headteacher who leads on Relationships, Behaviour and Attendance.

He exhorts us to outweigh negatives with positives, aiming for at least 5:1. He reminds us of the impact that the smallest chat or acknowledgement can have on a young person. For example, a child who finds attendance hard is greeted with, "It's great to see you – we're so pleased you're here." A child arriving late to lesson comes in and sits down, gets on with their work, before the teacher quietly acknowledges their late arrival and welcomes them. We don't operate a tariff system, where for the sake of consistency a particular misdemeanour always results in a specific consequence. With the exception of a very small number of very rare incidents, we expect that an issue can be resolved at the lowest possible level and relationships strengthened and preserved.

All of our pupils wear a school uniform, for the vast majority this presents no issue or barrier, but where it does we apply some creativity and respond to a child in need or in crisis, removing a barrier: allowing for a hoodies, some trainers, no tie. Again, this means that our pupils remain in school, feel listened to and are dignified by the response of adults. Where adults are discomforted by this or see it as giving in, we explain. Sometimes it doesn't go quite to plan. With the young people for whom deep-seated trauma, for example, is triggering a regular and strong emotional response that means they find it hard to meet those demands of school that others find easy, how could it always go well? It certainly isn't linear – this is wild looping, iterative, joyful approach and we're always trying to do better.

Celebration and Recognition

We don't do rewards, but we are keen on celebration and recognition. No-one is given a certificate for 100% attendance, but we do send home letters acknowledging improvement and we do so carefully, very aware that for many children it is simply a matter of luck and circumstance. We celebrate young people's achievements, their virtues and the little things they do: their quirks and personalities. This is important to emphasise: we are seeking to reduce or eliminate perceptions of judgement or shame, always considering how the most vulnerable or marginalised child will feel. A great deal of simple recognition and celebration must be spontaneous: laughter, a quiet word, phone call home. As far as possible we try, through our communication with staff, to build a school where laughter and fun are welcome and encouraged, not stifled by quotidian rules and routines.

Everyone Is a Teacher

Schools rely on a team of "support staff" (we are reviewing that somewhat demeaning nomenclature) to make them work. We are very fortunate to have a Director of Finance and Operations and an HR Manager who both see their role as leaders in an organisation that exists for the benefit of young people. Consequently, recruitment and the allocation of resources or the setting of budgets are keenly focused on the development of an environment that ensures young people's psychological safety. Moreover, the development of the school estate has contributed to this in the creation of spaces of safety such as a library, wellbeing provision and the Francis Centre for autistic children.

Our strategies for recruitment and retention are driven by a simple principle: the ideas that are good for young people are good for staff. Hence, we have enhanced our approach to wellbeing, flexibility, diversity, inclusion – all contributors to a professionally safe workplace. Our HR manager is currently leading the professional learning of "support staff" so that the gigantic and vital role they play in building relationships is fully realised and is properly developed.

I think our schools are chock-full of brilliant people. When I walk around the place I work I am often deeply moved by the interactions I see between staff and pupils, by the swell of decency and humanity that carries us all through each day. A great many schools are, by accident or design, working to be places of psychological health, where people can flourish and where child development is on an equal-footing with academic attainment. This is impeded by the agendas emanating from government over the last 14 years, not least because it means acknowledging our limitations and seeing that for some young people school is a place of distress and difficulty. Acknowledging that and adjusting what we do takes humility, courage and (something of a theme here) love.

Change has not been easy or straightforward. At the start I alluded to the upset caused by attempting to build a more inclusive, psychologically healthy school at the wrong time and in the wrong way: for the change to happen and stick it must take place at the right time, with the right people and a strong, shared vision. It is a genuine partnership of staff, pupils, families, community and others; it demands constant tending and powerful communication of challenging ideas; it requires staff development and great skill.

However, it is worth it. The richness and strength of community is a strong foundation for education. In the words of one of our Year 8s when asked how she felt about attending our school: "I know I am loved here."

Summary

- There are schools which have deliberately chosen to focus on relationships and meeting the psychological needs of their pupils.
- This is not done easily and requires a commitment across the school to doing things differently.
- Looking after and training staff well is an essential part of this.
- These approaches do not eliminate challenging behaviour or difficulties with attendance, but they do change the ways in which adults respond to these issues.

4

When Things Go Wrong

> In this chapter you will find:
>
> 1. The Journey to School Attendance Problems
> 2. Making Sense of Behaviour and Attendance
> 3. A Behavioural Lens
> 4. A Mental Health Lens
> 5. What Can We Do Now? The Trust Test

Introduction

We had an attendance bear. Whichever classroom had the best attendance, they would get the bear, and I remember all of the other kids used to come to me and tell me, "Look, this is a problem because you've always been the reason that we never get the bear."

Which was obviously a problem. I remember when we did the attendance certificates at the end of the year for kids who had perfect attendance.

They also did another section for the children who didn't have perfect attendance, but it wasn't their fault. There were about two children who had that, but they both had physical disabilities. Then they wouldn't have any other children go up. I thought, "Okay. Well, they have a category for children who don't attend all the time, but it's not their fault, and I'm not in that category, so it must be my fault, wasn't it?" It's logical when you're a child.

All the input I was getting is, "This is your fault." So I was very confused because obviously, you've got all the doctors saying it's not your fault, then all the kids saying, it's definitely your fault.

When Things Go Wrong

Obviously, they were kids, they didn't understand. But all that they understood was that I was the reason they weren't getting this pretty little attendance bear. I have no resentment towards the kids. But I do lament towards some of the teachers who allowed that to happen, I'd say.

As told to Naomi by Alice (13) who stopped attending school to become home educated when she was eight.

Here is where this book changes pace. We've been talking so far about schools and how schools interact with children – and how this affects children's wellbeing. We've described seeing problems with behaviour and attendance as signals that something else is not working well. We've introduced self-determination theory, a psychological model which suggests what makes an environment one in which people can flourish, and we've given some examples of how schools and teachers can promote that.

Now we are coming back to the individual. This chapter is about what happens when a young person is struggling to attend school, and in particular, about the unintended consequences of that and the downwards spiral that can happen for some children. It is our argument that well-intended interventions can have side effects which ultimately make problems worse rather than better.

In this chapter and the next we'll focus in on what happens to children at school when their attendance and behaviour starts to cause concern. This chapter is not a "how-to" guide for common interventions for attendance problems and school-related anxiety. If that is what you are looking for, you can find that in other books (Thambirajah, Grandison and De-Hayes 2008, Garfi 2018, Rae 2020, Kearney 2021).

Instead, it's a look behind the curtain to show what families and young people say about these strategies. As always in this book, the stories here don't imply that these are everyone's experience. They are the voices of those who whom the interventions haven't worked, the most vulnerable.

The Journey to School Attendance Problems

One of the clear differences which we see between parents and professionals is at what point they think that school attendance difficulties begin. Schools see the moment when a child does not attend school as the start of the problem. Parents often talk about school attendance problems as being at the end of a long journey of unheard distress and strategies which have made things worse. They sometimes describe distress which has gone on for years and which has got worse over time. They see behaviour and poor attendance as the result of this.

This means that parents and schools are seeing the situation in a very different way. When a child stops attending school, schools and professionals will sometimes talk about "nipping the problem in the bud" by which they mean, getting that child back to school as soon as possible. To parents, this makes no sense because the problem as they see it started years ago, and they think that getting the child back to school won't solve the problem of the child's school-related distress. They often feel that they asked for help to "nip it in the bud" years before when the child first started to express their distress and weren't heard.

There are particular things which parents and young people describe as contributing factors when they talk about school-related distress. Transitions are clear vulnerability points, and the research shows that when the expectations of the school system are increased (such as when children move from reception to Year 1, or from primary school to secondary school), then each time a group of children start to struggle when they were coping before.

Other things which parents frequently mention include a new teacher who doesn't seem to "get" their child, use of class behaviour apps or charts which make the struggles of some children highly visible. Teenagers tell us about academic pressure in the form of assemblies where children are told things like "failure isn't an option here" or that there will be life-long serious consequences

What Can We Do When School's Not Working?

if they do not do well in their exams. We have talked to parents whose children were told in assembly that if they don't attend school every day, they are more likely to develop drug and alcohol problems and get involved in county lines. For young people who have physical and mental health problems which prevent them from attending school regularly, these assemblies are particularly distressing and can cause intense worry about their future.

Peer problems are often mentioned, with some children being rejected by their peers and bullying ranging from physical violence and attacks through to more subtle shunning in the lunch queue. Some of these young people describe school as a hostile environment, with no space to get away from other people, even during breaktime.

Some parents talk about a slow deterioration lasting years during which they asked for help and support, while others report a relatively quick decline, often following the transition to secondary school or the introduction of a new stricter regime at school. Children typically express their distress through

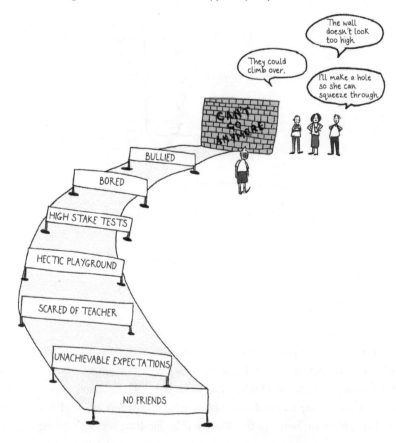

their behaviour, both inside and outside school. Parents see the way in which schools respond to these early signs of difficulty as something which can cause problems in attendance and engagement with school later down the line.

Freya is a parent. She describes her daughter's journey towards being withdrawn from school which she reports as having started two years before.

> My youngest daughter loved school. She has always been sensitive but with the right below and support she thrived. Loved her friends, the teachers and school overall. A change of head and teaching staff in Year 5 brought the start of her struggles. Split teaching, very harsh teaching assistants and a lack of consistency made her feel uneasy but we muddled through.
>
> In Year 6 the same teacher and teaching assistants moved up with her class and it was hell. The younger children, as young as three, were brought into her class to be punished by her teacher. They were told off in front of the Year 6 class, made to stand in corners, told to look at the floor and so on and she hated this. This was coupled with the harsh assistants again and my daughter started to not want to go in. When we struggled to get in, we were regularly left outside alone and told they were too busy and she would just have to come in on her own once she'd got herself together. When I started to complain about this her teacher took it upon himself to bully her in a passive aggressive manner when she was in. Her Year 6 was very traumatic until we decided to remove her.
>
> She was keen to start secondary so I asked them for help with a view of getting a plan in place to help her start in September (she was a shell of herself after Year 6) and was basically told no, there was zero help until she was on roll and that she would be fine.
>
> She wasn't fine and couldn't start. Once she was a blip on their records the pastoral care team offered their "help". This help consisted of telling me that I needed to be a stronger parent. That I needed to break her emotional attachment to me and that I needed to tell her: "You're a big girl now so to stop making a fuss." If she had a worry, to say things like "That's your problem not mine" and then to change the subject and distract her.

Making Sense of the Problem

The way that professionals respond to problems with attendance and behaviour depends very much on how they understand what is going on. At the heart of every intervention is an (often hidden) assumption about why the problem is happening. In Chapter 1, we talked about the many different ways in which problems at school are understood and how this affects both our attitude to these young people and the interventions which are made.

What Can We Do When School's Not Working?

This flow chart gives you a simple way to think about what sense is being made of any problem – and how that is guiding the interventions which are being put in place.

As will already be clear, parents, the child and other professionals make very different sense of problems at school. They see things through different lenses. We all bring our own biases to the situation.

When Things Go Wrong

This difference in opinion really matters, because it means that what professionals perceive as support is often perceived by families as inappropriate and even punitive. And it means that when parents ask questions about how things are done at school, schools sometimes respond defensively, feeling that the role of parents should be to support school policies and practice, not to question them.

Families tell us that they feel that their parenting is blamed for their child's behaviour and attendance, even if they have other children who have no problem in attending school. They say that they feel scrutinised during meetings and that they find the offer of parenting classes patronising. When parents become understandably anxious about their child's difficulties at school, they are told that this anxiety is "fuelling" their child's anxiety. This does not make them feel less anxious.

Invisible Power

There is an inherent power differential when schools work with families, and it's visible everywhere you look. In meetings and reports parents are often referred to by their first name, or even by their roles "Mum" and "Dad", while professionals are "Dr F" or "Mrs P". Parent-school contracts are written by the schools, not the parents, and parents are rarely given the chance to have meaningful input into what goes into them. Their role is to agree with school requirements, not to question. If they do disagree, they say that they feel others perceive them as "difficult" parents and they worry about the impact on their children. Many parents say that they start to feel like children again in the school context, with teachers "telling them off" if their child doesn't do their homework or isn't making it to school on time.

In diagnostic assessments, what a parent says about their child is generally given less weight than the opinion of a professional, even when that professional has only met them once. Professionals advise parents on what to do, but parents are rarely invited to advise professionals. Families are worried that they will be judged and are sometimes fearful that social services might be called if they were honest about how difficult things are with their child.

Professionals rarely feel this power differential and will (in my experience) sometimes deny it's there, saying that they have a good relationship with parents. Parents, on the other hand, often report feeling dismissed and stereotyped as neglectful parents because their child is not happy at school. This means that parents and professionals can have very different experiences of the same meetings. It means that a school may think a plan or contract has been mutually agreed, while parents feel that they have had no choice.

Politicising Attendance and Behaviour

Behaviour and school attendance are highly politicised in England. There are government "behaviour tsars" and national attendance targets of 100%, set by the Children's Commissioner – a government appointee. This means that any discussion of what might be causing problems in attendance or behaviour can quickly become ideological, with alliances forming around particular perspectives and interventions then being put in place.

In this chapter, we're going to discuss the main ways in which problems with attendance and behaviour are understood. We'll describe common interventions which are put in place and what families say about these interventions. We'll then discuss whether there are alternatives.

It's (Never) Just Behaviour

Human behaviour is complex, and children behave in distinctly different ways to adults. Psychology is the study of human behaviour, and modern psychologists see behaviour as a way in which people express themselves and react to their environment. Not necessarily intentional communication, but a response to the circumstances that the person finds themselves in and an expression of their internal experience. This is particularly the case for children. Disruptive behaviour and attendance difficulties, seen through this lens, provide us with information about what is going on with this child – and *en masse*, they give us information about the wider system. If many young people have problems with behaviour and attendance at school, then this is important feedback on the school system and how it is working (or not).

However, there's another way to see behaviour and it's one which has become increasingly prevalent in the English school system over the last decade. From this perspective, behaviour is something which needs to be trained into children (or established as habits), and a large part of "good behaviour" is that children need to accept adult authority. Behaviour is seen as a choice on the part of the child. As Tom Bennett, leader of the £10 million DfE Behaviour Hubs project puts it in his bestselling book for teachers, *Running the Room*: "In most *mainstream* classrooms, *most* misbehaviour is avoidable. Most students could, if they decided, do otherwise" (Bennett 2020, p. 44, italics in the original).

Since a lot of typical childish behaviour in school is often seen as misbehaviour (running instead of walking, shouting out instead of putting your hand up, not sitting still in your seat, forgetting what you are doing, not paying attention for the whole lesson, not following all instructions), this view essentially says that children can (and should) choose not to be childish, if they just wanted to enough. Maturity is redefined as an act of willpower. No matter what is happening in that "mainstream classroom", the children should be able to manage it. Defining "misbehaviour" as a choice removes any responsibility from schools and teachers to either engage children or to be developmentally informed.

Through the "behaviour is a choice" lens, children's behaviour is seen as something to modify through consistent feedback, structure and high expectations. If they are "misbehaving", then they need to be taught to do otherwise through consequences.

To clarify why this is a problem in education, think about different ways in which a primary education can be organised. Primary schools across the world vary enormously in what they expect of children, particularly between the ages of 4–8. In Finland (to take one example), children do not start school until they are seven, and everything up to that point is play-based. In England, children start school at age four, and by age seven are expected to be spending most of their day seated at a desk. English and Finnish children are in very different environments, the expectations put upon them are different and their behaviour should be seen in context. A Finnish six-year-old who wants to run around all day will not be seen as a problem, while an English six-year-old who does the same will find themselves in trouble.

To frame this behaviour as "a choice" ignores the different context, and puts the responsibility on children, rather than on the system around them. If English children are disruptive, don't sit still and aren't learning to read despite being taught to do so, there is no space in this model to see this as a problem in the way that English schools are educating young children. The problem (so the model says) lies with the children making poor choices.

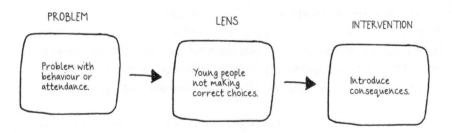

In Bennett's classroom the ideal is for adults to decide while young people comply. Or as he puts it, "My room, my rules." This perspective cannot see behaviour as feedback, even if many children are behaving the same way, and thus a lot of valuable information is lost. There is no space for children's behaviour to be a result of the way in which schools are organised or for questions to be asked about why so many children feel negatively about school. For Bennett, good behaviour is defined as compliance with school, by both young people and their parents. No matter what the school requires and how unreasonable young people and their families might perceive that to be.

Behaviourism

The "classic sanctions and rewards model of behaviour management" to which Bennett refers is likely to be familiar to anyone reading this book. You may not, however, be familiar with the assumptions on which it is based, which are those of behaviourism, an early form of psychology.

The origins of behaviourism can be traced to the early years of the 20th century, when early psychologists applied their observations of how animal behaviour could be changed through associative learning to human beings.

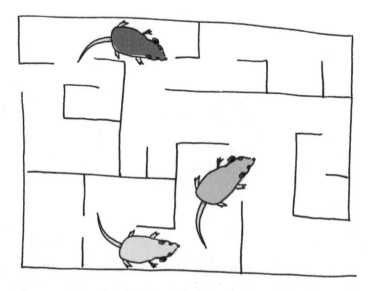

Behaviourism in its most basic form suggests that behaviour will be encouraged when a person is rewarded for it in some way, and then we will see more of that behaviour. If you want to see less of a behaviour, then the person should be punished or a sanction put in place. The person will then learn not to behave in that way in order to avoid the consequence.

Behaviourist strategies are commonplace in schools. Charts on the walls where children's names are moved from the sun to the rain clouds, peg charts, attendance awards, token economies where children win Golden Time if the class gets enough gems – all of these are behaviourist in origin. They attempt to change children's behaviour through changing the consequences. They introduce unpleasant consequences if a child does not comply, and pleasant consequences when they do.

Developmental psychology has moved on from behaviourism when thinking about children. It's too simplistic, and it became clear that it ignored some

very important aspects of child development. Children do not learn mostly through the application of pleasant or unpleasant consequences; learning is far more complicated than behaviourism would imply. In some places education, however, has been left behind.

The problem with behaviourism as used in many schools is that it introduces unpleasant consequences for those who are not compliant – and if it doesn't work, the consequences become more and more unpleasant. Longer time spend in isolation, more detentions, external exclusions. In some (not all) schools, we hear that the more this doesn't work, the more they are applied. If a child doesn't respond well to behaviourist approaches, they are often made very unhappy as a result and their relationship with teachers and school can break down. One young person ended up with more detentions than there were days in the school year. One mother told us that her son had so many detentions that she could plan her work schedule around him being late out of school every Monday. It's a basic truth that you cannot make someone thrive through punishment, no matter how hard you try.

When Things Go Wrong

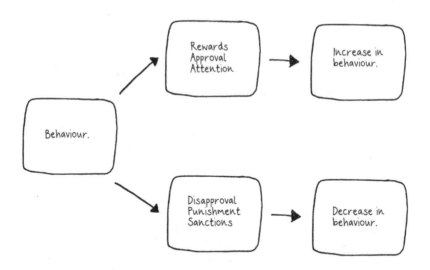

Figure 1: A Basic Behavioural Model, Underpinning Many Strategies Used in Schools

The other thing to bear in mind about the science of behaviourism is that it isn't simply about control. The aim is for people to be learning new behaviours which then continue when there are no longer external consequences. As an example, think of a child who is potty training. They may initially need lots of positive reinforcement (praise, stickers or even chocolate buttons) to use the potty, but the aim is always that in the longer term, the reinforcement can be withdrawn and they will use the toilet without the need for rewards. This is how behavioural interventions should work. If continual and controlling consequences are necessary in order to maintain a behaviour (like the threat of detentions for years on end), then the child is not learning how to behave themselves, they are responding (or in some cases, not responding) to external control. The likelihood is that the moment the consequences end, their behaviour will change too. Nothing has been actually learnt.

This distinction is important, because the point of education is for children to learn. Part of this is learning how to behave so that they can participate in society as adults when they leave. Punitive consequences and high control environments can give the impression that children are learning because their behaviour is controlled. If genuine learning is happening, then we should see a continuation of prosocial behaviour when the consequences are no longer in place. This isn't what teachers in high control environments describe.

The Side Effects of Behaviourism

Many schools now have awards for attendance and behaviour which can be parties, school trips and even book tokens. These awards are publicised around the school on billboards or even projected onto whiteboards from an app, meaning that those who do well are visibly celebrated – while those who do not, are visibly not. In some schools, children's behaviour is tracked and rated every lesson. Very young children are rewarded for staying in their seats or on the carpet and keeping quiet, and sanctioned if this isn't something they are able to do.

Schools tend to focus on the positive impact of these programmes, but parents tell a different story about what they see at home. They talk about the impact on children's self-esteem and of rising levels of anxiety, often culminating in refusal to go to school. Many of them describe their children developing stomach aches when stricter behavioural programmes are introduced, and of this starting them on a pathway to reluctance and then refusal to go to school.

Anna told me about her son Jack.

> In Year 2, his new school used "Class Dojo". The whiteboard defaulted to a screen showing everyone's monster, along with their individual Dojo tally. In the bath one night Jack told me how many Dojos Mia had – she was the top-flight Dojo earner, clearly very well suited to the school environment and expectations (I went on

school trips so had chance to observe his classmates). She had 120, and he seemed pleased for her. He then told me he had 60. I asked if he knew why Mia had so many Dojos and he said: "Yes, it's because she does all the right things."

I explained that it was easy for Mia to "do the right things", because she wasn't bothered by sounds, smells, temperature, people being in her space and so on, and said it absolutely did not mean that she was better than him.

"Yes, it does" was his reply.

Another parent, Kay, talked about group behaviour policies and the impact on children who found school more challenging.

The school employed "table points" where the tables in class were pitched against each other in behaviour, tidying up and getting work done. On one instance my son came home saying the teacher had said of his table that "one person was letting the whole table down". By now he was well aware of how they felt about his behaviour and told me: "I knew she was talking about me and so did the rest of the table."

This eventually led to him making comments about himself such as "I am a naughty boy" and "I am bad" and beginning to express a reluctance to go to school. He told a friend that the teachers make him feel naughty. The friend told the teacher and he was told to think very carefully about what he tells people in the future. He came home fearful of telling me things he thought might get him in trouble later.

And Kirsty told us this heart-rending story about her autistic son.

Near the beginning of his "school life", our son told me that he simply did not understand how to "get on the rainbow". He tried so hard to sit still but it hurt his back to do so. I spent months trying to help him achieve the coveted "rainbow" placement, which he did not make in his entire school year when he was aged four. Every day for months, he left the class looking downtrodden, accompanied by his support worker advising: "It's not been a good day, Mrs Jones." I started to thoroughly dislike the sight of her cheerful face telling me he had tried his best but, essentially, all efforts had failed.

I had to admire our boy's resilience, though, when he left class one day in that year. Our son encouraged his equally diagnosed friend to approach me and say that Peter had made it onto the rainbow. My boy followed, beaming, and I had absolutely no reason to doubt he had achieved his goal. I ruffled his hair, congratulated him on his hard work, and asked how it had happened. He looked confused. Then his friend looked confused.

I realised then they had made it up. Bless them. My son had encouraged his friend to lie and neither had expected any follow-up questions to aid in understanding where the success had occurred!

Very gently I said, "It doesn't matter to me about the rainbow, you are on my rainbow every day."

They looked at me and his friend, having served his purpose, ran off to his mum shrugging his shoulders. My son, bless him, said, "I just wanted to see what it would feel like. I wanted you to hear I had done it."

The Unexpected Results of Rewards

There is an extensive literature about the unintended effects of a reliance on behaviourism. In particular, self-determination theory, which we introduced in the previous chapter (Deci and Ryan 1985) suggests that intrinsic motivation (the internal drive to do something) is damaged by a reliance on rewards and sanctions (external motivation).

Self-determination theory came about because of unexpected experimental findings. Researchers thought that by adding a reward, they would make an activity more enjoyable. They took a group of children doing something which they enjoyed – drawing a picture – and gave them a sticker for it. Then they had a control group who were not given the sticker. You might think that the group with the stickers would report more enjoyment, that the sticker would work to motivate the children. It didn't turn out like that. In fact, when the experimenters stopped giving stickers, the children who had been given stickers drew fewer pictures afterwards, as compared to the children whose drawing hadn't been rewarded. Their joy in drawing pictures had been diminished by the stickers. They'd stopped doing it for the love of drawing, and they'd started doing it for the stickers, and so when the stickers stopped, they did less drawing.

An extensive evidence-base had repeated these findings in many groups, including school children, teenagers and adults at work. Adding external motivators can damage intrinsic motivation. It changes the reason why a person does what they do. The research indicates that high quality intrinsic motivation is fostered when the conditions support a person's sense that they can make choices about what they do, a sense of being capable and a sense of being part of something (Ryan and Deci 2017). When external motivators (such as prizes, behavioural charts or attendance awards) are added, the quality of that intrinsic motivation falls.

There's another problem with relying on rewards to motivate children, and it's the effect on those who don't get the rewards. As Alfie Kohn (2018) demonstrates in his book *Punished by Rewards*, the absence of a reward can psychologically act as a punishment. Being the child who is excluded from the annual Rewards Day and who therefore has to come to school while everyone else goes to a theme park, will feel like a punishment. Giving rewards rather than punishments feel better to adults, they feel positive rather than negative, but there is another side to them.

Sage told me about the way that her daughter, who is now home educated, responded to the Dojo points system.

> *We had to deregister my five-year-old after the first term of Year 1. She's an exceptionally bright child, always been quiet and seemed to tick all the teacher's boxes.*
>
> *By the time we deregistered she was a shell, picked her lips all day at school, would occasionally just burst into tears for no apparent reason while in class and we were seeing massive changes in her behaviour at home. Night terrors every single night and she used to do this thing where she'd talk herself to sleep, pretending to be someone in the class.*
>
> *The reward system stepped up a notch when they went Into Year 1. They used something called Dojo. I let the teacher know we wouldn't be doing homework set by school, we've got allotments, a big garden, a big family, and so on, so I felt time at home was for us as a family. She was told at school because of that she'd miss out on Dojo points.*
>
> *One night I remember her completely losing it, she'd been practicing for a spelling test but was just so exhausted she wasn't physically able. I told her she only had to try, it didn't matter what the score was and she was screaming she wouldn't get a Dojo point if she didn't get 10/10. The pressure of getting Dojo points on top of the ridiculous workload had her crumbling.*

What this means is that the more schools rely on sanctions and incentives to control children's behaviour and learning, the less they can expect children to be intrinsically motivated to behave well and learn. This is the opposite of what Tom Bennett argues when he suggests that external control is liberating for children. Instead, the evidence shows that too much external control will lead to a loss of interest in learning.

Self-determination theory poses a serious problem for the current model of behaviour management espoused in some of the stricter schools. For behavioural management can't continue for ever – the aim is surely for young people to want to behave well and to want to learn far the future. If the strategies that are being used directly undermine their internal drive to do so, then there is no way for it to work in the long term. The evidence shows that the more that schools try to change young people's behaviour and learning with rewards and sanctions, the less young people will be internally motivated to behave well and to learn for its own sake. The stories from parents indicate that these behaviour modification techniques also have an impact on some children's self-esteem and emotional well-being, which puts some of them on a path towards school attendance difficulties.

A Behavioural Lens

When school attendance difficulties are primarily seen as a behavioural problem, professionals (understandably) make recommendations which are designed to change the behaviour. If the child isn't attending school, they have limited power to put sanctions in place at school. Instead, many parents report being told to make home "less pleasant" so that school seems better in comparison. This advice is repeated in many of the books for parents and professionals, as well as in popular articles.

The handout for parents given at the end of a widely used handbook for professionals is a good example of this. Parents are told:

> Don't let the child watch TV, play computer programmes or enjoy other activities when he or she is at home during school hours and not at school. Create an atmosphere of solitary confinement as long as the child is at home.
>
> (Thambirajah 2008, p. 149)

What Can We Do When School's Not Working?

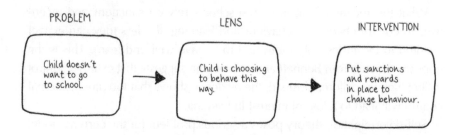

This is an unusual recommendation for mental health professionals, to say the least. I have never seen it in any of the (many) other books on child mental health which I have read. Solitary confinement is a serious punishment because humans find it very distressing, and for children who are being put into confinement by their parents it has the added element of damaging the relationship between them. It is likely to damage both the child's and parents' mental health if instigated for any length of time.

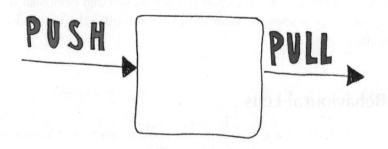

The reason that this is recommended is that the authors think that if home is boring enough, the child will choose to go to school out of sheer desperation. The problem will be "solved". This is sometimes framed as "pull" and "push" factors, with "pull" factors being things which pull a child towards school, such as rewards for attendance or promises of treats if they do well, and "push" factors being things which push the child out of their home, such as making home not allow them to do interesting things while they are not at school. The cycle below is drawn by Naomi and is based on similar examples which we have seen used by schools, and which indicates that "pleasurable activities at home" is part of what makes problems at school worse. To break that cycle, parents are told to make home less fun.

When Things Go Wrong

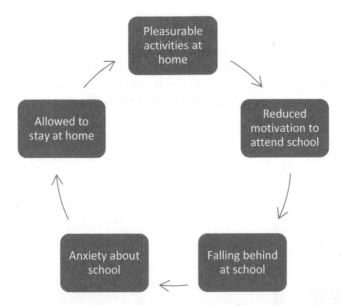

Figure 2: Cognitive Behavioural Cycle illustrating a hypothesis about how school non-attendance is maintained

Side Effects of Behaviourism at Home

Sian told us about her daughter Leila who had been out of school for 18 months. She would now be in Year 7 (aged 11–12).

> *In the run up to Christmas, Leila had a few winter viruses and she became tired, sad and less keen on going into school. She was very clingy in the mornings at the classroom door. She'd asked to come home a few times in the middle of the day, and was worried she would not be able to use the toilet at school.*
>
> *We talked to the pastoral team and one of them did some work with her to try and establish what was going on. Leila said she "just wanted to be at home with us", which we dismissed as she'd spent 2021 lockdown telling us she wanted to be back at school! Leila started having sporadic mornings off, though she mostly attended as she had a leading role in the school performance, and she wanted to keep this.*
>
> *School did very little to assist, and I believed their narrative of "she's fine at school", despite hearing accounts that she occasionally cried through the morning sessions. Leila would often refuse to go to her class after school rehearsals and one of her class teachers used to roll her eyes at me as she came out early.*
>
> *After the performances, which she loved, her attendance took a deeper nosedive. The deputy head offered sympathy but I know now her suggestions were deeply unhelpful.*

What Can We Do When School's Not Working?

She suggested making home unattractive. We did this, taking away Leila's iPad and making sure she was dressed and out of her bedroom each morning. Leila would say she didn't care and spent many hours sitting on the stairs instead of going into school. She then stopped attending altogether. The deputy head then marked her as unauthorised, suggesting we needed CAMHS evidence and that we should consider anxiety medication. She reiterated that Leila was fine at school.

Leila "burnt out" entirely in January 2022 and has been at home for 18 months, except going in for a few low demand sessions in Year 6 with her dad. Our perspective on the advice we were given has changed entirely! I do now believe that Leila will flourish when she is in the right environment and when she has the capacity to do so. It was never her that needed changing.

Sara told me the advice she was given about her son.

I was told that we had to make home unpleasant and boring for him so he would prefer school. They sent home worksheets they wanted me to make him do, told me to ban screens and toys until he did them, and when that failed, they told me to pick him up and force him into the car. There were several times when he was 7/8 years old where he tried to get run over by passing cars because he was so desperate to not go to school, and they said he was "just attention seeking".

Things got so bad that my usually chatty boy went non-verbal for several weeks and I home educated him for a full school year before he got a placement at an excellent SEN provision which meets his needs. The way he is now blossoming is wonderful, but it's an extra layer of pain, knowing that if ONLY the school had LISTENED to me and him, he wouldn't have been harmed so badly in the first place.

128

When Things Go Wrong

Anya's daughter was older, but the advice was similar.

> *We were told to get our 14-year-old autistic anxious child up at 7 am every day, get her dressed in her uniform and sit her on the sofa with no tv, no tablets, no entertainment, day in day out until she agreed to return to school.*

> *We were told that we as parents need to be harder on her and ban her from her tablet as she has it "too good at home". When the educational psychologist visited us at home she was shocked at how withdrawn, traumatised and shut down she was due to unmet needs at school. We were advised against sending her back to that school.*
>
> *She documented in her report how punishing an EBSA child is not effective.*
>
> *The way the school behaved towards us had such severe consequences I hit mental health crisis. It's taken my daughter a year to begin to show some improvement and trust in adults.*

All of these parents were given advice by professionals. Those professionals probably thought they were doing the right thing and the best thing for the child, but their perspective on children meant that they saw "behaviour" and prioritised behaviour change, with no regard for what was driving that behaviour. Undesirable behaviour had been defined as "not wanting to go to school" which means giving the child extra attention when they did not attend school is seen as reinforcing the behaviour. This had an impact on the mental health of children and their parents.

A Mental Health Lens

An increasing number of children with school attendance problems are being defined as anxious. Terms like "emotionally based school avoidance" or "EBSA" are widely used, with some parents telling us that their child's struggles with school are "because of EBSA".

It's certainly true that children who are struggling with school often show signs of anxiety, depression and other mental health problems such as OCD or panic disorder. What is less clear is whether those mental health problems are best understood as the *cause* of their attendance difficulties ("anxiety is the reason they can't go"), or a *reaction* to their experiences with school ("they feel anxious because school isn't a place where they can thrive")

For many professionals and parents, identifying anxiety as the cause of school attendance problems feels like a much more compassionate response. We have now defined this child as distressed, as opposed to badly behaved. This can feel like a great relief for some families. Many will understandably go to great lengths to distinguish themselves from those who are seen as "badly behaved" – the truants and those who are excluded.

As a mental health professional, however, there is something deeply frustrating about the focus on mental health. When a child who is anxious about school comes to see Naomi, the first thing she asks them is what happens to them at school. They tell her about things which would make anyone anxious – lessons which make no sense to them, having to sit still all day when they are desperate to move or behaviour policies which mean they could end up in detention if they forget their pen or talk to their friend. Some of the younger children say it feels like prison and they just want to run around and play. The teenagers tell her that they feel anonymous at school and as if they only exist when they do something wrong. They say that they worry about exams which they have been told will determine their whole future. Sometimes they talk about terrible experiences with their peers, including in some cases being attacked on the way home from school, videoed and having the video put on social media to be mocked and ridiculed by the other students.

When we define an emotional reaction as a "mental health problem", a set of assumptions come with that. We are essentially saying that this reaction is not an appropriate response to circumstances, and the reaction is beyond what would be reasonable. It medicalises the problem, defining it as an "mental illness" or "anxiety disorder". This way of making sense of a reaction often called *the medical model*. Emotional reactions are seen as a medical problem, in need of treatment to reduce their impact.

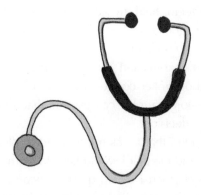

Although this might be, on the face of it, more humane than a behavioural approach, the medical model doesn't look at why the child is feeling the way they do. It implies the child's reactions are the problem, and that the pathology lies with them. This leads to the ideas (again from a medicalised perspective) that correct mental health treatment should resolve the problem, and the child will then be able to happily return to school. The child must be stopped from feeling the way that they feel.

There is no space for the possibility that this child's emotions may be an appropriate response to the circumstances that they find themselves in or that the problem might lie outside the child themselves.

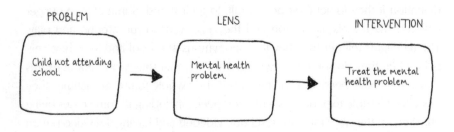

Naomi: To illustrate what we mean, let me tell you about my relationship with roller coasters. I really don't like them. They make me not just feel sick, but actually vomit very quickly. Even the baby roller coasters make me nauseous for hours. When my children were young I did sometimes have to go on a roller coaster because they had to have an adult with them in order to ride. We had annual passes to our local theme park which was only ten minutes away from home and we went a lot. I gritted my teeth, held my sick bag and endured. One terrible day we rode the Dragon about five times. I can still feel the queasiness in my stomach when I think of it.

I don't like roller coasters and I prefer not to go on them. However, I'm not anxious about roller coasters because I know that no one is going to make me go on a roller coaster, and that if I decide to go on one then that is my decision.

If someone decided that I was not allowed to dislike roller coasters, however, and told me that I would have to learn to overcome my fear of roller coasters then I would quickly become anxious. If they told me that the problem is really my avoidance of roller coasters, and that I needed a reintegration programme, telling me that from now on I would be going on a roller coaster every day, then my anxiety would really start to rise. Every night I would worry about the inevitable sickness which would come in the morning, and I would ask if I couldn't be let off, just this once.

Then someone might diagnose me with Emotionally Based Roller Coaster Avoidance (EBRCA). I would have lots of symptoms of anxiety if they insisted that I went on roller coasters every day, that's for sure.

But anxiety isn't the reason I don't like roller coasters. Anxiety is what happens to me if I'm made to ride rollers coasters against my will and when my preferences are over-ridden. I don't have a mental health problem. I just don't like roller coasters.

This happens all the time with children, where we assume that the "reason" they don't want to go to school is anxiety. We fail to distinguish between anxiety which is an appropriate reaction to being made to do something which you really dislike and have no choice about, and an "anxiety disorder", which is when that anxiety goes beyond reasonable response to circumstances. There is nothing disordered about not wanting to go to a place where you are deeply unhappy.

Emotional reactions are how our bodies and brains react when things aren't right and in many cases it is a natural response to circumstances. Being anxious is not always a sign of a mental health problem. The more pressure we put on young people, the more anxious some of them will become.

What Can We Do When School's Not Working?

Anxiety Treatments

Many interventions for school attendance problems start with the premise that the problem is an anxiety disorder, for which the primary treatment is cognitive behavioural therapy. Joanne Garfi defines the three main factors of school refusal as being "FEAR + ANXIETY + AVOIDANCE" (Garfi 2018). Training for professionals on the topic are typically full of anxiety management strategies, books have worksheets to help children challenge their anxious thoughts (Rae 2020). Many books include an anxiety cycle like the one below (which Naomi has drawn based on her clinical work).

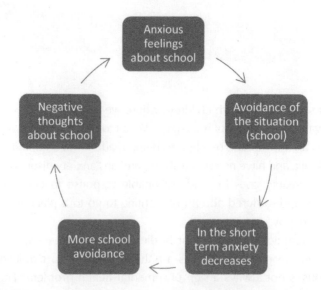

Figure 3: Cognitive Behavioural Cycle Illustrating a Hypothesis About How Anxiety Is Maintained

134

This cycle is based on cognitive behavioural principles (CBT). It is called a "maintenance cycle". In other words, it is a cycle which hypothesises about how anxious feelings are being maintained by thoughts and behaviour. These types of cycles are a common part of cognitive behaviour therapy. Intervention involves trying to break those maintenance cycles which usually means gradually exposing people to the things which they fear. This basic theory is well supported by research and Naomi has used it successfully with young people who have fears of (for example) dogs, public transport, being without their parent or even balloons.

However, there's a problem when it is applied to school attendance issues. The cycle frames not attending school as a behaviour designed to avoid anxious feelings about school. Within the CBT model, avoidance is likely to increase anxiety. However, there is no space in this model for school to be genuinely an aversive place for some young people. Their anxiety has been conceptualised as irrational.

The problem is that when they are used without an awareness of context, these cycles have the potential to make things worse.

Luke (15) told me what happened to him when he stopped going to school. His experience of exposure-based CBT was not good. To him it felt as though he was being deliberately made more upset by his therapist.

> *I saw a therapist and things got even worse because the therapist didn't understand. The whole attitude of CAMHS is go back to school. They treated it as if it's a dog phobia or something. They treated it as if it's something that you can do normal CBT with.*
>
> *They thought that by upsetting me more, that would make me feel better. The therapist was really not helping at all.*
>
> *I was admitted to hospital because I was suicidal. I went to hospital for not long, and then a psychiatrist came on an emergency visit and prescribed me risperidone.*
>
> *This was in summer 2020. All throughout the time I had very extreme depression. I was making my art throughout the whole time and had that. I obviously wasn't doing any work at that point.*
>
> *Then after the summer holidays (well, for everyone else, it didn't feel like a holiday at all for me) I didn't go back to school.*
>
> *Then they said it was a case of school refusal, emotionally based school refusal.*

The use of this simple anxiety maintenance cycle as an intervention for school attendance is a very limited form of CBT. It conceptualises school problems as a school phobia, an irrational response to a benign situation. But to young people like Luke, school does not feel benign.

What is missing from Luke's experience is an understanding of what is making him feel so terrible – and what is missing in the intervention is meaningful change which addresses the reasons why the anxiety is there in the first place.

When maintenance cycles are used like this without any consideration of causes, the consequences for young people can be severe. They can make things worse, as they did for Luke.

Identifying Possible Side Effects

Any psychosocial intervention can have unanticipated outcomes – and the behaviour and attendance policies which are being enacted by schools are psychosocial interventions. The first rule of any intervention must be *do no harm*. Or, to phase it differently: *don't do anything which makes things worse*.

We found that there are unexpected consequences to many psychosocial interventions and that these are often seen by parents rather than by professionals. Interventions which ignore the reasons for a child's reluctance to go to school have the potential to make things worse and push a child into deeper distress, as happened with Luke and Leila. Before implementing any psychosocial intervention, professionals need to think through the unanticipated possible outcomes.

It is particularly important that the impact on young people for whom any intervention does not work is thought through. No intervention will work for everyone. What will be the impact on the child whose behaviour doesn't improve due to the Dojo app, for example, or who never makes it onto the rainbow? What about those who, despite frequent detentions, find it hard to organise themselves and get their uniform correct?

Every intervention can go (at least) two ways, and a proper risk assessment needs to include thinking through the consequences if this intervention does not work as expected.

As an example, think about the very common advice which parents are given to "make home less pleasant". Professionals give this advice in the hope that it will quickly lead to the child deciding that school isn't so bad after all, and going to school.

However, it doesn't work like this for everyone. And for those for whom it doesn't work, the consequences can be serious. Withdrawing stimulation at home makes some children very unhappy and prevents them from learning.

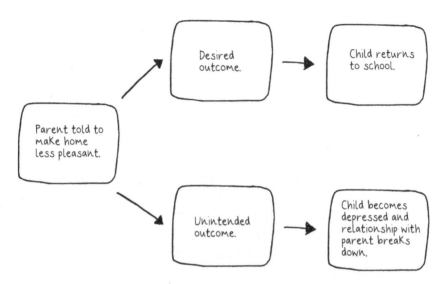

Figure 4: Unintended consequences of making home less pleasant

Many behavioural interventions work by leveraging unhappiness. They try to make a child who isn't at school feel bored at home, so they will choose school instead as the least bad of two options. Rather than making school better, they make home worse.

This means that already unhappy children become more unhappy – and very unhappy children are less likely to return to school. It can also damage the relationship between parents and children. From the child's perspective, adults are simply being unpleasant and are not listening to their distress.

Exposure Therapy Without Buy-in from the Child Is Not Therapeutic

The unexpected consequences of treating a problem as an anxiety disorder can also be negative. The reality of what is called "exposure therapy" or "reintegration" for school attendance is that it is often done against a child's will or with only reluctant consent.

If a child is told that there is no other option but to return to school and to undergo an exposure programme, then they cannot truly consent. For consent to be meaningful, there must be another option. This is often inconvenient for adults, but it gets to the heart of good therapeutic practice. In order for anxiety to reduce, the child must feel that exposing themselves to feared situations is within their control and not forced upon them. The desired outcome needs

What Can We Do When School's Not Working?

to be something that they want for themselves, rather than just something that adults want for them. Consent is a fundamental part of this.

This makes exposure therapy for school attendance problems very different to exposure-based cognitive behavioural therapy for adults. For adults, being in control is understood to be an essential part of the process. For children, this is often disregarded and instead parents are told that the child must learn to respect authority and do what they are told. Parents tell us that they were told that children must not be allowed to avoid school as it will make their anxiety worse – and that what happens next can involve them being forced into school and their parents told to leave. For some, this can create a trauma response (which we talk about more in Chapter 7). Being forced to go somewhere that you don't feel safe and then being trapped there is enough to cause trauma, even if the adults around you think that you are overreacting and that everything is fine.

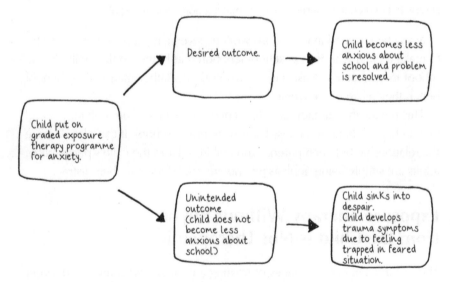

Figure 5: Unintended consequences of graded exposure

Putting in the Break Clause

Every psychosocial intervention should have a break clause. There should be a point where the adults check whether it is having the desired effect, and if it isn't, then something else should be tried. Otherwise children find themselves in a downwards spiral where the answer to "this isn't working" is "just keep going". This has a serious effect on their mental health and wellbeing.

When Things Go Wrong

Before any intervention is put in place (and any interaction can be seen as an intervention), a risk assessment should ask what will happen if the child does not react in the way which is intended. It should be decided when that intervention will be stopped and something else tried. If anxiety responds to exposure, this happens relatively quickly – in weeks or a few months. Exposure therapy which goes on for years is not working and can lead to hopelessness for everyone.

Here are some examples of unintended consequences.

Table 4.1 Unintended Consequences of Interventions

Intervention	Desired effect	Unintended effect
Tell child and parent of the terrible life-long consequences of not attending school.	Child returns to school, driven by fear of the future.	Child continues to not attend school and becomes hopeless about their future as well as the present.
Fine parents or threaten them with court/prison.	Parents put more pressure on child from fear of the consequences. Child goes to school.	Financial strain on families. Tensions increase between children and parents. Child becomes fearful that their parents may go to prison.

(Continued)

Table 4.1 (Continued)

Intervention	Desired effect	Unintended effect
Introduce rewards and consequences for school attendance.	Child goes to school, motivated by the reward.	Child does not go to school and is punished for it, leading to a deterioration in their mental health and a breakdown in their relationship with their parents.
Reintegration programmes based on principles of exposure therapy.	Child's anxiety decreases due to gradual habituation, and they are able to attend school full time.	Child becomes sensitised to school by repeated experiences of being highly distressed and not being allowed to leave – leading to "school trauma". Child loses trust in parents and school after experiences of being repeatedly forced to attend.
Parents told to stop interacting with child during the school day or allowing the child to do anything pleasurable.	Child is bored at home and so chooses to go to school.	Child becomes depressed, isolated and miserable at home. Relationships between child and parents are affected. Child is not able to learn when at home during the school day as they are prevented from engaging in activities.
School does not send work home.	Child is motivated to attend school so they don't fall behind.	Child does not regularly attend and cannot keep up with work either and so falls more behind.
Child is made to sign agreements where they lose their "privileges" such as seeing friends at weekends if they do not attend school.	Child is motivated to attend school to get the privileges.	Child does not regularly attend and the weekends are no longer a time of respite. Child is not allowed to engage in activities or see friends at weekends and becomes isolated and increasingly unhappy. Relationship between parents and child become strained.

(Continued)

Table 4.1 (Continued)

Intervention	Desired effect	Unintended effect
Parents are told to be consistent and follow through with all boundaries and agreements.	Child attends school.	Child does not regularly attend and parents follow through with consequences, potentially for months and years as no time limit is given. Child's social and extracurricular opportunities are affected and their relationship with their parents deteriorates.
Parents told not to allow children to avoid school as it will make their anxiety worse.	Child attends school and anxiety reduces.	Parents try to force children to attend school against their will, seeing this as anxiety. Child's distress increases and relationship with parents deteriorates.
Anxiety management strategies	Child feels more able to manage their anxiety about school and so is able to attend.	Child feels that their concerns about school are not being heard or addressed and becomes hopeless about the possibility that a professional can help them.

One way of considering the unanticipated consequences might just be about asking inconvenient questions in meetings. It's about asking: "Does this have the potential to do harm?" as well as "What is the outcome we want?". It's about thinking through the risk to this child and whether the intervention might be pushing them further along a path towards serious mental health difficulties.

What to Do Now: The Trust Test

We hope that after reading this chapter you may have a new perspective on the way we understand difficulties with school attendance and behaviour problems – but you also be feeling quite hopeless. You might be thinking that this is the only way you know. You are now more aware of unanticipated outcomes and side effects but you still don't know what to do differently or how to avoid them.

There are professionals taking different approaches and we'll be talking more about them in the next chapter. There are schools doing amazing, psychologically informed, work for the young people in their care and young people flourishing and learning both in and out of school.

Our main recommendation here is that before any intervention is initiated (including a simple suggestion to "make home less fun"), take some time to think through the consequences if it doesn't work as adults hope. It's a human tendency to focus on the desired outcome and not to think through what will happen if that does not materialise. We've developed a tool to do this – the Trust Test.

The Trust Test is a way to evaluate the likely harm before you start.

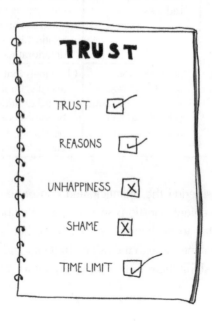

Table 4.2 The Trust Test

☑ **Trust**
Will this intervention build trust between the child and adults?
Will this intervention lead to the child feeling that their voice is heard and matters?
Will this intervention improve relationships between this child and the adults around them?

(Continued)

Table 4.2 (Continued)

☑ **Reasons**
Does this intervention look at reasons, or just reactions? What are the causes of this child's distress? What are they telling us with their behaviour and emotional reactions? If we saw their behaviour as communication, what would we be hearing?
✗ **Unhappiness**
Does this intervention use unhappiness to try to persuade the child into behaving differently? Telling parents to ignore their child while at home is deliberately making a child unhappy – this can have long-lasting consequences. Putting a child in isolation uses unhappiness and can have consequences for how they come to feel about school and themselves.
✗ **Shame**
Does this intervention use shame to try to make the child behave differently? Shame-based interventions include public consequences, for example a child being excluded from a school trip or the prom due to their school attendance record. Other shame-based interventions include making children sit in the corridor where they can be seen, or writing their name on the board, or moving their name to the Red zone. Increasing shame is likely to lead to a deterioration in emotional wellbeing and an increased reluctance to return to school.
☑ **Time Limit**
When and how will you evaluate if this intervention has made a difference? When will the break clause kick in? Interventions which aim to reduce anxiety or change behaviour should work fairly quickly – a few weeks or a month or two. If there is no change after a couple of weeks, it's likely that it isn't working and something else should be tried.

Summary

- When children aren't fine at school, it's usually framed as either behaviour or anxiety.
- Reactions are confused with reasons, and so interventions focus on changing children's reactions without considering the reasons.
- Many well-intended interventions have side effects and unintended consequences.

- Any intervention should be risk-assessed for the unanticipated consequences as well as for the desired outcome.
- The Trust Test is a way to evaluate an intervention for possible harm.

References and Further Reading

Bennett, T. (2020). *Running the Room: The Teacher's Guide to Behaviour*. Melton, Woodbridge, UK: John Catt Publishers

Deci, E. and Ryan, R. (1985). *Intrinsic Motivation and Self-Determination in Human Behaviour*. New York: Plenum Press.

Garfi, J. (2018). *Overcoming School Refusal: A Practical Guide for Teachers, Counsellors, Caseworkers and Parents*. Melbourne: Australian Academic Press Group Pty Ltd.

Kearney, C. A. (2021). *Getting Your Child Back to School: A Parent's Guide to Solving School Attendance Problems: Revised and Updated Edition*. New York: Oxford University Press.

Kohn, A. (2018). *Punished By Rewards: The Trouble with Gold Stars, Incentive Plans, A's, Praise and Other Bribes*. San Francisco, CA: HarperOne.

Rae, T. (2020). *Understanding and Supporting Children and Young People with Emotionally Based School Avoidance (EBSA)*. Northampton, UK: Hinton House Publishers Ltd.

Ryan, R. M. and Deci, E. L. (2017). *Self-Determination Theory: Basic Psychological Needs in Motivation, Development and Wellness*. New York: Guilford Publishing.

Thambirajah, M., Grandison, K. and De-Hayes, L. (2008). *Understanding School Refusal: A Handbook for Professionals in Education, Health and Social Care*. London: Jessica Kingsley Publishers.

5

What Can We Do Instead?

In this chapter you will find:

1. Changing the Lens
2. Different Ways to Intervene

   Engaging Those On the Margins
   Relationships On and Off the Pitch
   Self-managed Learning
   Kids Do Well If They Can
   Building Self Worth

Introduction

In Chapter 4, we talked about common interventions used with children who are struggling with school attendance, and outlined the pitfalls of these approaches. Whenever we talk about this, teachers ask, so what do we do instead? This is completely understandable. The stories of those who are trying to do things differently are often unheard, going on in small projects and pockets around the country without much fanfare. There are, however, many innovators who are trying to do things differently, and this chapter shines a light on some of them. These stories are examples. They aren't meant to be comprehensive. We found as we talked to more people that their stories had very similar themes, and it is those that we have tried to pull out here.

Here you'll read about different ways to intervene with children who are struggling with school attendance and behaviour. As with earlier chapters, it uses stories of personal experience (in this case, from professionals) with evidence-based interventions.

Changing the Lens

Before you think about doing anything at all, take a deep breath. From the perspective of this book, the most important shift you can make is in how you make sense of the problem. That will inform everything. In the previous chapter, we described what happens when a child's attendance and behaviour is seen as the problem and how these can contribute to a pathway where things get worse instead of better.

Behavioural interventions aim to change the child's behaviour by manipulating the consequences, anxiety interventions aim to change the child's emotional reactions by desensitising them to school or teaching anxiety management. Both of these interventions position the child and the family as the people who need to change.

We've suggested that both behaviour and attendance can be seen as a signal that something isn't going right between the child and the school. From this perspective, attendance and behaviour are just the visible signs of an invisible problem which may date back years. The children themselves aren't the problem, they are pointing out a problem.

Seeing problems as a signal means that it's very unlikely that the long-awaited referral to CAMHS is going to work magic. Counsellors and therapists often (but not always) focus only on the child and family, and not on the interaction between the child and the world around them. Changing what happens at school is usually beyond their scope.

Our starting point is that the best way to improve a child's learning is to address how the child feels about their school and themselves, tapping into their internal drive to learn and do well. This doesn't mean an intervention focused on solely changing what the child thinks and does, but an intervention focused on changing what happens at school. Self-determination theory provides an evidence-based structure which suggests where the focus should be.

If we accept that the environment is part of the problem, then we can't plan to "fix" the child, send them back into the same environment and then expect things to go differently. If that really worked, then there would be no frequent offenders in schools. We wouldn't hear about young people spending a month in isolation. Young people would "get the message" when given a detention or isolation, they would change their behaviour and all would be well.

Different Ways to Intervene

What Can We Do When School's Not Working?

In the following sections, we will use case studies to show how different organisations are working with those who are struggling. These interventions aim to help children learn and they use different methods in order to do this. The case examples here are not meant to be a comprehensive list. There will be many more ways to do this well.

The approaches you'll hear about come from different perspectives. Some are ex-teachers, others are psychologists or counsellors. As we listened to their stories about working in different contexts, we were surprised to hear recurring themes each time. None of them talked about putting more pressure on young people, there was no mention of punishments and rewards and many didn't focus specifically on individual at-risk young people at all. None of them identified young people as the problem or set out how they must change. Instead, they focused on changing the way that things worked around the young people to create situations in which they could feel better about themselves and about learning. They described a focus on connection, collaboration, empowerment and competence – the pillars of self-determination theory.

Some practitioners were explicit about using self-determination theory while others weren't. No matter what their methodology (and these are quite different), they talked about the same priorities. Helping young people feel competent and valuable, giving them a voice, working collaboratively with them and prioritising connections and relationships.

You'll read several stories in the chapter but we could have included many more. There are organisations who use music, drama and art to engage at-risk young people, and those who meet young people in skateboarding parks. These stories are meant to be examples to give you ideas, not templates to follow.

What Can We Do Instead?

Engaging Those On the Margins: Nurture Is Not Enough

"Finding My Voice" is a one-to-one and small group project based in the south of England, which works with children and young people in mainstream school who school staff identify as vulnerable in some way, such as those considered as at risk of exclusion or struggling with attendance. There is also a whole school approach with the same name, which you can read about in Chapter 3. It seeks to offer something more than a nurturing approach, and aims to identify and remove barriers these individuals are facing, and help them change their own narrative. It is firmly grounded on the principles of self-determination theory, and focuses on building relationships, supporting their autonomy and developing feelings of competence. (You can find out more about the project at higginsoncreativeeducation.com and www.findingmyvoice.co.uk.)

Abigail sat down with Rachel Higginson, the founder of the project and heard about their work.

> *I was concerned with a theme of the group on the "outside" when I went round schools across the country, a group for whom education wasn't meeting their needs. Children at risk of exclusion, school refusers, anyone who was vulnerable and on the margins. I would always ask what support they were getting, and they were always getting something. The interventions were very nurturing and therapeutic, but not necessarily very practical. There wasn't something they could walk out of the room and then use in their life. I saw there was a need for something deeply applied, that those kids could learn about themselves and about life and then apply in the classroom. We are trying to change the narrative for these young people, find out what those barriers are.*

We've been running this one-to-one and small group project for about six years now. We work with individuals for around 4–5 weeks. We bring them together into small groups of around 6–8, and run projects with about 20 in each school for two terms. Then we have a final project – it can be an exhibition or a performance, a product, it can be a speech day. We've made lots of films. We then developed a transition project because we found that kids were really making much stronger choices, feeling really empowered in their school life and then going to secondary school and it would all change and revert back. Our transition project has worked really well and has a positive impact and a good success rate.

The theory which shapes it all is self-determination theory – relatedness, competence and autonomy or agency. When we talk about relationships in school, it's often very one-sided and it's like a parent-child thing rather than that we bring mutual value and I really like being around you. I think that twist is really important. Quite often with children or anyone who's at rock bottom, they see people being compassionate to them and feeling sorry for them. They don't see that they've got value or what they bring to others. For a lot of these young people, beginning to give them nuggets of responsibility and the message "I need you" is a really powerful way in. When you have young people who are constantly failing in school, the impact that has on their self-determination and their motivation is just catastrophic. That feeling of being incompetent. That became a really important element to consider in the project.

The foundation of the project for me is building really strong relationships with "hard to reach" families. We do a trip to Exeter City Football each term because I found that is one activity that all the parents will come to. Parents come whom schools have never managed to interact with before. This is an intentional culture of belonging, community-centred. I think for some young people, they are victims and they give themselves that label and the world gives them that label. I think changing personal narratives is really important. I'm really passionate about creating something that you belong to and you've got a sense of a tribe. I know there's lots of layers of belonging in school, but for me, having something that you feel connected to, you bring value to others.

When I first met Oliver, he was not in class. He was really destructive, throwing furniture, jumping out windows, really unhappy. He wasn't allowed in the classroom because he was deemed unsafe. The school were very caring towards him, but something wasn't working. I came in to work with him one to one and we were slowly getting to a place where he was opening up. He was passionate about flight and planes.

I managed to get him a visit to the Air Traffic Management Centre. It was absolutely fascinating; he just thought the whole thing was wonderful. We spent the whole day there, wandering round the different rooms. At the end of the day, we sat in the café and David who'd shown him round said, "So, Oliver, do you think

What Can We Do Instead?

you'd like to come and work here one day?" Oliver replied, "I would love to, but I can't because I've got ADHD and I'm autistic."

David sort of chuckled and said, that's ok, most of the staff here are neurodivergent, you would fit right in. The really unbelievable part was that the next day he asked to go back into class. He completely reintegrated from the next day, no challenging behaviours, no dysregulation. It was as simple as that for him.

Oliver was very loved in his school, but nobody was working with him in this practical change of life kind of way. Those conversations and that slant weren't occurring. It just goes to show the sort of misconceptions that our young people can be harbouring. The barrier for him was the labels he had been given, he perceived that they meant he couldn't be a normal person in the world. He did his SATs, he did well, he felt proud.

Football Beyond Borders: Relationships On and Off the Pitch

Football Beyond Borders (FBB) as a concept developed after the London Riots in 2011. The founders wanted to connect with disenfranchised, angry young people, and thought they were likely to be football fans. There are now 150 programmes in schools, in London, Manchester and Birmingham. Young people who are passionate about football, but who are disengaging from school and at risk of exclusion follow a specially designed weekly programme over four years. This long-term, intensive support is built around relationships, and underpinned by attachment theory, understanding of developmental trauma, adolescent neuroscience and humanistic theory. This work is in mainstream schools.

FBB practitioners become part of the school pastoral team, funded by the school, and work with groups of young people over four years, from the age of 12/13. Groups are formed of a balance of those at risk of exclusion, passive learners and a few role models. Far from focusing on solely football skills, FBB teach socio-emotional learning, and work on self-regulation, responsible decision making and social awareness, both on and off the pitch. They teach a life skills curriculum for an hour in the classroom each week, and then use reflective questioning to explore and apply the lessons on the pitch. Football is a safe context where the young people are able to express their emotions and work through difficulties with guidance. The football is, by their own admission, a "Trojan horse".

Preventing exclusion, attainment in English and maths and social and emotional learning are the stated goals. Students graduating from the programme make powerful statements about the impact of the programme on their life and the development of key life skills. Evidence from FBB's impact report reveals that 95% of those who were at-risk of exclusion/managed move remained in school. Those who had attended the programme were 11 times more likely than their peers (in a matched comparison group) to pass their GCSEs. (You can read their impact report, and find out more about their work at www.footballbeyondborders.org.)

In addition to working directly with young people, FBB work with the adults in school, running a fortnightly programme offering a reflective space for senior staff. Abigail met with Stefan, who runs groups for teachers which he describes as often emotional, with the aim of freeing them to develop best practice in a non-judgemental environment.

Stefan was a secondary teacher for 10 years. He subsequently did a counselling qualification and an MA in group and individual psychotherapy. Here he explained how he works.

> I am running reflective practice groups for senior leadership teams, pastoral leads and heads of year. It's a processing space for the staff. When you do this work in schools there's such a tension. The conditioning is, "I haven't got time to be doing this and if I start reflecting on things, I won't get my books marked, so go away."
>
> It takes about six months for groups to really fully get it. Then they adopt it as this way of being and then they say, we really need this. You cannot work with this concentration of children with a range of complex needs and not have a space to reflect on the emotional impact of the work. No other professional working with children like that would be expected to do that.
>
> It's a space to think more reflectively and creatively about the most challenging young people that they work with. If something organically arises out of it which is a solution, that's great. But the primary purpose here is just about being reflective. For the majority of these groups, we run fortnightly for up to 75 minutes with pastoral leadership teams, heads of year, DSLs, there'll usually be some SLT in there. Those groups are more about bringing the most challenging children, that elicit strong reactions from adults. Those are the children most at risk of being excluded.
>
> It is our remit to start with relationships. My argument is that in order to have any real deep and sustainable impact, we have to be working with adults as well. In schools, we can't just work with the young people because the experiences, feelings and practices of the adults are inseparable from the experiences of the children. We've worked with leadership staff who've never sat and asked themselves "What is going on here? What's happening between us that's potentially being mirrored in the wider school community?"
>
> It's been mind-blowing stuff. We combine a classic Reflective Practice structure, based on the work of Dr Arabella Kurtz, with principles from humanistic group therapy. It's like a group supervision, where each week there's an informal rota and a staff member is expected to bring a particular young person to discuss. We're

saying that these children are so complex that we have to slow down. We have to really go into trying to translate and make sense of what's being communicated in the behaviour. Even if it's experienced as really obnoxious and really triggering.

It's not about saying you should feel bad because they've had difficult lives. It's that they can't make sense of what's going on for them. We're the adults. We have to try and be reflective and give ourselves space to think about these children, because they often can't find space in their own chaotic lives to think about what's happening for them. If we can't even do that, we may as well exclude them now.

There were these two boys that a head of year was on the verge of excluding. They were saying these boys were going to be excluded, there was nothing we could do for them. And myself and my colleague, who worked at the school asked them to tell us a little bit about them. All this stuff came up, and we decided collectively it was important for their particular context and circumstances to be considered before any decisions were made. We're still met with the understandable defence of "loads of people have had hard lives" but these children were eliciting really strong responses in these adults, because they were projecting what they'd picked up in dysfunctional relationships, usually with their caregivers. We were like, "Well, let's slow down, let's breathe, let's come back into the felt response. What are you feeling as you talk about these two children."

We are constantly getting them to come back to and stay with their experience. It's hard to even capture it in words, really, but it moved them into their sadness and a sense their own rejection as an adult that "I can't reach these kids" and "what is it that I'm doing wrong?" And then the person who'd brought them to the circle was really upset and explained they had had a similar experience to one of the boys, but had never talked about it. They were almost jealous that this child could meet it by acting it out and being like, "Fuck off" to adults. It was a process of discovery and reflection on these children.

We came back two weeks later and the member of staff was saying that they'd given the boys 20 minutes of their time every morning since she had last seen us and subsequently had decided that they didn't need to be excluded. And 18 months later, they still weren't excluded. It's not what we said, it's obviously about her putting in the time for them. She said, "what I'd never given these boys is a chance to just speak and to be listened to". She brought in a bit of food for them, they sat in this room together. First couple of days, it was a bit weird, then something shifted, and the teacher felt she could manage the relationships and find ways of supporting them that meant that they didn't need to be excluded. I think that's incredible.

Sometimes we get pushback, saying we didn't sign up for therapy, this is just about the children that we work with, it's not about our feelings. And I say, I wonder if it is that simple, to separate your feelings from these vulnerable children you work with. But I often say that I don't think you can completely separate professional

What Can We Do Instead?

and personal. While I'm not asking anybody to disclose personal things, it may well be that something that happened to you in the past or even recently is connected to what you're experiencing in the relationship with this child.

Another example is about how the team was being run. In this school, nobody talked about how anybody felt, and that message spilled out into the school's practices with children. There was an interesting dynamic in senior leadership, with one person who avoided all conflict, and another behaving like a bully, and ruling with an iron fist. People kept leaving and everybody was absolutely terrified of that teacher. Everybody agreed with each other all the time and was trying to be nice, but you could cut the tension with a knife. The school organism was deeply damaged.

When we came in, something about being external facilitators meant that we had a vantage point. We didn't collude with them. We asked, what on earth is happening here, nobody really says what they think. They shared with us in the group that when they first started at the school, they were appalled by how the staff member spoke to children and adults. But they thought maybe that was just the way things were done, and no one ever really challenged it. We named all of that, and there was a complete revolution. In the end there was a vote of no confidence and the staff member left.

Self-managed Learning: Metacognition and Purpose

Many of those of those who are trying to help children struggling with school end up working around the outside, as something which happens in addition to lessons-as-usual. They try to increase student voice and promote a more compassionate approach, but they don't directly challenge the way that learning happens at school. Dr Ian Cunningham has done something different. He has tried to bring empowerment and autonomy right into the process of how young people learn. He has used his evidence-based "self-managed learning" (Cunningham, 2021) with adults in organisations ranging from British Airways to Sainsburys, and in the last 30 years has extended the model to young people.

The idea of self-managed learning is that it empowers young people to start to make choices about their lives, and to feel like they are in the driving seat of their learning. The method advocates a holistic approach which is akin to coaching, looking at the whole person rather than just their next academic qualifications. It asks "How can we help these students to lead a good life, as defined by them?"

The approach is deceptively simple. It is grounded in five key questions which young people answer and discuss in small groups. There are: Where have I been? Where am I now? Where do I want to get to? How will I get there? How will I know if I've arrived?

The key is the values underlying the simple structure. The five questions and progress towards them are discussed regularly. Within their groups, pupils are known and cared for, and they are given the freedom to make decisions about their learning, while also sharing this journey with others. The goals are their own, and the aim is to help them to create a meaningful life for themselves.

Self managed learning for young people can be used either within mainstream schools or in alternative educational settings. Cunningham established the Self Managed Learning College (SMLC) for young people aged 9–16 in Brighton and Hove in the 1990s, and it still runs there today (www.smlcollege.org.uk). It runs for only a few hours a day, because it is not a school. Young people (who are all home educated or have EOTAS packages) attend in either the morning or the afternoon. Many of these young people have had unsuccessful experiences at school. Some of them have

been excluded while others have become highly anxious. Others are there because their parents wanted an alternative education.

The Centre for Self Managed Learning have carried out research with parents and young people, who said that the aspects of self-managed learning which made a difference to them were the focus on autonomy and choices, feeling seen as an individual and finding a sense of purpose in life. Young people who participated in self-managed learning programmes in schools talked about the important of having time to think, of being able to talk to adults as equals and of feeling that it had increased their confidence. They also said it helped them think about their future and to see learning in a wider perspective.

Cunningham explained their approach:

> *Our approach is about metacognition; we want them to think about what they think about. We do that by asking these questions. They have to think about their beliefs and values. We separate the two. Values are what you care about and beliefs are what you hold to be true.*
>
> *Somebody might say, "Well, I want to live in a nice house and have a family." So we ask, "And what does that mean? And would you want to travel?"*

"I'm not really interested in travelling."
"Do you want to make lots of money?"
"Well, I just need enough."
"So what? You're going to need some work, which will get you that money?"
We'll say things like. "Well, that type of work might give you how much?"

And this might be coming from a person who is in care, or who lives in a squalid flat. You have to deal with all that complexity. But it's always just the person in front of you. If you don't know something you just ask them.

In school, teachers ask questions because they know the answer. At SMLC we ask questions because we don't know the answer. We ask, "What do you like? What don't you like? What do you want to do with your life? What help do you need? What would be useful to you?"

We ask questions because we don't know the answers. These are real questions.

Some people get it very quickly. But others take time. They can't undo the damage in a week. They've been at school for six or seven years, you can't expect them to recover immediately. They come in sometimes not trusting what we say. We say, "We value what you want." They imagine there's a hidden agenda, they think we can't really mean it. The main thing is the peer group, that's what makes the change. Their friends start to say, "They're for real, you can actually do anything you want." Then they start to get it. We know that the peer group is the biggest influence on teenagers. What we want to do is establish a positive peer group.

We want parents to know that these are the principles we work from. These are the non-negotiables. They need to come to the meetings and to the learning groups and to sign up for the principles. They have to buy into the structure in some way, because that's what the college is there for. If they don't want that, that's fine. Quite a bit of my time is advising parents on other choices that they've got.

One of our current groups when he first came only wanted to talk about wrestling. He would sit in the office with the co-ordinator and they would be chatting about wrestling. The co-ordinator was prepared to learn about wrestling from him because that was all he wanted to do. Then he gradually learned to branch out and to engage more in the community. Now he is doing great within the community. Very active in many other things.

We had a girl who was excluded for taking a knife into school and threatening to knife somebody. I met with that girl and said, "Well, if you actually bring a knife in, it's against the law. We could suspend you." She gave an explanation for what had happened. She'd been threatened by other girls and she wanted to scare them. She came to SMLC and she was okay. We never had any issues with her. We've had students who've been excluded from school in some cases for violence like that and it's worked out fine. They realise that we're different, and that the way that they've been violent has been inappropriate.

What Can We Do Instead?

In collaboration with the University of Sussex, Cunningham has run small groups in East Sussex using self-managed learning in schools. At the time of writing, you can watch some highlights from the project on YouTube (search for Self-Managed Learning in Action). The exciting thing about this project is how little time it takes up, and how it can be integrated into current curriculums and systems. Trained learning advisors facilitated small group discussions with six pupils for an hour every three weeks. Pupils set themselves goals according to what they want for themselves in the future, they make decisions and work collaboratively, helping each other reach their goals.

Collaborative Problem Solving: Kids Do Well if They Can

What alternatives are there for those whose disruptive behaviour at school means that they are being secluded, excluded or restrained? Collaborative problem solving (CPS) is a methodology based on the principles of cognitive therapy which has been tested (and found to be effective in randomised control trials) in mainstream schools across the USA.

Dr Ross Greene, clinical psychologist, is the originator of this approach (which he now calls Collaborative and Proactive Solutions™) for working with children and young people with behavioural challenges in school. It has been used with children with the most extreme behaviour, including those with diagnoses of oppositional defiant disorder. He argues that behavioural approaches assume the problem is that the child does not want to behave (or is choosing to misbehave), and so consequences are used to try and motivate the child to change. Instead, he argues, we could assume that children do want to do well but can't always do so because they are lacking the skills – and so a more effective approach would target those skills rather than the behaviour.

The method is outlined in detail in *Lost In School* (Greene 2014) as well as other books for parents and professionals. Recent studies show a significant and sustained decrease in restraint and seclusion used in schools after the CPS approach was introduced. Lists of the current research can be found at www.livesinthebalance.org and at www.thinkkids.org/research along with links to resources and training.

The CPS lens sees behaviour as the result of "lagging skills". By this they mean some children have skills behind those which are expected for their age group and this causes them problems at school. We see the results of those problems in their behaviour. These skills are in areas such as emotion regulation, difficulty maintaining focus, difficulties in appreciating the perspective of other people and difficulties in transitions. This fits well with the developmental perspective we outlined in Chapter 2. Children develop at different paces, and these differences – particularly for those with a "spiky cognitive profile" – can cause problems at school.

CPS suggests that challenging behaviour is a signal that the child is struggling to meet expectations due to developmental differences and skills they have not yet developed. Consequences do nothing to change this, because they do not help children to develop the skills they are lacking. Central to the CPS ethos is the idea that "all children do well if they can" – so if they aren't doing well, then adults need to work out what the problem is, and the most effective solutions to that problem will be found by working collaboratively with the child. Unsolved problems cause challenging behaviour, and focusing on the behaviour does nothing to solve the problem.

In his book, Greene uses the example of academic skills to show what he means – if a child can't yet multiply fractions, introducing harsher consequences for failing to do so will not help them learn more effectively. The child would prefer to be able to multiply fractions, the problem is not a lack of motivation on their part, the problem is that they lack the skills.

What Can We Do Instead?

The CPS approach is highly practical and can be applied by classroom teachers. They suggest that teachers do an assessment of a child's problem areas and lagging skills (for which they provide a free template) and then take a problem-solving approach collaboratively with the child. This problem-solving approach does not address behaviour directly, but instead addresses the unsolved problems which are assumed to be behind the behaviour.

This approach has three main steps.

1. Empathy. The goal of this step is to understand why the child can't meet a particular expectation and what their concerns are. It involves the adult taking a non-judgemental and curious approach to what is going on and asking the child for their perspective.
2. Define Adult Concerns. In this step, the adult adds in their own concerns – not their preferred solutions, but their concerns about how this problem is affecting the child and other people.
3. Invitation. Now that both the child's concerns and the adult concerns have been identified, it's time to generate some potential solutions to address the concerns. The adult invites the child to suggest their solutions, starting with something like "I wonder if there's a way for us to do something about (your concerns) which takes into account (my concerns)."

Then the task to choose a solution which both child and adult are happy with and give it a try. If it doesn't work, then it's back to the drawing board.

What Can We Do When School's Not Working?

If you want to know more about this approach, the process is elaborated in several books and trainings which are listed at the end of this chapter. It can be used for young people with a wide range of problems and reasons for their difficulties at school.

Building Self Worth through Co-Production

States of Mind is a social enterprise working in secondary schools and sixth form colleges in inner London. One of their long-term projects is called Breaking the Silence and involves working collaboratively with young people to co-construct how education could be evaluated. The project mostly takes place during 1½ hours on a normal school day, in mainstream schools, and it is up to the young people involved to what extent and how they participate. In each phase, which lasts a year, a new group of sixth formers choose to be part of the project, and decide together, without a curriculum, how to take the project forward.

The project is the brain-child of Dr Chris Bagley, an education psychologist who is passionate about working with those who are let down by the education system. He sees how young people's sense of self-worth is damaged by schooling leading, for some, to incarceration and lifelong harm. He helps young people regain their sense of competence through open ended projects which they work on together.

He told Abigail about their journey.

> States of Mind reimagines what education can look like and takes action to promote change. Our work mostly takes place in lesson time, in mainstream schools across the London borough of Newham. The approach has been successful in regular schools and can be used by anyone, though it requires surrendering control of the curriculum and being open to co-constructing projects alongside student participants.
>
> In 2019, at a time when Ofsted were conducting a public consultation, we ran focus groups with about 80 young people, and asked them: "What do you think education evaluation could be?" What emerged was a tsunami of critique and possibilities from young people who never get asked their views about what education should be. Teenagers said things like "Teachers don't like us", "We're not learning, we're memorising" and "I feel like a robot".
>
> For the young people I have spent most of my time working with, those held in the secure estate (prison) sector or attending pupil referral units or "alternative provision", schooling is often an alienating, marginalising experience that leads to considerable emotional damage. They spend their entire life, from being on the giraffe table in Year 1, all the way to being kicked out of school in Year 10, feeling "stupid" or "dumb". Some say things like: "I'm a retard" or "I'm a spastic". These are words you hear all the time when you meet these kids. People think setting {by ability} is fine, even though the academic evidence shows that it causes psychological distress, particularly for those placed in "bottom sets". In the countries that have mixed ability classes, the attainment is as good, if not better, and it's certainly better socially.
>
> There are a number of underpinning elements in regard to States of Mind. Self-determination theory is at the core of everything because it's very well demonstrated over decades of research. I think the other thing at the core is a worldview around co-production. We conduct action research holding this tenet central. The education system tends to hold a neoliberal ontology; one where everyone and everything is positioned as being in competition. A space where there must be winners and losers and both curriculum and assessment are pre-defined and standardised. At States of Mind, we take a completely different view and take a social constructionist approach. The idea that everyone exists in the world and creates meaning by dialogue and discourse with others and where we co-develop a sense of truth. Taking this approach, what constitutes success is not forced upon people but developed together in a responsive community. If everyone perceives that they are able to interact with a project in a way that allows them to relate to others in a

much more honest, authentic and open way, they don't perceive that they have to be something they're not and can relax and learn fruitfully.

If you want to co-create a successful community, or learning space, the best way to do that, in our experience, is to position everyone on an equal playing field as participants – not subjects of research. Some of the feedback we get from young people is amazing. They feel seen, heard and "in control" because we're promoting authentic collaboration and that creates genuine relatedness and a strong sense of belonging.

Due to the Covid-19 pandemic, much of our project work took place on Zoom and even in this context, collaboration and belongingness can be fostered – this was surprising! If projects are grounded in this worldview you can create something really wonderful. As part of Breaking the Silence we are demonstrating that you can evaluate your school community using this approach. If we treat education evaluation as a collaborative, community-based endeavour to facilitate change, rather than a process of external "judgement" (as promoted by Ofsted) we can be responsive and make it flexible. We can make changes to our environment authentically. Nobody knows their community better than the community members themselves.

The Breaking the Silence project is a completely different way of conceptualising curriculum too. Over a number of years, working with young people for 1.5 hours a week, in school lesson time, they propose their own research questions, read research, generate data and decide how to disseminate their findings. Everything is consent based. Students opt in and then engage in participatory action research with us. There's usually 12-15 young people working with myself and sometimes, another psychologist or teacher. They build their understanding about a topic of significant interest (in this case school evaluation) by exploring, listening, discussing and reflecting. Then, they take the next step and consider how to "act upon" this learning. What might happen if children were socialised to learn in this way rather than by imbibing a set curriculum?

Generic school curricula are grounded in a different proposition, what we might label the "Tower of Right Knowledge". This is an idea that there's a prescriptive set of knowledges that must be learned in a certain way in a certain order, and using a certain pedagogy, and if you don't enforce this upon children, the world will end. Mostly, throughout history, it's elite white men deciding on behalf of the entire universe what constitutes right knowledge. "I know what's true. I know what's right. I'm going to tell you what that is. Either you accept that what I'm telling you is the truth, or I'm going to marginalise you, whether you're a teacher or a student." Self-appointed ideologues filter what should be learned and this presented as ideologically neutral, as "just the way things are". Anyone disagreeing will suffer. "You're out. We don't like you. We pathologise you."

At States of Mind our understanding about knowledge creation, our "epistemology", is characterised by what we call "deep documentation". That is, participants explore research questions that are decided in collaboration, then co-construct their own appreciation of knowledge, about what has been learned. This can be captured, though not in the usual format of standardised scores or grades. In this case, young people co-created a documentary (https://vimeo.com/725602882), devised an alternative education evaluation framework – the Review for Progress and Development – wrote articles, took part in podcasts and worked on a piece with The Guardian *to share their perspectives. They have planned and delivered numerous presentations at national and international conferences. All of these are "outcomes" but they demonstrate "deep" rather than shallow learning. Nothing is standardised, everything is meaningful to the participants. The way things are recorded are aimed not at credentials, grades or badges but at personal growth and building a sense of power and capacity to change their lives.*

Self-determination theory and belongingness are massively important here; when everyone perceives that they are able to interact with the project in a way that meets their needs and allows them to interact with the work in a way they find motivating, it allows them to get creative, take risks, absorb challenge and relate to others in a more honest, authentic and open way. They grow; they flourish.

Each research phase lasts a year, with a new cohort of young people passing the baton to the next. In Phase 1 – Young people reflected upon the conversations in focus groups with their peers and wrote to Amanda Spielman (Head of Ofsted at the time) outlining their findings. They received a patronising response that did not address their concerns.

In Phase 2, they decided they wanted to ask other young people and teachers, "What's the impact of schooling on your mental health? To what extent does schooling prepare you for real life? To what extent does schooling promote personal development?" A number of papers, co-written by a psychology doctorate student, were generated and shared.

During Phase 3 another group of young people devised an alternative education evaluative framework. They asked what's the impact of Ofsted on young people? They interviewed ex-inspectors, headteachers and academics and did focus groups with teachers and students. They decided that the best way to structure school evaluation could be through a school self-evaluation approach in partnership with a similar local school. It's about collaboration and trust rather than scrutiny and judgment. That came from everyone they'd spoken to, and emerged from careful, sensitive work over nine months.

It was fascinating that the project brought teachers and the students closer together. For example, the young people recognised that they wanted to evaluate teacher autonomy because when they spoke to the teachers, they realised the reason that their teachers were so focussed on delivering a tight curriculum is that they have no choice. They realised through meeting school staff that they need to perceive a sense of autonomy to feel good about their work and hence, this is a crucial element of any school's makeup.

Seven areas were identified that would be evaluated as part of the Review for Progress and Development. See below.

Phase 4 – This involved focus groups with teachers and young people based upon the following research question – "How can we meaningfully evaluate the following areas?" 1. Student mental health, 2. Student-teacher relationships, 3. Student interactions, 4. Teacher autonomy, 5. Student satisfaction, 6. Life skills, 7. Personal development.

Phase 5 – A core group of young leaders worked with the NEU on their "Beyond Ofsted" campaign; this included writing a piece to capture their findings. It is revealing and shameful that despite States of Mind contacting Ofsted repeatedly, they have refused to take part in the study. They are the only professional group approached whose views on school evaluation are not part of the Breaking the Silence project.

Phase 6 – This is the current phase. We worked with another group of young people in Autumn term 2023. They felt that an appropriate final phase in drafting the Review for Progress and Development was to engage with parents. They proposed the following research question: "What do parents think school evaluation should look like?" We will soon be conducting another round of action research

What Can We Do Instead?

with a group of parents to answer this. Once this is complete, a fully drafted alternative evaluation framework will be ready to trial in schools.

The Review for Progress and Development is not owned by anyone, it is a flexible evaluation approach that places trust and collaboration, rather than judgement and scrutiny at the centre and can be used by all in a way that suits their community.

Find out more about States of Mind: https://www.statesofmind.org/

In this chapter we have presented several different ways in which professionals are working with young people at risk of attendance and behavioural problems at school. There are common themes which emerge from the work of all these people and they are around familiar, evidence-based themes. Autonomy, a sense of competence and connection with others.

The importance of all three of these domains is something our interviewees highlighted. Sometimes when young people are struggling, interventions are

What Can We Do When School's Not Working?

put in place to alleviate distress through taking a more caring approach. Perhaps nurture groups are set up, or hubs where they can go and talk to pastoral workers. These can be very helpful for many young people and may help them to continue to attend school. However, ultimately this isn't enough. Those are things which are done to (rather than with) young people, and in some cases they can inadvertently make young people feel different, or singled out, without helping them to feel empowered and more confident about their abilities.

We have heard from families who have been told that "just being in school is enough", and while we understand that this comes from a place of compassion, it isn't true. Just being in school doesn't mean that a young person is learning or developing, and sometimes a young person can be in limbo for years, attending school but not learning anything. Some of the most despondent young people we meet are those who attend school but who find the classroom unmanageable and so spend their days in the corridor or Reset room. If a young person isn't able to learn from formal classroom lessons, then adults need to be thinking about other ways for them to learn.

The interviewees in this chapter talked about different ways of engaging young people so that they could feel more autonomous and competent. Self-managed learning, collaborative problem solving, co-production or small group projects, these are all ways in which our interviewees tried to help

children feel like they could make choices about their lives, and that they could be good at things. They tried to help young people feel differently about themselves and their learning.

All young people need to be challenged and stretched in order to learn, and many of the professionals in this chapter have described ways that can happen for those who are struggling. None of the approaches suggested here are "quick fixes" and that might disappoint you. You may be looking for a six-week-plan, or a road map to get children learning. It's our argument that the way to sustainable change is for the adults around a child to rethink their approach, and to shift their priorities from attendance and behaviour to learning and flourishing. Essentially, rather that expecting flexibility from the child in fitting into a rigid system, think about how adults can be flexible and do things differently.

The interventions described in this chapter are very intentional. Sometimes alternatives to strict behaviour polices and high control environments are caricatured as "doing nothing" or "leaving kids to get on with it". These accounts demonstrate how far from the truth that is.

Summary

- In order to work with young people who are experiencing difficulties at school, we need to move beyond a focus on behaviour and mental health.
- Effective interventions vary from individualised problem solving to collaborative open-ended projects, interest-based programmes (such as football or skateboarding) and reflective groups for teachers.
- Those who work with children who are at risk or already experiencing school distress emphasise the importance of starting where the child is and forming relationships.
- Practitioners described working with young people in different ways to help them develop their sense of autonomy and competence, whilst also focusing on connection.
- All three domains of self-determination theory are important if children are to thrive. It isn't enough to focus solely on relationships and nurturing, as children also need to feel empowered and competent and have opportunities to learn.

References and Further Reading

Cunningham, I. (2021). *Self Managed Learning and the New Educational Paradigm.* London: Routledge.

Greene, R. (2014). *Lost At School: Why Our Kids with Behavioural Challenges Are Falling Through the Cracks and How We Can Help Them.* New York: Scribner

Football Beyond Borders. www.footballbeyondborders.org

Lives in the Balance. www.livesinthebalance.org

Rachel Higginson. www.higginsoncreativeeducation.com

Self-Managed Learning College. www.smlcollege.org.uk

States of Mind. www.statesofmind.org

6

Deciding Not to Go Back to School

In this chapter you will find:

1. Stuck in Between
2. Making the Decision Not to Go Back
    Young People Deciding
    Adults Deciding
3. What Happens Now?

Introduction

Emily (15) told us her story:

> It's been a year now of not really going to school. I would get taken in for lunchtime because everyone's goal was always just to get me back in school. That was the main goal. That was the big achievement.
>
> I had loads of different things for anxiety. I had counselling in school, out of school, loads of things like that. All of it would be based around my anxiety in school.
>
> I would talk to my counsellor about things that I was finding difficult in school, like the busy corridors, things like that. They'd come up with solutions for that to get me back into school because that was the only thing people really focused on.
>
> I did this online counselling that was really great for a while because the main focus was just my anxiety in everyday life. But then at the end, it was back to school. Probably the last month of it was just school, school, school.
>
> All of that was just working up to get me back in school. All my conversations with my mum were about different timetables to get back in school. The conversations with school were different timetables to get back in school. No one was actually thinking about other things.

I felt really overwhelmed, to be honest. I think deep down I knew that it didn't matter what the plan was. I knew that if it was in school, it wasn't going to work. But every plan that people came up with, I would just agree to it because I felt like I should, and I felt like I should try it because then when I didn't, I'd have people saying, "Well, you're never going to know if you don't try."

Everyone was so sure that the more I did it, the easier it would get, because that is the case for most things. I would go in and I do it once. We had quite a few arguments over the fact that I would do the plan once, and I wouldn't go in again. My mum said, and other people said, you need to go in again because it will get easier. I said it was so hard that time that even if it gets a bit easier, it's going to still be awful, and it doesn't get easier for me anyway. I didn't know how to say that because everyone would be like, "Well, you've only done it once, so you don't know if it's going to get easier."

When I wasn't at school I was at home. I like being on my own, and I like being at home, but it did get a bit lonely and a bit boring sometimes. I think people thought that if I couldn't go to school that meant I couldn't do other things during the day. They'd say, if you're okay enough to do that, then you're okay enough to go to school.

Both of my parents have said that at some point. Because obviously, they got frustrated, which is fair enough because they didn't know what to do, and they didn't know what was going on, and they didn't know how to help. Everything they tried, it just didn't work.

It was really difficult because I hate disappointing people. I've done a lot of that this year. I've done a lot of it because I had to, because there was nothing else I could do. But then I hated it because I hate my mum being cross with me.

I think my not going to school was always considered by everyone else to be a choice, and I think in some ways they still think that.

When the Only Solution Is School

Up to now, we've focused on schools and how children can be helped to thrive and learn at school. Every book and article we have read on school refusal assumes that the successful outcome is for the child to return to regularly attending school. Each list of "tips" or "strategies" assumes that the aim is full time school. More school is the treatment for not being happy at school. It's not surprising that that was Emily's experience.

This is the stance taken by the professionals who write about school attendance problems.

Thambirajah et al. are a clear example: "Many professionals may not realise that successful and sustained return to school and attention to factors that

Deciding Not to Go Back to School

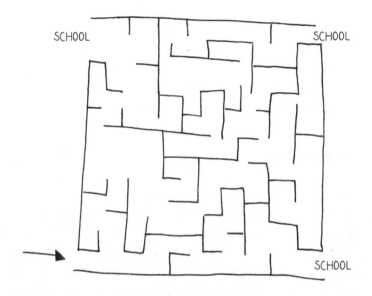

contribute to the school refusal is *the* treatment of the anxiety associated with school refusal. Many children . . . do not need other forms of 'treatment'" (p. 72).

Garfi, in her book for parents and professionals, also makes it clear that the only possible outcome is a return to school: "Just as the swimmer is slowly **encouraged** and **expected** to master their water skills so must we **expect** the school refuser to return to school" (p. 5).

That's what happened to Emily. She was expected and encouraged to return to school for a year, but then it didn't turn out like the books say it will. It didn't get any easier for her. In that year, everything in her life was dominated by her difficulties with school. Her relationships with her parents, the way that she felt about herself and everything else that she did were all affected. She's not alone. Many other families and young people tell us similar stories.

Stuck in Between

Those who insist that a return to school is the only possible outcome usually have good intentions, but there is an unanticipated consequence to their stance. It leaves young people like Emily stuck. The adults in Emily's life were trying to get her back to school for a year, a year which she describes as miserable. She told me that there was always a new plan, she would try it, it wouldn't get any easier and then there would be an argument. We have met young people who have spent two or three years or more attending some school, trying to do more, but finding that it never gets any easier. The reintegration plan isn't progressing. They lose faith that adults can help and their parents become highly frustrated.

Strategies which focus continuously on a return to school offer nothing for those for whom it doesn't work. These young people aren't learning at home and they often aren't really learning when they are at school either. Many families describe losing hope because multiple attempts to return their child to school have not worked and the interventions have made things worse. When they express this they are often told that they must try harder or be more consistent. They feel as if they are in limbo. Each new professional who they meet assumes that they must get the child back to school in order to move forwards, so they try the same interventions, they fail again, and nothing changes. Because returning to school has been defined as the only positive outcome, the child who does not return to school is left with nothing, just as Emily describes.

Emily was sent to talk to counsellors, but she felt that they focused on solving small problems while missing the bigger issue.

> *I really, really didn't like counselling in school or out of school, either of them, because it was very much I'd tell them what I was struggling with and then straight away there'd be a solution.*

If I said to the person who was counselling me in school, "I find it really difficult to leave the classroom," they'd say, "Right, well, we'll put you at the front. We'll give you a card that you can hold up. We'll do this, we'll do that."

But then I'd be like, "Well, I still have to walk out of the classroom, and I still have to hold that card up, and I still have to do those things." It was always the same. Every problem I had, there was a solution, and I was like, "It's not going to work."

I felt like I had to try for my parents and also for myself, because I felt like I had to be in the school to get a proper education. My parents were worried about my education as well because they were like, "Well, you're not going to get a good enough education with the work that you're doing from home."

I felt like I had to. I just did it once, and then I just stopped, and then we would make a new plan, and then would I do it once, and then I just stop. I kept agreeing to things that I should have just said no to, but I just couldn't do it.

I was worried that I was going to be really far behind. I was worried about going back into the classroom because of the fact that I felt really far behind. I think now, because I'm not in school, and I'm learning, I don't have to be doing the same stuff as

What Can We Do When School's Not Working?

everybody else because I'm doing other things on different websites with different organisations. I don't have to be doing the same thing.

I always measured myself against what my friends were doing and how far they were going. Then, when I was at home as well, trying to work, at that time, I only had stuff that my teachers put into OneDrive, and the majority of my teachers didn't even bother. I had very little work.

I did the best I could, but I was worried that I wasn't going to get a good enough education. I knew that my parents were as well, but I didn't really know what to do about it.

Every time I was in school, I learnt even less than I did at home because the time that I spent in school, I was just so focused on just getting through it. I didn't really do any work. Even if I did write stuff down, I wouldn't take it in. I was just writing words without really knowing what they were meaning.

They would always say, "Well, school is the right place to be, so we can do this in school." It was never, "Well, how about we do this instead of school?"

They were definitely seeing me as just a pupil in the school. They weren't seeing me as someone who can do other things. I think because they were so focused on that, I had to work out by myself how to find a proper solution. They just found the little solutions. They didn't think of the overall picture.

Deciding Not to Go Back to School

They didn't think of the fact that my time at school would be lunchtime and a lesson, and then I'd go home and be miserable until next week until I had to do it again.

Everything that I said that was difficult, they'd give me a reason why it was now easy. They'd say, "Well, you don't have to walk out the classroom very far because you're at the front end, so it's fine." It made me sound like I was being difficult. I think that made me feel like I needed to try it because maybe I was just being difficult.

You can hear in Emily's account how it felt to be on the receiving end of well-intentioned efforts to reintegrate her. She started to feel that she was being difficult, and that this is how everyone saw her. She wasn't learning and she wasn't happy – but that didn't make attending school any easier. She was worried about her future and her education. Her problem wasn't lack of motivation. She wanted to learn, but she couldn't do that at school.

While professionals and parents assume that school is the only way for this child to get an education, this becomes a self-fulfilling prophecy. No other education is arranged for them. No other learning opportunities are offered. It's school or nothing. If this message is passed onto children, it becomes something that leads to despair and depression, and often to feeling terrible about themselves.

Max, who was 15 when I talked to him, told me what that was like for him:

> The Head of Pastoral Care said, "No, you should definitely not be doing school work." But then the SENCO phoned the Educational Support Unit, and they said: "Oh, it's very unusual for someone not to be doing work. They must need work sent home."
>
> Then the SENCO told the Head of Pastoral Care and they pressurised us with schoolwork and it all got even worse.
>
> I was doing a couple of pieces of school work a day, but it really didn't help at all and made me feel even worse. I was feeling really bad. At school, no one really knew why, they just said what helps is to come back to school and let's meet.
>
> At that point, I couldn't really go out of the house. For reasons other than school, some anxieties and sadnesses I've had all my life. The therapist was making things much worse and I was actually seeing a psychiatrist as a temporary support.
>
> She was nicer but could be unpredictable too and say things that made things worse. She said [that the problems with school attendance] felt half on purpose, half by accident. I felt very unsafe at that time.
>
> At the end of November, I was pressurised by the school to come and meet the head of year. He didn't really know what he was doing. I think he was just saying what the Deputy Head and the Head of Pastoral Care was saying but mixing it all up.
>
> I was very depressed and anxious and it just got worse and worse and that went on for a bit. I was doing a couple of bits of schoolwork each day and sending them back. But what really made it a lot worse was going into the school which brought up all the memories of before.

Parents told us similar stories of how awful it was to be stuck. Jade told Naomi about what it was like when her daughter was having difficulties with school attendance.

> A typical week would look something like this...
>
> Sunday was a day of stress. My daughter would be so anxious, her OCD would set in. Her day would be spent tapping, touching and repeating herself all day long. Begging me, crying, not to send her to school the next day. While I was desperately lining socks up hoping to find a pair that would not cause distress the following morning and making the perfect packed lunch, in the hope it would bring her a little happiness the following day. Sundays she would finally cry herself sleep about 1 am.

Deciding Not to Go Back to School

Monday morning would be a morning spent on eggshells, knowing she was struggling and at any moment she would become so distressed she would be fighting for air. The getting dressed and shoes process would start at 7 am and finish at 8.30 am. The shirt, the tie, the feel of her skirt, her cuffs not level, her socks touching her toes, shoes too tight, hair being tied back, the feel of the bobble on her neck, the smell of the spray on her hair, all would trigger distress and all had to abide by the school uniform policy. She would grip my hand so tightly in the playground, repeating herself about 40 times before finally being able to walk through the school doors. With the look of pure fear on face, like being sent into battle. Eyes wide in fear and red from crying all morning, skin all blotchy from getting so distressed and her head down to the ground in defeat because she had been forced into school. Her coping mechanism in school, when the fidgets and chew toys didn't work (which some teachers didn't allow her to use because it wasn't fair to the other children in the class), was to repeat statements in her head over and over again and she would hear my voice reassuring her that it's okay.

The rest of the week would continue on the same path, with the added pressure of trying to get her to read every night, because that's what her teacher insisted. This was because the other children in her mainstream school were rewarded with stickers and stars every morning if they read the night before but *the children who never read were told off in front of the whole class. She was having to finish work at home, because she was so overwhelmed in school and struggling academically, she wasn't finishing it at school.*

I had been in repeatedly and made it clear she was not to be forced to miss her break times because she couldn't keep up. The pages upon pages of homework she was expected to complete from the age of six, after spending all day long at school masking, then coming home to continue school/home work would be torture, not only to her but for all of us as a family. Watching her sobbing, having panic attacks begging us not to have to do the work because she was mentally exhausted.

It was like that every single day, except school holidays, for five years.

When young people are struggling to attend school, they are typically told that not attending school will lead to certain lifelong failure. Any alternative means of education is devalued. Parents and professionals are sometimes warned against allowing a child to settle into a "halfway house" such as part-time school, or tutors and work at home, lest that encourages them to think they can stay out of school and still learn. Garfi states this in her book: "While I understand that these programs [distance learning and home education] resolve the issue of the student's anxiety and school attendance in the short term, they also delay the inevitable. At some point, the student and their family will have to address the anxiety and learn to manage it effectively" (Garfi 2018, p. 48).

Garfi's point is one which is often raised: Don't young people have to get used to school, in order to prepare them for the real world? Won't allowing them to do something different just make their anxiety worse in the future?

This question only makes sense if you think that school is the best place for everyone to learn. That is a cultural assumption which you may have never questioned. But if this was a workplace, we would not say that every adult must get used to one particular type of workplace, in order to be able to function in all future work places.

Naomi: Several years ago, I got a job in a specialist service for children and young people. It was in a lovely setting, with friendly people. However, there was a problem. Our desks were in an open-plan office. Ten of us crammed into a small space, with telephones going constantly. I sat next to people whose job it was to find future placements for the children who would not be able to return home. They would be on the phone, describing what had happened to the children. This was a trauma service. The stories were often terrible. I started to feel highly anxious. My skin started prickling in the mornings. I would wake at night, hearing the phone ringing or with pictures of the trauma in my head. I started to dread going in. I got noise-cancelling earplugs, but it wasn't enough. I could still hear what they were saying sometimes, and I felt trapped in that room, trying to complete my admin. There was nowhere else for me to be – my manager said that everyone found it tough at first and that I'd get used to it.

I ended up leaving that job when I stopped being able to sleep. I felt better instantly. I got another job where I had my own office, and none of the same problems recurred. Since then, I have avoided jobs with open-plan offices. I know they don't suit me.

Why am I telling you this story? Because if I had been a child at school, the advice might have been that I should not have been allowed to leave as that would make my anxiety worse and might affect my future career. The onus would have been on me to "get used" to it. As it turns out, I don't have to get used to open-plan offices to have a successful life. Avoiding something isn't always pathological.

My anxiety wasn't irrational. That environment made me feel awful. Because I was an adult, I could find other environments which worked better for me. But when it comes to children, we don't give them that choice. For some children, the school environment makes them feel terrible. Being anxious about that isn't irrational, and pushing them to keep going won't solve the problem.

Deciding Not to Go Back to School

The negative impact of this assumption that a return to school is the only positive outcome is rarely discussed and for many families is highly significant. Families of children who are out of school are often despondent about not only the current situation, but the child's long-term prospects. They feel hopeless. In our experience, this leads many young people to despair. They know that school feels terrible, but they are being told that not attending school will lead to their whole future being blighted.

What's the Alternative?

The reason that most professionals want to get children back into school is because they think that this is the only way that they will be able to access education. They are concerned about the long-term implications of the child not attending school.

However, inadvertently a focus on school attendance as the only outcome can leave some young people with very few opportunities to learn. Poor outcomes are not inevitable for this group, but if they are not offered alternatives then they become so.

At some point, the focus needs to change from attempting to return the child to school to working out how this child can learn and get an education, whether or not they are at school. Being in between is the worst place to be.

Educators can help support this by sending work home or helping young people and their parent access educational resources. They can move away from the stance that says that home should be made unattractive in case this dissuades children from returning to school, and instead prioritise building children up so that they see themselves as capable people who can learn. This is more likely in the long term to lead to reengagement with formal education. They can avoid making dire predictions of what will happen if they don't return to school, and instead focus on how to help each young person learn and move towards a positive outcome for themselves.

Making the Decision Not to Go Back

School is not the only way to get an education. We know from the research with home-educated young people (many of whom go onto university and to have successful careers) that school is not necessary in order to get an education. Long-term outcomes for young people who are out of school will be highly variable depending on what is offered to them and what they are able to access out of school. In the final chapter of this book, you will hear some stories of young people who have left school. Some of them were home educated, others remained on the school role but had tutors at home, and others received an EOTAS (Education Otherwise Than At School) package, funded by their LA.

It is never easy for families who decide to find other ways for their children to get an education, and we are often asked how they manage it financially. One answer is that it is already financially hard to manage when you have a child who is not attending school regularly. Parents describe being called to school so frequently that they lose their jobs, or having to give up work because their child is not reliably at school. They say that while it was financially and practically hard to manage when their child stopped going to school altogether, at least the element of uncertainty had gone and they no longer have the threat of fines hanging over them. School only works as childcare (and therefore enables you to work) if your child can attend reliably.

Some families make it work by working shifts, where one adult works during the day and then takes over during the evenings while the other goes to work. Some parents find flexible work which can be done in the evenings. Others swap childcare with other local families, or set up groups where a few parents get together and hire a room and find a tutor. Some single parents move in with their own parents, or we know of single-parent families who have combined their households to cut costs and to have two adults around to cover childcare. As children get older, some parents say they can do a bit of work from home with the children there. They arrange online playdates or in-person playdates to meet children's social needs. There are no ideal solutions, and most families find a mosaic of different ways to make it work which change over time.

Many families describe a moment when they decided that they would not continue to try school, and that, rather than being a closing of options, this led to an opening of new opportunities.

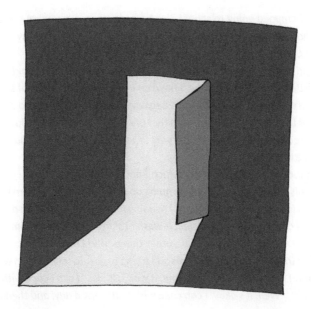

Young People Deciding

Emily, whose story started this chapter, explained what it was like for her.

> It was such a relief when I said I wasn't going back to school. When I was trying to go to school and I felt like I had to, that was so overwhelming. By the end of the week, I was like, "Well, I can't do anything else. I'm so tired and so overwhelmed." I never really did anything.
>
> Then in that half-term holiday, I just realised that I don't want to go back to doing that again. Over the holidays I was going out, and I was seeing people. We

went and stayed with my mum's friend and her two daughters, who were some of my best friends.

The last time I saw them, it was the first week after I had a week of school, and I had a meltdown before we left, and I really struggled that weekend. This time, it was the holidays, and I went up, and I was absolutely fine, and I had an amazing time, and we went out with them, and I had a really nice time.

I went to loads of places and I did loads of things in that holiday, and then I realised I don't want to go back to not feeling like I can do that again.

I had agreed to so many things and I tried. I think a lot of people thought I could have tried harder, but I think I really tried. When I finally said, I'm not going to do this anymore, it was like, well, that's that. Done. It's over. I don't have to do it ever again.

Since I stopped going to school, I've been doing so many more things. So this week, I had my alternative provision on Tuesday. I went to help my mum's work yesterday.

I found yesterday really difficult because she's a primary school teacher, and I am a little bit of a germaphobe. I have an incredibly good sense of smell. It was really overwhelming, but I felt like... Because I was okay, because I'd been relaxed the rest of the week, I could deal with that one day of it being hard. But I know that if I was already overwhelmed from trying to go to school, I wouldn't have been able to manage that.

Then today I'm talking to you, which I never would have done. I'm seeing my cousins this afternoon, and then I'm going up to the stables, and then I'm going to meet my friend's horse on Saturday. I'm doing loads more things. I'm a lot happier.

When I cut school out of my life, it wasn't taking up so much room in my head any more. I'm a lot more able to do other things, and I'm a lot more able to cope with other things as well. When I was still trying to go into school, then when I tried things that I find difficult out of school, it was just like, "I can't cope with this." But now it's like, "Well, it's okay. I can cope with it. It's just a day, and then tomorrow I can relax."

Deciding Not to Go Back to School

When it's clear that a young person isn't going back to school, it can be hard for the people working with them. There has often been so much emphasis on getting back to school as the answer, and now that it's clear that this won't be the solution, the question is, what now? It's common to feel adrift and without a focus – or like an intervention has failed.

Just the decision to stop asking about school can be a significant one. The focus can shift from "How can we help you go to school" to "How can we help you learn?" which immediately opens up a different conversation.

Adults Taking the Decision

Not every young person wants to leave school, even when it is clearly not working well for them. Alice was 13 when she talked to me and had left school when she was eight. She had become situationally mute and had difficulty eating to the point where she was on a liquid diet. Her parents made the decision to home educate her out of serious concern for her mental and physical health and initially they made this decision against Alice's wishes.

> When my parents decided to home educate me, I was absolutely avid that I wouldn't leave school because I thought that was completely failing.
>
> On that last day there, I tried to stay there as long as possible, but then as soon as I left school, I loved it and I would never, ever go back.
>
> My parents decided against my will. I completely understand why they did it. Because at that point, I was convinced that all of those things were my fault because that's what I was being told. They were like, "I don't think you have the ability to make that decision anymore." Also at that point, I was very, very suicidal. They thought: "We've got to do something now."
>
> I think they brought it up to me right before the end of Year 4 [age 8-9], and I was adamant it wouldn't happen. I was adamant it wouldn't happen because that would be failing. Because at that point I was convinced that it was my fault. I thought, if it's already my fault, then I can't have accommodations for being a bad person.
>
> I thought, "Why would you accommodate me being bad?" Because in my mind, that didn't make sense. Then they did make me leave school, and I was really, really angry for about three months. Then I was extremely happy.

Leaving in Crisis

For many families, the decision to stop going to school happens quickly in a crisis, when it's clear that things are not going to improve.

Anita is a parent. She told us about her son's journey. He had become severely anxious about school after his friend left. "Reflection" is a term used for an isolation room, something some schools use as a punishment.

In January we agreed it was time to get him back into school. We'd done a self-referral to CAMHS and were having discussions with the school SEN team. I dictated that I would bring him in for an hour and build up the time; this worked well and although he didn't make it into lessons (he was in their support classroom) he was there and his feedback was quite positive. The next week I said we needed to take things slowly, but after day two the head of year phoned and said he couldn't support that approach and what Jon needed was "tough love" and he'd be made to go to all his lessons the next day. I totally disagreed with the approach and expressed how unhappy I was with the situation.

After Jon was forced into his lessons the next day (he was taken from lesson to lesson) I had a call from the head of year to say how well he'd got on. That wasn't representative of the 100+ text messages I'd received throughout the day begging me to collect him, saying how he couldn't do it and his head was going to explode!

Amazingly I managed to get him back the next day, but after two lessons he broke down and said he couldn't go into the lesson so he was told he had a choice, go to the lesson or go to reflection. He chose reflection. Afterwards, for his choice, he got an afterschool detention!!!

That was the end of going into school for him.

What Happens Now?

What actually happens, when school stops and there is no plan to go back? There's a period of adjustment for everyone. A time of sorting out how things will work. Some families deregister and become home educators, which means they have no access to funds for their child's education. Others stay on a school roll and either make arrangements with the school or apply for a package of funded EOTAS. Some use alternative provision or part-time learning communities. Others sign up for online schools.

The first important thing is that education doesn't have to look like school to be successful. Most of us were schooled, and we tend to think that school is the best way to learn. However, the home education research shows that it's not necessary to replicate school at home, and a young person doesn't need to be studying for all the hours that they might be at school. Young people often learn informally out of school, and this is not inferior to formal learning. Many young people out of school will spend very little time sitting at a desk, and may, particularly in the primary years, do very different things to what their peers in school are doing.

The research indicates that it isn't helpful to compare the progress of children out of school directly with those in school. They will learn at different rates and in different ways. Their learning will often not progress in the linear fashion expected at school. Being out of school can be an opportunity to do something very different – and presenting it as such to young people can help turn despondency into hope.

The adjustment when the decision is taken that a child will not return to school can be a worrying time for families. It's common for things to appear to get worse before they get better. Young people sometimes withdraw for a while and may show absolutely no interest in any sort of learning. Teenagers may hardly emerge from their bedrooms. Parents tell us that children sometimes stop putting clothes on, spending their days either naked on in their pyjamas. This is particularly likely if they have felt forced to attend school or are scared that this might happen. This period can go on for months before they start to show an interest in the world again.

Home educators call this period "deschooling", and it starts to come to an end when children start to show an interest in the world. This might not look anything like school – children might ask to go to the shops, want to try cooking something or find a passionate interest in murder mysteries, vampires or lock-cracking.

In this chapter we've talked about how young people get stuck when they are not attending school but when all the interventions available assume that they must. We've talked about how this can feel like limbo for young people and their families, and how this can be damaging both for the young person's sense of self and their relationship with adults. We've then shown you how some families have made the decision to stop trying school, and how hard that is. It is never an easy or convenient decision, and often includes significant financial cost when a parent has to give up working or reduce their hours. However, having a child who is struggling to attend school is also not easy or convenient, and can include a financial burden when parents are not able to continue working.

What emerges in place of school will look different for every young person and will evolve over time. Many families find eclectic ways for their child to learn, bringing together a variety of different options. They may use online courses, local mentors or tutors, with days spent volunteering or at an alternative provision. Some sign up for full time online school. Young people meet others at Scouts, climbing, band practice or youth clubs. Some parents set up board game clubs or social clubs for their children. Some children, particularly those who are primary aged, will learn entirely informally for several years.

Some children are more seriously affected by their experiences, particularly if they have gone on for several years. These children may show signs of trauma or burnout, and may take longer to recover and need more help to do so. It's this which we will turn to in the next chapter.

Summary

- Most interventions for school distress assume that the only successful outcome is a return to school.
- This leaves young people for whom this doesn't work in a perpetual state of limbo.
- Deciding not to return to school can be the start of really moving forward.
- Working with young people who will not be returning to school requires professionals to think differently about their work and priorities.
- There is always a period of recovery when it is decided that a child will not return to school.

References and Further Reading

Boles, B. (2010). *The Art of Self-Directed Learning.* Summertown, TN: Book Publishing Company.

Fisher, N. (2020). *A Different Way to Learn: Self-Directed Education and Neurodiversity.* London: Jessica Kingsley Publishers.

Garfi, J. (2018). *Overcoming School Refusal: A Practical Guide for Teachers, Counsellors and Parents.* Brisbane: Australian Academic Press Group Pty Ltd.

Llewellyn, G. (2001). *The Teenage Liberation Handbook: How to Quit School and Get a Real Life and Education.* New York: Holt Paperbacks.

Thambirajah, M., Grandison, K. and De-Hayes, L. (2008). *Understanding School Refusal: A Handbook for Professionals in Education, Health and Social Care.* London: Jessica Kingsley Publishers.

Thomas, A. and Pattison, H. (2007). *How Children Learn at Home.* London: Continuum.

7

School Trauma and Burnout

In this chapter you will find:

1. Can School Really Be Traumatic?
2. What is Trauma?
3. Helping Young People Recover from Trauma
4. School Burnout
5. Helping Young People Recover from Burnout

Introduction

Apparently my daughter was "fine in school", the difficulty was getting her in. The implication from school was that it was just a transition or an attachment thing.

The things that we were encouraged to do were to actually physically take her in, guide her in with a hand, which to me is actually physically pulling her in. I would get her to the gates every morning and if she was reluctant to leave me there would be lots of coaxing. There'd be lots of "Come in and do this."

There were times where her desire for social interaction with her friends was used. I thought at the time that that was a better option than physically taking her in and just getting it over and done with as quickly as possible.

When you look at it though, that's all quite manipulative, really. There's this place you don't want to be and the only bit of it that you like is the social bit. The social part actually isn't really the purpose of it, and they're using that to entice you in, so we can force you into some learning at the same time. It's a bit warped when you look at it from the other side. It's actually really inappropriate.

I know from my work with dogs that coaxing into fearful situations has huge potential fallout – it seriously undermines trust and can end up creating aversions to the very things we may later need to feel "rewarding"

> *In terms of what happened to my daughter, she became sensitised to going to school. In a sensitised state, her whole sensory system went into overdrive, and every sense, smell, sight, every single one was on complete overload. Nothing good was ever going to come from being in that position, until that level of arousal had come down. You can't just keep trying something else. There needs to be a break first, some respite and a chance for the system to come down from overdrive.*
>
> *Nobody seems to grasp this.*

Kim (animal behaviour expert) is talking about her daughter Ella who now has an EOTAS package and no longer attends school.

When children stop going to school the emotional impact of their experiences can continue for years. Some children retreat to their bedrooms. Others refuse to go anywhere near the school they were at and become very fearful if they think they see a child who used to attend the same school as them. Some won't leave the house during school hours, in case someone asks them why they aren't at school. Others develop an aversion to things they associate with school, like reading books, black shoes or the smell of the dining hall.

Education professionals are often quite sceptical that a child can be traumatised or burnt out by school, particularly if nothing that they consider to be "really traumatic" happened. School is thought of (particularly by professionals who work in education) as something which cannot cause harm, a good place for all children. It doesn't seem to make sense when some young people have an intense emotional reaction to their experiences and then go on to develop mental health problems.

It has been our clinical experience that some children show signs of a post-traumatic reaction to their school experiences, and that others experience something which is akin to adult "burnout". In this chapter we will first discuss trauma and what school trauma can look like. We will then move onto school burnout and how young people recover from burnout.

It is of course the case that some children will come to school having experienced trauma at home, and this will affect their behaviour. Some will be experiencing ongoing adverse situations which will affect their ability to engage at school, resulting in poor attendance and behaviour. While this is a highly significant part of the picture for some children, in this chapter we are going to focus specifically on school related trauma and burnout. That is because it is our experience that this is an area which few people have written about and which is often misunderstood.

Can School Really Be Traumatic?

We're going to take a guess, and that is that most people reading this book did okay at school. You might not have loved it, you might have found some parts boring, but at the end, you probably came out with adequate exam results and perhaps some friends who you kept in touch with. You may have learnt to think of yourself as capable at school, or someone who was a hard worker. We're making that assumption because this is a book for professionals, and those who do well at school are more likely to go on to get professional qualifications. For you school paid off. It was all worth it in the end.

Professional groups are full of people who succeeded at school and who learnt to think about themselves as capable and worthwhile. This leaves us with a problem. There's a serious lack of professional voices of those for whom school was not a positive experience, who dropped out or who failed all their exams. They are simply not well represented in professional walks of life – which means that their perspective is rarely heard.

This type of diversity is not often talked about – it's rare for people to complain that the teaching profession needs more people who failed all their GCSEs, for example, or that we need more members of parliament who stopped attending school when they were 12. The very idea seems laughable. One of the things that many of us learn at school is that our self-worth and value to society is determined by our academic results – and that the worth of other people is also defined by how well they do at school and how many qualifications they got.

This leads many of us to assume (without ever thinking too much about it) that the perspective of those who did badly at school has less value than the perspective of the successful. We assume that the voices of the successful should override the voices of those who did badly. We think it's fine for important decisions to be made by the school successes, because (implicitly) we think their views are more valuable than those who were failed by school.

When it comes to education, this can mean that most professionals assume that the way that they experienced school is the way that everyone should experience school. They got positive feedback and learnt to feel good about themselves, and they think it could be like that for everyone. If only they could persuade children that school is a good thing really, and their ticket to a fulfilling life, then all will be well.

For a significant number of children, this is not how school is. Their experience is of a series of events that shows them they aren't good enough, that they aren't trying hard enough and that there is something wrong with them. This happens particularly when there is a developmental mismatch between the child and the expectations of school.

This developmental mismatch can happen for a number of reasons. Some children will have neurodevelopmental differences which means that they acquire skills at a different rate to many others. Others will have had difficult early experiences and may have disrupted early attachment. Others will have conditions such as foetal alcohol syndrome (FASD) or have physical illnesses or disabilities. For many children, the Covid-19 pandemic had a significant impact on their early social and emotional experiences, meaning that they were less ready to manage the demands of school than earlier generations.

No matter the reason why, some children enter school and immediately find it challenging. They discover that they are expected to be able to do things like hold a pencil with a tripod grip, sit quietly on the carpet and listen and put their hand up when they want to answer a question, all of which are a struggle for them. They are told to try harder and sometimes sanctioned if they don't conform. They start to feel that they aren't good enough and their parents start to worry. Some parents tell me that at the end of that first year, they are presented with a report of all the things their four- or five-year-old child can't do yet, and it's demoralising for both them and their child.

Others manage the early play-based years, but then start to struggle when school becomes more about formal learning and less about play, at around Year 1 or 2 (age 5–7). They aren't yet able to sit at a desk without wanting to get out of their seat, and the task of learning to read doesn't make sense to them yet. They may learn that they are not as clever as the others. Some of them learn that they are disruptive, or spend a lot of their time in the Red Zone, or sitting outside the headteacher's office.

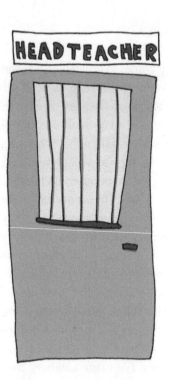

School Trauma and Burnout

There's another group who manage through primary school, but then things go wrong at secondary. At this transition, there is a withdrawal of support at the same time as an increase in the demands on the child. They are now in a school where many adults won't know their face or their name, and they are expected to get themselves from lesson to lesson and to remember all their equipment. There is usually less flexibility than at primary school. Many teenagers report only having negative interactions with adults during school hours, and for some it all goes wrong at this stage. Parents say "it was like falling off a cliff" or "the wheels came off".

And the final group start to experience serious problems with school at the age of 13 or 14, when the pressures of exams start to increase. There's often a lot of talk in school at this stage of how important these exams are and how the rest of your life will be determined by them – and for some children, the pressure is too much. They drop out, they start truanting or they do something unacceptable and they get excluded.

There is in fact another group as well. This group is those who appear to manage through school but then who find the transition to the looser structure of work or university extremely difficult. They're have managed in the tight structure of school but have very little sense of how to make decisions for themselves, and sometimes have a breakdown in their early 20s. This group are outside the scope of this book.

For some of these children, an obvious thing might happen which causes a trauma reaction, but for many more, it's more subtle. That's because trauma isn't just about what happens to you, it's about how you experience those events – and how others help you to make sense of them.

What Is Trauma?

When we hear the term "trauma", most of us think immediately about terrible events. Car accidents, plane crashes or tsunamis. It's true that it's those types of experiences which get you a diagnosis of post-traumatic stress disorder (PTSD). In order to get an official diagnosis of PTSD a person has to have experienced what is called a "Criterion A" event. This means an event which involves exposure to death, threatened death, actual or threatened serious injury, actual or threatened sexual violence. This exposure can be direct or indirect. Only a minority of children experience something like this at school (although a certain number do). However, understanding trauma is about a lot more than this.

Psychological trauma isn't, however, just about exposure to injury and violence. It's about the way our brains and bodies react to events. And for that, it's not so much what actually happened that matters, it's what you experienced. If you feel that you are in danger, that can cause long-term negative effects, even if actually you are objectively not at risk. Many small events can result in a nervous system which is constantly on alert.

This is because of the way our survival system works.

School Trauma and Burnout

The Survival System

We all have a system in our body designed to keep us alive. When our brains think that something dangerous is happening, this survival system gets triggered. It prepares our bodies for fight, flight, freeze or fawn – essentially, all ways to keep ourselves safe from an attack by a wild animal or other threat. The survival system is more complicated than I will outline here, but this is a simplified model which might help you to make sense of what is going on.

This response is triggered by the amygdalae, two small-almond shaped parts of our brain. The amygdala is triggered what it perceives to be dangerous – and it's a quick-fire system. There's no time to lose if you might be attacked by a lion. Your brain needs to react before you can think it through. Your life could depend on it.

In order for our amygdalae to effectively predict the things which are dangerous, we collect memories of times when we felt under threat. If you've ever been in a car accident, or been mugged, those memories will have been stored in your amygdalae.

The amygdalae use those memories as clues in order to better detect danger in the future. Our brains scan the environment looking for matches between those memories, and the world around us. If there's a match, then the survival system is triggered.

This is why, after a car accident, many people are scared to get back in the car, or to walk along a busy road. The amygdalae are reacting to every car as threat. The alarm goes off and your body goes into fight, flight, freeze or fawn. From the perspective of survival, it's much better to run away from a hundred things which aren't dangerous than to miss one truly dangerous situation.

Memories in the amygdalae are storied in a different way to other memories. They are more chaotic, fragmented, and often there is not much of a coherent narrative. Our autobiographical memories – memories of times when we didn't feel under threat – are stored in our hippocampus. Memories there are stored in a way which we can think of like a filing system. We can choose to think about them when we want to. When we think of those memories, we can tell that they are in the past – it's like they have a date attached. Something which happened yesterday feels different to something which happened ten years ago.

Amygdalae memories are different and not at all like a filing system. Those memories are retrieved by matches in the environment, and when that happens, it can feel like the threatening event is happening all over again. The amygdalae are more like the cupboard under the stairs, where the memories have been crumpled up and shoved in.

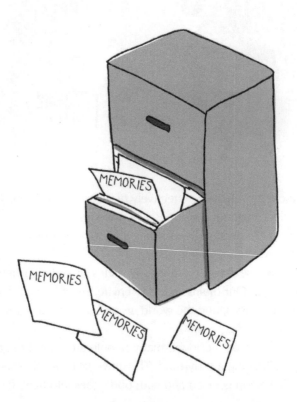

Can you think of a time when you had a frightening experience, and then afterwards you were scared of something which before you hadn't found scary? This can happen for all sorts of things. Lifts, buses, spiders, the sea – Naomi has even worked with someone who was scared of baked beans after a nasty experience where one got stuck up his nose . . .

This is your amygdalae doing their job. Your brain is trying to keep you safe, by using your past experiences to predict what might be dangerous in the future. It would rather keep you alive than let you stay calm and relaxed.

Vulnerability

When it comes to psychological trauma, our perception of an event is more important than what actually happened. If a person feels under threat and that they can't escape – even if there was no real threat – then they are at risk of being traumatised. If they have repeated experiences of feeling under threat, then these memories will lead to their brains perceiving more experiences as dangerous, and they will feel under threat more of the time. It's a vicious cycle.

Some children have experiences at school which lead to a trauma reaction, even when those experiences don't seem to be traumatic to an observing adult. This is particularly likely to happen for children who have developmental differences, perhaps because of neurodiversity, learning disability or early traumatic experiences. These children are vulnerable.

A Child's Experience

There are three main things to think about when considering how a child experiences school.

The child's **individual characteristics** can make school more challenging. Their development may be out of sync with what school expects. They may be autistic or neurodivergent in other ways. They may not get along well with their peers and they may find the demands of school highly stressful. They may struggle to follow a lesson in the classroom or they may be less articulate than other children their age. They may find transitions very hard, and school is full of transitions. As school has become more pressured, more children have found it challenging. There is less leeway to develop in a slightly divergent way when expectations are constant and standardised. The child who isn't reading is likely to flag up concerns early in England, for example, because of the phonics screening check at the end of Year 1 (age 6). They will know that they are "behind". In other countries, children are taught to read later and six-year-olds aren't expected to be able to read yet. A non-reading six-year-old would cause no alarm at all.

The way that the child **experiences the world** can mean that the way that school works feels unpredictable and chaotic. They may experience school as too loud, too noisy, too chaotic and too smelly. This can put them in a state of high arousal. Their experience of life in the world outside school can mean that they expert adults to behave in particular ways – both positive and negative.

Then there is the way that the **world responds to this child**. Some children are bullied or harassed at school. Their peers are more likely to be hostile and teachers are more likely to get frustrated with them. Their way of being may be invalidated by others who just don't understand why their experiences are different. Their behaviour might be seen as intentionally disruptive, rather than as a sign of their distress, and so they are sanctioned for it.

All of these can combine to mean that the child doesn't feel safe.

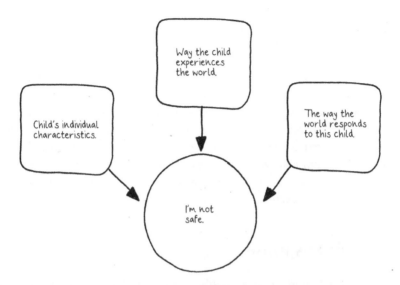

Once a child doesn't feel safe, then everything that happens can start to feel like a threat. A "firm voice" may sound to them like a shout, or a gentle telling off will feel devastating. They start to accumulate memories of difficult experiences, and each one will be stored in their amygdalae as an example of a threat.

Laura told me about her son's experience at reception. He was her third child and the older two were already at school. This is an example of how a child's differences – in this case, autism and sensory processing differences – meant that school was an intensely traumatic experience for him, to the point where he stopped speaking.

> We got about three weeks into reception. Even now it makes me feel a bit sick thinking about it. When you go to do pickup, and you're at the door, and you're trying to get as much information as possible out of that teacher in five seconds. And you can see on your child's face the pain that they've been experiencing. Suddenly the teacher said,
>
> "Oh, we've had a real breakthrough. He nodded today."
>
> And I thought "Why? Why is that so noteworthy? Why are you reporting that to me as an achievement?"
>
> At this point, it became evident that my child was mute entirely in the school setting, and that no one had seen fit to mention this to me.
>
> I had repeatedly said, "Look, he's struggling, and he doesn't want to be here." They'd been saying, "Oh, no, he's fine. Honestly, once you've gone he's fine."

Their idea of fine was clearly very different than mine, because my idea of fine is not a verbal child going mute.

At that point, I knew that we weren't playing this game anymore; attending school. This is absolutely not going to happen because, sadly, even those few weeks did untold damage that took me about five years to help him recover from.

It was so distressing to be in that place and to feel that all of this was avoidable. We just found ourselves there. We had trusted and we'd gone along with it. School would say things to try and put your mind at ease. Clearly they had absolutely no clue of the reality that I was living, of how our home life was, because he wouldn't sleep, he would just cry from the minute he was home till the minute I took him back, because he was so depressed at the idea of going to school.

The Adult Response

Trauma is about more than a child's experience. Difficult and distressing things happening to children (and adults) do not always result in psychological trauma. Social support and context can make the difference between something which causes long-term problems, and something that the child is able to successfully integrate into their life story.

This means that what adults do can make the difference between a child making sense of their experiences and feeling safe enough, or being traumatised (and continuing to feel under threat).

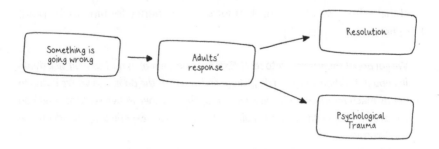

As we discussed in Chapter 4, the way in which adults understand a child's problem will affect how they respond. Many adults understand a child's difficulties at school as either "behaviour" or "anxiety". When a child's distress is seen as behaviour then it is unlikely that they will be helped to make sense of their experiences.

When schools take a behavioural approach to school distress, they often tell parents they must continue to bring the children to school or they punish children who are struggling with school. The more the child protests, the more parents are told not to give in. Parents are threatened with education welfare officers or social services and they feel blamed and caught between their child and the professionals.

Professionals usually hope that insisting that a child attends school will lead to them being desensitised to school. The idea is that they will learn that school is not dangerous, and that they are safe. However, when a child is forced into school repeatedly, they can form lots of memories of feeling under threat associated with school. These memories are stored in the amygdalae, where they are used to predict future danger. The effect is that school feels more and more threatening. Each time they go in they feel more under threat.

The strategy which was mean to make things better, makes things worse.

School Trauma

Our clinical experience is that one result of repeatedly forcing children to attend school can be a post-traumatic reaction to anything which reminds them of school.

What does it look like when a child has a post-traumatic response to school?

- Fear of anything related to school.
- Shame about learning and reading.
- Anger and aggressive behaviour.
- Anxiety.
- Nightmares and sleep problems.
- Avoidance of things they were made to do at school (e.g. reading, homework, sitting at a desk).
- Low self-esteem and self-blame.
- Meltdowns before and after school.
- Separation anxiety.
- Toileting problems.
- Eating problems.
- Situational mutism.

What Can We Do When School's Not Working?

Nora told me about what that looked like for her son Kai.

Towards the end of Y1 (age 6) they started to get more formal and sitting down, staring at the board, eye contact, not fidgeting. He went from being the teacher's pet practically to being the naughty kid. He really, really struggled with it. Years later I was like, oh, that makes sense. At the time we didn't connect the dots. When we took him out, we just chilled, that whole kind of recovering from school.

Slowly but surely, he opened up about things that happened at school that he hadn't thought to mention at the time. We were like, that isn't normal. Kai thought that because he told the teacher, he didn't then have to tell us about things like bullying. It never got dealt with, and Kai never thought to tell us.

It was really quite distressing because he was getting into trouble for misbehaving at school in a way that he never would at home. With hindsight, it was because the rules didn't make sense to him. We were getting sad faces and smiley faces, those punishment and shame-based behaviour controls. The shame of getting a sad face and being put on red on the traffic light system, and things like this. We were having meltdowns at home. The moment you walked through the door, all hell broke loose. Every morning was hellish, getting into school, and every evening was hellish.

School Trauma and Burnout

> *The biggest thing that made me say yes, let's home educate was he went from being a lover of stories (we had to have about three bedtime stories every night) to one who hated reading. They push reading and it becomes a chore. Every single night you have to read and your mum and dad have to sign the book. He came to just despise reading. My ex and I are big readers. A child that's grown up around stories and round books, saying I hate reading and in tears about it.*

School trauma is family trauma. It isn't just about the child. It can affect everything about how a family works and can cause distress for parents which lasts for years.

Nicole told me about the experience when her two autistic children were at school.

> *There's a lot of regret and guilt that I have about putting them through school. I've got some images that are really upsetting when I think about them. Eva being pretty much held down and the teachers shouting "go". My gut was saying no, I always tried to ease them in. I was never wanting to be pushed out the door but in this one particular case, as I left I thought "What on earth is going on?" You're almost bulldozed into it, they say: "You're making this worse by staying", all of this kind of stuff.*

207

These are the symptoms which parents tell me about which they experience themselves.

- Becoming tearful when asked about school.
- Waking at night and nightmares.
- Finding meetings with professionals very anxiety-provoking.
- A "threat response" to emails from school or messages in the parents' WhatsApp group.
- Avoiding talking about it.
- Shame and guilt.
- Anger.
- Feeling negative about themselves and their parenting.
- Very low mood.

This means that when you meet a family, the parent as well as the child may already be hypervigilant. They may be highly anxious and they may be waiting for you to say that their child must return to school as soon as possible, or to tell them off for not pushing hard enough.

In order to work with school traumatised families, we need to establish a trusting relationship with them. This is challenging to do when families have had many bad experiences of professionals. They will be primed for us to say things which they find distressing, and they will be highly sensitive. They may not expect to be understood or listened to.

Recovering from School Trauma

The good news is that trauma memories can and do resolve over time when the conditions are right. Not everyone needs trauma therapy to do this. Memories can move from our alarm system to our filing system – psychologists call this "processing" and this is a natural process. We are all doing it, all of the time. When people talk about an event afterwards, and compare experiences, that can be processing. When children play about things they have seen and done, that can be processing.

There's a caveat here. Children and adults can only process past traumatic memories if they actually are safe now. You can't calm down and feel safe if you are still under threat.

Most of us try not to talk about difficult things when things are calmer. We don't want to upset our children again and we think it's better just to move on. The problem with this is that memories stay bottled up instead. Avoidance works in the short term – it means we don't have to think about difficult things, or experience difficult emotions – but in the longer term the memories just stay in the amygdalae, and this can cause problems.

Many things can keep those memories bottled up – not having anyone to talk to, feeling guilty about what happened, feeling ashamed of what happened or perhaps a fear of how overwhelming the memories might be.

Thirteen-year-old Alice told me about her experiences after leaving school aged eight.

> When I first left school, then anything that looked like school – so sitting in a circle during groups – was a no. Anything that felt like school was awful. I've also had a problem ever since school with trusting adults that I meet that have some sort of authority. For example, I was terrified of police. I was terrified of teachers. I don't have that really anymore. I used to be just really scared of all adults because, obviously, I'd pretty much lost trust in all the adults at school by that point.
>
> Because obviously, in the morning, you've got to come in and drag me into school building, lock the doors. It was a really big problem with them, the trust.

> I think it really upset me to be dragged into the school building. Also, I've always had a very high level of independence, when I was eight months old, I refused to be fed anymore. I would eat only adult food. I wouldn't let Mum hold my hand. She had to make a rule saying stop at roads and I'd just go, "Okay, I can run but I have to stop at roads."
>
> I've always just wanted to be in my own little world. I think having so many adults at school come and impose that on me led me to lose trust in them. I was terrified about being around adults for a long time, anything that looked like school. But I'm fine with that now.

Taking School Off the Table

There's a consistent finding in the trauma research, and it is that we need to be in a place of safety in order to recover. Without being emotionally and physically safe, a child will not be able to start to recover – and the possibility of being forced to return to school can make it impossible for a child to feel safe. In general, in order to recover from school trauma we have found that it's important to say explicitly that a return to school is not the goal unless the child wants to make it one. It's important to note that this doesn't necessarily mean that the child won't return to school, but that the pressure to do so is lifted. Many children feel able to return when they know that it's something they can choose.

In order to feel safe, children need to be able to show how distressed they are, but they can't do that if they are afraid of upsetting adults. Adults need to reassure children that they will not be forced to go back into school against their will again and that they are listening to them. They need to be safe on a physical, emotional and psychological level.

At this point, the work for professionals is about helping parents to make home a safer place for their children. It might involve helping the parents tell some of their own story. It might involve helping parents access support or find others locally who are going through similar experiences.

Talking About Emotions

Talking to both parents and children about emotions is important – and your work might be encouraging parents to talk to their children about emotions, even if they all find that upsetting.

Children often think that no one else feels things as intensely as they do, because they can't see the feelings from the outside. Parents can help by making the invisible visible and describing their own feelings and body sensations. One way to do this is for parents to talk about themselves and their emotions in a child-appropriate way. They might say things like "I get really nervous when I go to a new place, but then I feel better."

When children talk about feelings, it doesn't matter if children label them correctly, just encourage them to notice any sensations. You don't need to whip out an Emotions wheel (particularly since this might remind children of school). Some children I know talk about "fizzy" feelings or "heavy" feelings. The important thing is for children to learn that feelings come and go and they don't need to be scared of their feelings.

Feelings often get more intense before they are resolved. It's common for children to start out numb (or claiming to be numb), and then become angry and then sad as they start to let themselves get in touch with their feelings about what happened.

Telling the Story

Making sense of what happened is an important part of moving on. Memories of feeling under threat are usually fragmented – it's like they are in pieces. They don't make sense. If we can help children make sense of their experiences, then this goes a long way to helping them recover and move on.

Stories are a great way to help children make sense of what happened. Stories don't have to be formal or lengthy. They just need a beginning, a middle and an end – and the end needs to be a resolution.

Here's an example story for a young child.

When you were little, you started school and at first it was okay.

Then when you went into Year 1 you didn't like it. You would shout to tell us that you didn't want to go. For a while we didn't understand and we made you keep going. You were really unhappy and angry.

Then we worked out that the school was too big and noisy for you and we moved you to a smaller school where you are now. You were much happier. I'm sorry that we didn't work it out earlier.

Older children might write their own stories – or make a recording or draw a picture of their experiences. It doesn't really matter how they do it. What matters is that they get a chance to make sense of the experience and perhaps to discover that it's not just them. Making connections with the experiences of others can be particularly important for teenagers, who may feel that they are the only ones to whom this has ever happened.

Some children talk all the time about what happened, but it never seems to end anything. They seem stuck. For them, you might need to help them move on and end their story. This can happen with drawing, play or acting something out.

You can end a story however you or they want – Superman coming in or the Pokémon can arrive. The child can fly away. It doesn't have to be real.

Some questions you could ask to help end the story.

- Could we write a different ending?
- What would you like to be able to say to your teachers?
- What would you say if this was one of your friends?
- If we could go back and change it, how would you like it to be different?
- What would this story be like from a different perspective?
- What advice would you give the parent in this story if you could?
- What happened next?

Reclaiming the Future

After a trauma, it can feel like the future has been cancelled. This can be particularly true when a child isn't going to school anymore. School provides a road map for the future and many children may not be able to imagine life going on. We need to help them deliberately start imagining a new one.

> **Exercise**
>
> Make a plan together for what the child would like to do. It doesn't have to cover the next five years – but maybe the next few months would be a start. What do they enjoy? Can you do more of that? Can they plan to meet people they like, or do activities they have liked in the past? Would they like to try out something new? Try to get excited about the future together.

School Burnout

An increasing number of parents are describing their children as "burnt out" by their school experiences. They say that when the children stop going to school, they don't bounce back to their former happy selves. Some become seriously withdrawn and may rarely leave their bedrooms. Others are highly anxious and situationally mute. Recovery can take months and years.

Chloe left school when she was seven after what she described as years of constant stress. She and her mum Tracey told me about it in this interview when Chloe was 14.

> *Chloe:* Straight after school it was instant meltdowns every day, crying, crying, crying, crying, crying, fighting stress, complaining about tons of things, offloading all of my trauma from that one day alone. Not being able to sleep.
>
> *Tracey:* She wouldn't leave the house. We couldn't go anywhere else. Our house became a prison. All our family are in Wales and visiting family was difficult. If we did do a holiday we had so many things we had to bring, we were essentially bringing the entire house with us to make Chloe feel safe someplace else. We had to have a caravan rather than something more glamorous so she could see every room. There were all those steps to be taken into consideration.
>
> Once she left school I'd say it took nearly a year for her to acclimatise and realise that she didn't have to go back to school. We would just do short walks to the park. It was very small things we had to do. It took a very long time to build her confidence and her trust with certain people. It took us time to find our tribe of home educators. It took us a good year of transition.

Sometimes, like Chloe, young people just seem to have nothing left. They stop going to school, and then they stop being able to do almost anything. They seem to regress and stop doing the things they used to do. They don't seem to enjoy anything. Their parents get very concerned, and they often are unable to access any support because they won't leave the house or talk to anyone. One way of thinking about this is burnout.

Burnout happens when children have been in a state of chronic stress for so long that they lose the ability to come back to an emotional place where they don't feel stressed. They can't return to a place of feeling okay at all. They can't soothe themselves and others can't soothe them. They never feel emotionally relaxed and engaged with the world.

This sometimes seems to happen unexpectedly for young people. They often appear to be coping and may even be doing very well at school. Then something small happens – maybe being told to get a haircut, or a friend leaves – and they crack. And once that has happened, there's no going back. It's like something has broken. They stop going to school, they often stop doing anything. They sometimes won't leave their bedrooms.

Andy and Claire told me about what happened to their daughters who are both autistic. Beth attended school until Year 5 (age 9–10) and is now home educated.

It was so hard to get all of the basics done, to eat food, to wash and brush their teeth, to do uniforms and all of that. There was no room for anything else. There wasn't the room for discussion. We were just dealing with it, trying to get them from A to B. As I look back on it now, I felt like I disappeared as a parent when they went to school. I feel like I'm a parent again now. In the school years my humanity and any sense of play or fun, all of that just became irrelevant, there's no room for it. You just had to get from A to B every day, it was just a cycle of that.

The final straw was to do with homework. Beth got monumentally stressed about it and just in floods of panicky tears. We reduced it. We spoke to the school and said, does she have to do any of this? They said, No, it's fine. But she became completely irrational. She was still panicking on a Sunday night. She'd think that the teacher might forget and she'd get shouted out for not doing the homework that didn't exist. She was a panicky wreck.

We just got to the point where there was no way we could enter school in the state that she was in. We took her to the doctor. I guess we were wanting to get her referred. I remember carrying her in and she was just a shell. She was an absolute shell. She actually couldn't speak, it was like carrying a ghost around. She just disappeared. There was no way that we could ask her to go into something that was doing that to her.

What Is Burnout?

The World Health Organization defines burnout has having three parts:

Exhaustion or energy depletion.
Feelings of negativity or cynicism
Feelings that you can't do anything well or be productive.

What Can We Do When School's Not Working?

Table 7.1 Burnout in Young People

Signs of Burnout in children and teenagers
(None of these in themselves are enough to indicate burnout, it is when there are many signs and they persist for several months that they might point to burnout)
Emotional flatness or numbing. Extreme compliance: "I don't care what I do." Constant exhaustion/fatigue, lasting for more than a couple of weeks and not alleviated by sleep. Hypersensitivity to noise/light and other sensory stimuli. Negativity about everything including self. Hopelessness about the future. Not able to concentrate on things they used to enjoy. Physical symptoms such as headaches, tummy aches, aches and pains which are not to do with medical reasons. Physical sensations such as buzzing, prickling or numbness. Never seeming to get into "flow". Feeling like requirements of everyday life are too difficult to meet – perhaps stopping showering or changing clothes when they could do it before. Volatility (flying off the handle about apparently minor things). Physically tense. Difficulties eating, or severely restricting what they eat. Tired all the time but can't sleep. No interest in anything. Not speaking in some environments. Spending all their time doing something like scrolling on social media but not seeming to enjoy that time. Losing their "spark".

The WHO is clear, however, that burnout is not a medical condition. They class it as an "occupational phenomenon" – meaning that it is a direct result of the chronic stress of a workplace. They also say that 'burnout' can only be the result of work, not other activities, but there doesn't appear to be a logical reason why other occupations (such as school) can't cause burnout.

The implication of the WHO saying that burnout is not medical is that we shouldn't be trying to help people recover from burnout in order to return them to the same, highly stressful, environment which burnt them out in the first place. The environment is the problem, and it's that which needs to change.

This is a really important distinction for young people. Everyone wants to patch them up and get them back to school – but the burnout model suggests that if it's the environment which caused the problems, then it will cause them again.

Unfortunately what happens when young people have burnt out is often not helpful. Adults often respond with pressure, fear and threats – all of which make things worse. I've heard of young people who have been told their parents will be sent to prison if they don't keep coming to school. Many have been told they'll never amount to anything and school attendance is essential for their future. It makes them feel terrible, and it stops them from getting better. They can't get any space away from the pressure to recover.

Schools often put on extra pressure without meaning to. The table below shows some of the subtle (and not so subtle) ways in which teenagers tell me they feel pressured.

Table 7.2 Ways in Which Adults Put on Pressure

Pressure Techniques	Examples
Emotional	"Your mum could go to prison if you don't attend school."
Comparisons	"Your brother is doing so well at school." "No one here should be struggling with this."
Future predictions	"If you don't work harder, you are going to end up working in McDonalds' your whole life." "If you fail your exams, you could end up under a bridge."
Labelling of things that young people do or enjoy	"Those video games are such a waste of time." "Only lazy people lie in bed until 10 am." "Only boring people get bored."
Praise (with a kick in the tail)	"You're so talented when you put the time in." "You're so good at French, it's such a shame you gave up the GCSE course."
Minimising the effort something takes	"It's just a spelling test." "There's no need to make a fuss. Everyone else can do this." "We only ask you to read for 30 minutes a day, it's not much."

Burnout Recovery

There are four stages to recovery from burnout. Parents and schools usually want to jump in at stage 3 or 4, but when the young person is still at stage 1, this is going to backfire and stop them from recovering.

The four stages are:

Breakdown/Crisis
Repair
Analysis of what went wrong
Planning for the future

At each stage, adults can help, but it's important to know which stage you're at because the strategies will be different.

At the first stage, breakdown, it's about providing a safe space and cutting out demands and pressure. It's about protecting the young person's space and making sure they are not pressured to return to school. It's about creating a safe place for them to land and keeping them safe. That might mean working on drug or alcohol use if they have been using these to regulate their emotions. It might mean working on eating problems or self-harm. Any work with young people at this stage needs to focus on connection and engagement. Success is them allowing you to come back next week. The relationship is everything.

The next stage is more active. It's when the young person is coming out of total crisis mode and is starting to show some interest in the world around them. At this point, they might be helped to find things they enjoy and do more of it. This is unlikely to be school work. Young people I know have been interested in fashion, horse-riding, video gaming, going out with their friends, ice-skating and writing novels. The return of their interest in the world is what matters, not what they are interested in.

Nurture those green shoots and don't put the pressure on or you'll scare them back into their bedroom. Join them in doing whatever they are doing which they enjoy – even if that is a video game. Show them that you are interested in the things that they value.

Stage 3 is when it's then time to think about what went wrong, and this can be an angry phase. This usually happens naturally as the young person starts to go over what happened. Parents are often surprised because they thought things were improving, but now that the young person is coming out of the burnout they start to feel emotions intensely again. They might be very angry about what happened and why no one noticed. Adults may need to keep quiet and listen. Young people might want to tell their story it through writing, music, recording, designing games – whatever works for them. If young people don't want to talk to their parents, they may need other people to talk to at this stage.

The next stage is planning the future, and this is where you put things in place so that it doesn't happen again. Don't just assume that if they go back to school then all will be well. It went wrong once, things need to be different for it not to happen again. They might need to be home educated, or do online school, or go back to somewhere different. They might need to cut the number of exams they are taking or school may need to offer a reduced timetable. They might be able to tolerate some challenge again, but on their terms. Too much pressure is likely to push them back into burnout again.

This whole recovery can take months or even years. It can't be rushed. Everyone involved needs a lot of patience.

Alice told me about how she recovered from her experiences. She had stopped speaking outside her home while at school, and had stopped being able to eat anything solid. She also had panic attacks. She stopped going to school after Year 4 and talked to me when she was 13. Her parents removed her from school because of their concerns about her mental health. She had wanted to stay at school as she thought, otherwise she would be a failure.

> Once I was out of school, I slowly started speaking more. I would speak at home, but it was very basic. "Yes", "No". I wouldn't really speak much at home but I would speak there. I was having hospital appointments about trying to get me to eat more because I was on a liquid diet.

I got to a point where I could communicate with my parents and realised why they'd done it [taking her out of school]. I think I also reached a point where I turned nine when I developed a complete obsession with books. I read tons and tons of books. Not nine-year-old level books, a lot of philosophy and politics type of books. I read loads of those. Then I realised that maybe it was the headteacher's fault and not my fault.

I realised when I looked back on everything. "Oh, that's definitely not normal behaviour. Definitely wasn't my fault, I don't think."

I think it was the perspective change that did it.

Up to that point I just felt awful that I'd been taken out of school and I thought that was me failing. Why should I be doing no work and these happy things at home when this was all my fault anyway? I think it was the perspective change of realising it wasn't my fault and then realising that school was awful.

Everybody always says that it's a slow realisation, which don't get me wrong, it normally is, but for me, it was very, very extreme. Just wake up and was like, "Oh yeah, yeah." For another year after leaving school, my anxiety and eating problems and speaking problems were still way up there, even if they were getting better progressively.

One day I woke up, and I was like, "I'm very, very sick of this." I tried to do one thing that was very out of my comfort zone, and then I did it. Then I decided, "Wow, I can do anything." On that euphoria, I signed up to these things and then just did them because they were already commitments.

I went to a group for socially anxious girls. I went there and I found my people. I found them! The main room was way too busy, and I was upset because I thought, if this is the group of socially anxious people and this is too much for me, then where am I going to go now?

I ventured off into a cupboard to hide away from the scariness, and I saw these three girls in this cupboard. One of them was wearing noise-cancelling headphones. One of them was wearing these light-blocking sunglasses, and one of them was sitting there with all these fidget toys. They all went, "Hello?" This was probably the first time I'd spoken apart from at the Calvert Trust.

That really helped as well. I went into this room with these girls, and they went, "Is it too loud out there?" I went, "Yeah." they went, "Come sit down." I sat down with them, and then I suddenly had three new friends.

Five years later, I still go to that group, except I go there now because it's shifted after Covid-19 to being for younger children. Now I go there to help the new, younger children.

I think the nicest thing for me, if I ever get sad again and need to see the progress, is that about 90% of the groups that I started doing, I now volunteer to help all of those little mes that started coming.

Table 7.3 Ways to Support Burnout Recovery

Take the pressure off.
Make it clear that recovery doesn't mean straight back to school.
Start where the child is and help them do more of that.
Find the things which make them feel good about themselves (or used to) and do more of that.
Find available adults who can come and be around without pressure (these people might be called mentors, tutors or music teachers, or they might just be friends).
Find examples of other people who have left school or failed at school and gone on to leave meaningful lives.
Challenge your thinking about what a meaningful future looks like.
Focus on offering opportunities but do not compel them to do them.
Protect them from judgement.
Find opportunities for them to feel in control and to make choices.

What If It Isn't Working?

Burnout recovery takes a long time, possibly years, but sometimes a young person just doesn't seem to be getting better. Things seem stuck. This is when it might be helpful to find a therapist who can help to unpick any beliefs that young person may have which stops them from recovering.

If you are looking for a therapist, then it's critical that that therapist does not see success as a return to school. They need to focus on helping the young person recover and discover for themselves what that might look like. Some young people are very clear that being able to say no to school is an important part of their recovery, while others are able and want to return, often to a different school.

When young people aren't recovering, it's often because the pressure hasn't really been removed. They may think that if they recover they have to go back to school, or they may think that without school, they'll be a failure. They may be worried about their age, and aware that everyone else is progressing while they feel left behind. Adults may be talking to them and about them in ways which make them feel bad about themselves without even noticing.

They may still have beliefs about how "school drop outs" will never achieve anything and so they think their life is over. Or they may be hearing toxic messages about themselves from others who are still at school.

At this point professionals might need to find out what recovery would mean for them. If recovery is associated with going back to school, then they could be in a double bind, unable to move forwards. Finding other young people who have succeeded without attending school can be helpful, as can hearing from adults who have gone on to live fulfilling lives despite having found school very challenging or having stopped attending school.

In this chapter, we've talked about school trauma and burnout. These are all reactions which parents and young people describe after leaving school, and are often poorly recognised by professionals. In particular, both trauma and burnout can be caused by the way that adults react to a child's difficulties, rather than the difficulties themselves. Recognising that parents and children may be traumatised requires professionals to be mindful as to how families might react to another person coming and (perhaps) trying to persuade them to try something new.

Summary

- An increasing number of young people are showing symptoms of trauma and burnout following difficult experiences at school.
- Interventions which force young people into school or make home less pleasant can exacerbate these problems or can cause a trauma reaction.
- A trauma response is a fear-based response, when the young person experiences things to do with school as a threat. It can lead to avoidance of anything to do with school, including reading, other children, people in authority and school buildings.
- Burnout is a state of chronic stress, brought on by an extended period of environmental stressors. Burnout happens when a person can no longer return to a less stressed state of mind.
- Recovery from both of these things can take an extended period, with parents and young people reporting that it can take years.

References and Further Reading

Fisher, N. and Fricker, E. (2023). *The Teenage Guide to Burnout Recovery*. London: Robinson.

Haines, S. (2016). *Trauma Is Really Strange*. London: Singing Dragon.

Morgan, F. and Costello, E. (2023). *Square Pegs: Inclusivity, Compassion and Fitting in: A Guide for Schools*. Carmarthen: Crown House Publishing Ltd.

8

Working with Children Who Are Not Attending School

In this chapter you will find:

1. Safety, Opportunity, Autonomy and Relationships (SOAR) Framework
2. Phases of Recovery
3. SOAR in Practice
    KITE Specialist Tutoring Service
    City Wall Alternative Provision

Introduction

There is an oft-quoted body of research which shows that there is a strong correlation between poor school attendance and poor educational outcomes. This research is used to insist that all children must attend school. These findings are unsurprising. Those who find school easier are more likely to attend regularly and to feel successful there, while those who struggle with school are more likely to also find it hard to attend and to do less well in their exams.

As any psychology undergraduate knows, a correlation is not the same as a causation – and in the case of school attendance difficulties, the relationship between attendance and outcome is complex and multi-factorial. Those who thrive at school are in many ways a different group to those who struggle. They are more likely to be advantaged in other ways, and to find the way that school operates easier to navigate. Their school experience is only one part of that.

Yet it's often assumed that this research means that attending school is the cause of better outcomes for everyone, no matter what – and all that is necessary to turn a person who is struggling at school into one who is not, is to insist that those who are struggling return to school.

This is not the only way to interpret the research.

It's not really feasible that school creates better outcomes for everyone, even those who are very unhappy or failing there. We know that school in itself isn't necessary to get an education, since evidence from home educators shows that children can learn and become educated outside of school. We know that attending school isn't sufficient for a child to do well, because many children attend school for years and do very poorly at the end. The school building is not infused with magical properties. Not everyone can learn there and for some, insisting that they attend every day prevents them from learning.

Another way to interpret the research is that as a society we are letting down the children who struggle to attend school. We are not providing them with accessible opportunities to learn – and consequently, they have poor outcomes. This perspective opens up new possibilities, namely whether it could be possible to change what happens when a young person struggles

What Can We Do When School's Not Working?

to attend school. The insistence that school is the only way to learn excludes many young people from education.

It is probable that for some children at least, it's not the absence of school *per se* which causes the poor outcomes, but the fact that no other educational opportunities are being offered. Parents frequently tell us of their frustration when their child is not able to attend school, and how they feel forgotten by the system. They and their children want to learn, but they can't do that at school, and it seems like there are no other options.

Young people who do not attend school lack opportunities to learn and are often told that they are failures or losers. These young people have frequently had very bad experiences at school, and may have learnt to think in ways which block their learning, for example thinking about themselves as worthless or as incapable.

It is a big shift to let go of school attendance as the primary goal and to consider what else might work for these children, but for some that is exactly what they require. For this to happen, the adults around each child need to

think about how else they could move forwards in their lives, even if that doesn't include returning to school. That is the focus of this chapter.

Research shows than when a child is educated at home, a straightforward replication of school at home is unlikely to be successful. In the absence of the structure of school, young people will rarely sit at a desk from nine until three. Learning will be far more interwoven with the rest of their life and much more of it will be informal. Most adults, however, were schooled, and they unintentionally approach education outside school with all the assumptions of school. It's just what they know.

This means that it can be hard for professionals to understand and frame what they see when a child is being educated out of school. It can also be difficult to recognise and measure the learning which is taking place when a child moves away from the formal curriculum.

This chapter is about ways to work with children who are out of school. It provides a framework for thinking about the work that we might do with these children. It includes stories from tutors, charities and local authority educational psychologists working with children out of school. As we have done throughout this book, we have included stories from a range of young people who have struggled with school attendance, including those who have been excluded or who have been in trouble with the law as well as those who have been identified as having emotionally based school avoidance or non-attendance. We include these together because the methods that professionals describe when working with these young people are strikingly similar.

SOAR: A Framework for Working with Young People Out of School

We have developed a psychologically informed framework for setting priorities when working with these young people. This structure is based on a combination of self-determination theory (already discussed in Chapters 4 and 5 (Ryan and Deci 2000)) and trauma-informed practice. Self-determination theory is a theory of motivation, and it suggests the conditions which nurture high quality internally driven motivation. We have found that with young people who have stopped attending school, finding (and nurturing) their internal motivation is the key to their reengagement with life and learning. However, this needs to be paired with a sense of emotional safety, and this is where trauma-informed practice comes in. It isn't enough to focus on motivation and learning. If a young person doesn't have some level of safety, they will not be able to learn effectively. Equally, safety is necessary but not sufficient for learning. We sometimes meet young people for whom all the emphasis has been on safety, with not enough thought given as to how they can access new opportunities and venture out of their comfort zone. Safety can become a trap if you can't tolerate the discomfort which comes with new experiences.

Engaging with a young person's internal drive means stepping away from content delivery and teaching. It may mean that progress looks quite different to what you expect. It means deliberately putting less pressure on young people and instead focusing on helping them feel in control of that situation. In practice this means that someone who is employed as a tutor or support worker will need to focus on connection and relationships before they make suggestions or do organised activities.

This framework has the acronym SOAR, which stands for Safety, Opportunities, Autonomy and Relationships. It's a way of thinking about how to engage young people, but also can be a way to evaluate whether enough is being offered to an individual young person when they are being educated outside of school. It may also be useful when thinking about how to engage young people who are still in the school system but who are not thriving and where things are at risk of breaking down.

We'll describe the detail of what these letters stand for and what progress looks like when using SOAR. You'll then hear some real-life stories of working with school non-attenders, from tutors, alternative provision and educational psychologists.

Safety

Physical Safety

Making sure that a young person is physically safe is a prerequisite to any work. Young people who are not attending school can be vulnerable and safeguarding needs to be a priority. If a young person is out of school, this will mean finding out where they are, what they are doing instead and whether there is a responsible adult looking out for them. Part of this work will be with parents, helping them to see that this is unlikely to be a short-term problem and that the family will need to reorganise around the reality that a child is not attending school. For many families, this is not at all what they had planned and it is very difficult to accommodate around work schedules. Some families have used the analogy of illness – if a child becomes ill and can't attend school, then everything has to change and this isn't a choice. This is unlikely to be an easy process and may involve thinking outside the box. It will require everyone to stop thinking about this problem as a choice or bad behaviour on the part of the child, and instead to see it as something which they cannot help. Many families are justifiably angry when there isn't an alternative school or childcare provision offered which will work for their child.

We know of parents who have negotiated to take their (older) children into work for a couple of days or who are self-employed and who have their children with them at their business. We also know of families who have changed their work patterns so that one parent works during the day and the other works evenings and weekends. Some families are able to call on extended family support, while some are able to pay for child minders. Some single parent families have moved in with relatives in order to have more adults around for children during the day. Some children attend part-time learning communities established for home-educated children while others go to forest school for a couple of days a week. Some families find other local families in the same situation and swap childcare. The resources available to each family will be different.

Emotional Safety

Establishing yourself as a safe professional is a key part of any work. The family may have had repeated experiences of professionals suggesting interventions which have made things worse, or which have felt blaming. Being safe will mean being non-judgemental and curious, and going out of your way not to come across as parent-blaming. You may need to listen to the previous bad experiences they have had with professionals with a non-defensive stance.

Part of being a safe person is seeing the child in the best possible light, and making the assumption that they will do well if they can. Children who have had traumatic experiences will often express this through what looks like disruptive behaviour or total withdrawal. They may be extremely hard to connect with. The challenge for you is to take none of this personally and to see it as an expression of how the child is feeling, rather than as behaviour which needs to be sanctioned.

A Low Demand Approach

Many children who have had a difficult time at school will react very badly to being told what to do or any attempt to teach them. They become very sensitive to pressure, and this can be a barrier to learning. These children will often say no in response to any suggestions which is deeply frustrating for adults who work with them. This 'No' is usually a sign that they don't feel safe. The no is like their shield, protecting them from the possibility of things going wrong. One way to support them with this is to adopt a "low demand" approach which takes some of the pressure out of interactions. The table below outlines some simple low demand strategies.

Table 8.1 Ways to Reduce Demands

Higher demand	Lower demand
Instructions (Get out your book and turn to page 5)	Statement (The thing I'm looking at is on p. 5)
Using rewards (If you do this, I'll give you a sticker)	Not using rewards (You can have a sticker if you want, whatever you do)
Adding emotional pressure (It will make me sad if you don't do this)	Reducing emotional pressure (You can do this or not, I will be okay either way)
Expecting them to join you (Can you put your tablet down and start the lesson now?)	Joining them where they are (You're playing Minecraft, is that your house?)
Not giving them the option (You need to do this right now)	Building in a get out clause (You could do this or we could do something else)
Lots of choices (How about doing X or Y or Z?)	One choice at a time (We could do X)
Authoritative (You need to stop doing that right now)	Collaborative (We've got a problem because you can't keep doing that, I wonder what we could do instead)
Threats (If you don't do this, then you'll be going back to school)	Reducing the threat on purpose (I won't be making you go back to school unless you want to go)
Rigidity (We're going to sit here until you do it)	Flexibility (We can go somewhere else and come back later)
Adding an expectation (I've got a great idea. I'm sure you're going to love this)	Reducing expectations (I have an idea. You might like it or you might have a better idea)

Table 8.2 Opportunities for Learning and Social Interaction

Local groups such as scouts or guides
Youth clubs
Dungeons and Dragons
Board game cafes
Music lessons or jamming sessions
Drama groups
Looking around charity shops
Going to car boot sales (either to sell or buy)
Volunteering at local cat rescue
Sea Cadets
Pottery painting
Bouldering
Climbing
Swimming
E-sports
Writing and recording music
Drawing
Writing stories or a novel
Going to the theatre
Going to the cinema
Running
Video game tournaments
Comic Con
Cooking and baking
Learning how to use a sewing machine
Learning how to do stage make up
Customising clothes from charity shops
Making jewellery with polymer clay
Learning how to code from YouTube
Creating their own video games using Scratch or other languages
Learning how to do magic tricks to put on a show
Going to the library
Making their own YouTube videos or podcast

Opportunities

Young people need opportunities to learn and to feel good about their capacity for learning. Those opportunities don't have to look like formal lessons (although they could do at some stages). They need opportunities to read and be read to, to play games, to meet others and to exercise. They need opportunities to discover things outside their immediate world and to be stimulated.

What those opportunities will look like depends on the young person. We can't give you a definitive list because what seems like a fascinating opportunity for one young person may be a total bore for another, but the following table gives some examples of opportunities which young people have found interesting.

The most effective way we have found to engage young people who have stopped attending school is to start with whatever they find interesting and to help them to do more of that. No matter what that is. We know young people with interests in pirates, film-making, fashion and beauty, traffic-calming measures, animal behaviour and locksmithery. Others are motivated by making money, becoming an artist, making stop motion films or learning how to code computer games. All of those are great places to start – and you don't have to have brilliant ideas or start teaching them about it. You just need to start by showing an interest. They will almost certainly know more about it than you.

Many young people may not want to talk to you about their interests because they have had experiences of these being used to control them in the past. Some young people tell us that professionals asked about their interests and then used that to design reward systems where they were only allowed to do things they enjoyed as a reward for attending school. You will need to establish yourself as a person who isn't going to do this before they will trust you with the things which matter to them.

Opportunities are non-compulsory by their very nature, and this means that you need to make your peace with rejection. Resist the urge to put the pressure on or to tell them that you're sure that they'll enjoy something if they try it. In particular, don't use your emotional responses to try and encourage the child by saying things like "I made a big effort to prepare this for you and now you're refusing to do it?" or "I've travelled all this way to see you and now you can't even come out of your room?" Flexibility is key. The less flexible a child is able to be, the more flexible adults need to become.

Autonomy

Autonomy is often misunderstood. People think that it means "independence" or leaving children to get on with things by themselves. Autonomy isn't the same as doing things by yourself and it's possible to be autonomous without being independent – for example, a person with learning disabilities may need significant help in their daily living, but can still be supported to make autonomous choices. Autonomy means feeling that you are able to make meaningful choices about your life. It's a crucial part of being motivated to learn and also safety. When people feel that they can make meaningful choices, they are more likely to be engaged and interested, and their learning is likely to be of a higher quality.

Most young people who have stopped attending school feel hopeless about their ability to make decisions. They may have been told repeatedly that they make "poor choices" or that they are "choosing" not to attend school. They may have been excluded from school for their "choices". Developing their sense of themselves as a person who can make decisions is a crucial part of the process of recovery.

Autonomy does not mean that a child or teenager makes all their own decisions, including those which put them at risk. Safety has to come first and autonomy is about making meaningful choices within boundaries. Balancing autonomy and boundaries is one of the most important tasks of parenting as children grow into teenagers and adults.

Having said all that, most of us aren't good at helping young people make autonomous decisions. When adults try to motivate children with rewards and punishments, this can interfere with their autonomy. They are no longer making choices based on what is important for them, they're making choices based on what an adult will do to them in response. These techniques take autonomy away from the child, whose decision making is now influenced by what consequences an adult has put in place rather than by their own internal compass.

Autonomy-supportive adults will help children make decisions, without being emotionally attached to the outcome. For some children, it's useful to make it really clear that they can say no to your suggestions. This could involve saying things like "We could play this game or you might have a better idea" or "I had thought we could go there, but somewhere else could work too." It isn't autonomy-supportive to simply say to the child "What would you like to do?" if they don't know or don't have any ideas. The idea is to make suggestions but to leave open the option of refusal without shame or guilt. Being able to say no is a skill to practice, and many young people need the confidence that their no will be accepted before they will be able to say Yes.

Relationships

The final part of the SOAR framework is supportive relationships. Although this comes last, it should never be thought of as something which comes afterwards or is an add-on. Supportive relationships are essential and you will get nowhere without forming a connection first. The young person needs unconditional relationships around them, and a sense that they belong somewhere.

This is particularly important for young people who have had a very negative experience at school and who may have been excluded, because they have often felt unwanted and rejected by the school community. They may also have disrupted relationships at home, or parents may have been told to use their relationship as a form of punishment, not interacting with the child if they do not attend school. All their relationships have become conditional on their behaviour, and so as their behaviour was considered to be less acceptable, their relationships became less supportive.

Relationships are affected by years of school distress, and rebuilding family relationships without school at the centre needs to be a priority. Parents sometimes say they don't know what to do now that their focus is not getting their child to attend school each day, and the child is often angry about having been forced into school. This anger can emerge years later, often leading to distress for parents who were doing the best they could at the time.

This is an area where a professional might be able to help parents adjust their expectations and focus on seeing their child's strengths as well as their weaknesses.

Moving outwards from family relationships, the child needs opportunities to have relationships with people outside their immediate family. For many young people, spending time with same-age peers feels like too much pressure and may remind them of school, and so finding adult mentors can be helpful. Youth workers, football coaches, tutors, music teachers or Scout leaders can all play this role, as can relatives and extended family.

Table 8.3 Summary of the SOAR Approach

	Questions to ask
SAFETY	**How can we increase their sense of safety?** What helps this child feel safe? Physical (environment) (e.g. space to get away, place in the playground where footballs don't fly around) Physiological (body) (e.g. food they can eat in a place they can eat it, access to toilets and water) Psychological (thoughts and emotions) (e.g. do they feel it's okay to feel the way they feel, are there people who will listen to their feelings?) What makes this child feel shamed or anxious? Are adults using shame or anxiety to control this child's behaviour (e.g. through behavioural charts)? What environments are overwhelming for them on a sensory level?
OPPORTUNITIES	**How can we bring more opportunities into their life?** What opportunities do they have to do things they enjoy and find meaningful? Are the things they are good at valued by the adults around them? Are their opportunities being restricted because of their behaviour? How could we overcome that? Are opportunities being presented in a way which means they can access them? Could we change that?
AUTONOMY	**How can we enable them to make meaningful decisions?** Does this child have a chance to make real decisions about their life without being shamed for it (e.g. to give up doing something they don't enjoy)? Are they being made to do things against their will? Where does this child feel in control of their life (for many children, this only happens in video games)? How can we help them do more of this? Does this child see themselves as someone who can make choices? If not, why not?
RELATIONSHIPS	**How could we improve the quality of their relationships?** Who are the key relationships in this child's life (in and out of school)? Are there people who "get them"? Do they have available adults they trust? Are there people who see them the best in them, even when they are at their worst? If a child struggles with peers, can we find older mentors for them?

Phases of Recovery

When we implement SOAR with children who are not attending school, progress typically goes through three broad phases. Adapting your approach to the phase which the child is at is crucial. When you first meet a child they may be in Phase 1, but if you arrive with a plan of activities for the session and a checklist for them to complete then you are coming in directly at Phase 3. The likelihood is that you'll be disappointed. You may also not get another chance to try as they will withdraw more as a result of your efforts.

You can't get to Phase 3 without first establishing safety and focusing on relationships. This means that if you are working individually with a child, no matter what role you are in, you need to focus first on relationship building, and building trust with the child or young person. If you come out of your work with a young person feeling "we got nothing done" then it could be that the child is still in Phase 1, but you're expecting to be in Phase 3. Or it could be that you are focused on content rather than on the process.

SOAR in Practice

It's striking how similar the accounts are of those who work with children who have stopped being able to go to school. Everyone we talked to (and we didn't coach them first!) gave examples of how they connected to young people first through their interests and through establishing themselves as safe and non-judgemental. They did not replicate a school timetable. They did not use rewards or punishments to try and motivate them. They described young people gradually re-engaging with life and learning but said that this sometimes took months and years. There were no stories of quick fixes. We're including two examples here but they represent many more.

The first example here is of individual work with young people who have EOTAS (or EOTIS) (education otherwise than at/in school) packages, while

Table 8.4 Phases of school recovery.

	What it looks like	What professionals can do
Phase 1	Child is withdrawn, may not be seeing anyone or doing anything. Child may not be leaving the house and may also be preventing other family members from leaving the house. Family may be in crisis. Child may exhibit self harm or suicidal ideation. Child and parents may express feeling "numb". There may be a lot of family conflict.	Lift the pressure off the child in terms of returning to school. Listen to parents and encourage them to tell their story. Try to foster a sense of hope and to let parents know that you have seen things this bad for other families and things have got better. Make sure that the child is safe. Establish relationships with parents if not the child. Encourage the parents to see the child is in recovery from difficult experiences as opposed to behaving badly. Use low demand language and help parents to learn to do the same. Focus on helping the child regulate their nervous system, perhaps using sensory strategies.
Phase 2	Child is starting to show an interest in learning things on their own terms (which may well be nothing to do with school). Child may start to be angry and to express that. Child may express interests but then not follow through. Child expresses boredom and frustration but doesn't like any suggestions which are made.	Follow the child's lead. Get involved in what the child is doing. Show an interest in them and the things which they find important. Encourage parents to support whatever the child is interested in and to see the interest itself as the positive sign. Be prepared for interests to come and go and don't expect projects to be finished. Respect the child's no's as well as their yeses. Provide a listening ear for the child and parent's story.

(Continued)

What Can We Do When School's Not Working?

Table 8.4 (Continued)

	What it looks like	**What professionals can do**
Phase 3	Child is showing curiosity and interest in the world around them. Child starts to be able to reflect on adult suggestions and to try new things (but still needs the option to say no). Child starts to be able to think about future goals.	Bring new opportunities into the child's life, even if they don't take them up. Help the family to think about ways forward which could mean some formal learning online or at college or might mean apprenticeships or informal learning. Look for opportunities for the child to expand their experience – whether that is online learning, local groups or mentoring and tutoring.

the second is of an organisation who work in Alternative Provision and with young offenders.

Facilitating Learning

Laura Kerbey is an ex-teacher who has worked as a tutor for those who are educated outside school for many years. She runs Kite, a specialist tutoring agency and here she describes the progress of two young people. These stories are shared with the permission of the families involved.

> *As an ex-teacher, I have many concerns about our education system, but one of my biggest concerns is that education that takes place in a school is seen as superior to education that takes place outside of it.*
>
> *My experience has shown me that this is not the case for so many young people.*
>
> *Since I began supporting neurodivergent children and their families I have seen time and time again how damaging school can be for some of our young people. But, I have also seen the flip side of this which is the incredible impact of alternative types of learning.*
>
> *There are two examples that stand out to me, although I could write about so many more.*
>
> *I met R and his parents when he was in Year 8. R was still enrolled in his local secondary school. When he transitioned into Year 7, he managed the first two weeks, then was unable to go back for the rest of the year due to extreme anxiety and burnout. The same pattern repeated in Year 8, R attended for the first two weeks of term, then retreated to the safety of his bed and then became unable to leave the house at all.*

R is exceptionally bright, the word "genius" is mentioned in his EHCP. R wanted to learn and actually wanted to go back to school, but he just couldn't go as his anxiety was so high. Expectations placed on R were high due to his intelligence.

The first time I met R he was in bed. I entered the room with his mum and spoke very quietly to him about who I was, what I did and how I felt I could maybe help him. I wasn't asked to leave, but there was very little interaction from him. The second time I went to see R he communicated with me using a Minecraft pillow. I continued to work with R and his lovely parents, and eventually R accepted that school was not right for him right now and after a huge fight with the LA an EOTIS package was secured.

As soon as the EOTIS was agreed, I knew immediately which tutor would be best to work with R. Simon was not only a brilliant mathematician and computer geek, but he also had a strong passion for music and in particular drumming. These were interests that he shared with R. Again, the progress was very slow in building a connection between R and Simon, but Simon respected the fact that he needed to go at R's pace, and very gradually their interaction bloomed until they were having regular meetings online. Sometimes these meeting took place very late at night as R would often sleep all day and was at his most alert and most open to learning much later in the evening which Simon completely respected. Simon also said that he was not really teaching R, he was just guiding and facilitating R's learning as he was so bright and learning autodidactically.

In the summer of 2022 R sat his Maths GCSE and got a 6 after only eight months (of a two-year syllabus) working with Simon, showing the importance of what can be achieved with strong foundations, a trusted relationship and the breaking down of barriers to enable R to re-engage with education. He is now doing three GCSE Sciences, Computer Science A level and a Maths A Level. R also passed his driving theory on his 17th birthday and after two weeks of lessons passed his driving test. Again, this highlighted the importance of finding an instructor who worked with R and worked around his anxiety and burnout days.

Another young person who I will never forget working with was P. The first time I met P's dad he had travelled 300 miles by train and then bike to attend a PDA workshop which I was delivering. He told me he had to come to the workshop in Scotland as it was on a Saturday as he could not be away from home, and P, during the week when his wife was at work.

The pattern of P's journey through the school system was almost identical to R's and so many other young people I see. P had just about coped in his primary school, but again the transition to secondary was catastrophic for him and he ended withdrawing to his bedroom, unable to interact with anyone including his family. P did not have a diagnosis or an EHCP when I met his dad, but they fought incredibly hard to obtain both of these for their son. (Why do families have to fight so hard for what their kids need?)

What Can We Do When School's Not Working?

Like R, P was initially very reluctant to engage with a tutor. I managed to find an amazing tutor who shared many interests and experiences with P. She recognised that P was able to teach himself and had an amazing talent for photography. Like Simon, this tutor acted as a learning facilitator for P, not a teacher.

Sometimes P's tutor would go to the house and P was not able to engage with her, but she reassured him that was OK. She took it slowly, and respected his pace and eventually the most amazing, trusting relationship developed and the most amazing learning too. P ended up completing so many Open College Network (OCN) qualifications that they wrote to me to express their amazement and pleasure that no one student had ever achieved so many! With careful support P was able to transition to a college to study photography and has now been offered three unconditional places at university.

The success of these two amazing young men is not down to the education system. The success of these two young men is down to their intelligence, their bravery, their incredible parents who fought so hard for them and their amazing tutors who took their time to build safe, trusting connections which respected P and R's need for autonomy and autodidactic learning styles.

P's dad added his own perspective:

> I feel P was trapped in a schooling system that did not understand or care about his abilities or need to be with his peers. Consequently, frustration and a sense of

helplessness at having no way to influence what was, in effect, the abusive behaviour of the school system, led to his withdrawal and sense of misery.

Thankfully, combining the Kite approach and his tutors' dedication enabled P to regain confidence, self-esteem and vision for using his skills to go on to university. His school friends have also played an important part in including him in his peer group. Last summer P spent two weeks in rural Europe with the group of friends his school had separated him from at the start of Year 8.

The whole experience has highlighted the pressure the education system places on conformity over and above wellbeing, independent learning skills and real learning outcomes.

Thankfully, P's ability to stay focused and work independently has resulted in him being offered three unconditional places at university based on the quality of his work.

I feel parents need all the help they can get to stand up to the education system's narrow focus on attendance and conformity and fear of responding to children's individual approach to learning.

A Thousands-of-Strikes Rule

Citywall is a Manchester-based organisation providing rapport-based 1–1 and small group mentoring. The founders of Citywall, with experience as a former secondary assistant head and in health/substance misuse services, had both found that when they started by building relationships, young people were more able to engage with them. Through consistent support over time, mentors support young people using their strengths and interests as the jumping-off point. They now have intervention programmes in youth justice, education and wellbeing. You can find out more about the work and ethos of the organisation here www.citywall.org.uk.

Abigail met with Emma and Rachel, who told tales of going the extra mile, washing cats and sitting for hours underneath staging, all in order to connect with the young people they were working with. The conversation focuses on Citywall's work with young people in prison and their alternative provision.

> In the early days, Citywall was just working with young people in the criminal justice system. We didn't set up to be an SEN or specialist centre, or to specifically work with young people with neurodevelopmental differences. It is a relational programme to work with anyone, but we found that the way we work works particularly well for some neurodivergent young people who have found other settings very difficult to access. We ended up being asked to do more and more work as alternative provision because we were having more success than was expected through these relationships. We found that young people were comfortable to do and try things with us that they weren't in

other settings, because that relationship was there. We start slowly, take the time to invest in the relationship no matter how long that takes, and we put in the groundwork to show that we can be trusted.

Many of the young people we work with through our alternative provision work have a diagnosis of autism/ADHD and have had difficult school experiences, often school-based trauma. There's usually been some difficulties with professionals who we recognise are faced with working in an over-stretched system with limited resources. Families often feel like their child hasn't been understood and that no one understands what they're managing at home. Many of our autistic young people are experiencing very high levels of anxiety. The one-to-one relationship means you can create a sense of stability, safety and consistency.

There aren't really any typical stories, because we are so bespoke, but this is the story of one young person we worked with. We started working with him when he had been out of school for over three years. He was part of a specialist provision but was not able to access that either. He had diagnoses of autism and ADHD. His interactions with adults were often very positive but peer relationships were trickier for him, and he was very anxious. At our point of involvement, he hardly left the house, which is quite a common thread with our current cohort. I worked with him a couple of times a week for that first year. It started in the family home, often short sessions. He had older siblings who I also got to know and before long there were trusted relationships between myself and the family.

Very gradually he started to come out of his room more and started to play a few games, or we did a few quizzes. Things that were very low demand in terms of what was expected of him. We began taking little steps out, where he'd actually come outside and we'd sit in my car. Then we would have a little drive around and get some food and come straight back home. We did what we said we would do and we didn't ever do more than that. If we'd agreed to sit in the car, that was what we did, I didn't push it any further. We did what he had said he'd feel comfortable doing.

Over time, we saw this remarkable change to get to the point where every single session was out of the house. He was engaging in activities at our learning centre. He was beginning to engage in conversation with other adults that were around, sometimes with peers as well. He had aspirations around food and cooking and being a chef. We began to spend sessions cooking his family tea and so he had something to contribute for his family. As the relationship built, we began to more purposefully explore his anxiety through conversation. We used concepts such as riding the wave of emotion and the anxiety multiplier. We had a pictorial way of representing these concepts to support his understanding. He began to share things that he had never connected before, such as how anxiety feels for him physically. He was able to talk about what it prevented him from doing – things that he actually wanted to do, but didn't feel able to. He wants to have a Saturday job, he wants to be able to see his friends from primary school on Saturdays, but his anxiety stopped him from being able to do that. As he built confidence he began to realise he can do these things.

Ever so slowly we began to see his increased confidence and understanding of self drip into other aspects of his life, beyond our four hours a week together. His mum reported seeing him engage more in family activities, going out to celebrate things together, being able to go to the cinema together, things which hadn't happened for years. And that progressed, so he's now able to go out to visit different places and navigate different social settings. He's engaging in other provisions and is getting some qualifications. He can talk about how his anxiety feels. Our mentors are able to stand alongside him and support him.

We talk about building a trusted relationship all the time because if that's not in place you've not got a hope. You can't just automatically assume it's going to happen. This means we have to be ready to sometimes do unplanned, unexpected things in order to build relationship and get to know them. One young person I worked with had really got it in his head that his cat needed to be washed and wanted my help. We tried to wash the cat and it was a disaster, because the cat did not want to be washed. But this moment turned into such a comical thing that now he refers to it with warm affection, and we built a little bit of relationship, a shared experience in that moment. I hadn't gone in planning that I was going to attempt to wash a cat. I hate cats. But that's what he gave me on that day, so that's what I worked with.

Another time, I had a young person who was at a specialist provision and wasn't going to any lessons. He was going in every single day, but then disappearing. One day, when I arrived, I went on a search for him. I realised they had this stage that you could get underneath and he had hidden under it, at the really far end. I got down on my hands and knees and crawled in, far enough in so we could talk, but still giving him space. And that's where we spent our session. I couldn't even sit up properly, just curled up underneath the stage, talking in this incredibly uncomfortable situation, because he needed to be hidden in that place then.

We are committed to removing barriers. We vary session length, activity, we adapt the way that we work to the needs of the young person constantly. Sessions often initially happen at home, and we work with families to decide where in the house is a good place, and it's not in their bedroom. So often, with services, there's a two-strike rule – you miss two appointments and you're gone. We have a thousands-of-strike rule. We have young people where it takes months and months and each time we turn up, at the time when we say we're going to, we stand outside the door, we leave a note saying, "Really sorry we didn't get to see you today. We'd really love to have a chat next week if you feel like you're able." We show through our words and actions that we are reliable, trustworthy and safe.

We invest a lot of time early on, and we get to know these young people really well. We pick up on small physiological signs sometimes, which might be the first indication that they're uncomfortable, though they might not be able to express it. We had one student whose top lip used to sweat whenever they were being pushed beyond their limits. They would never say "I don't want to do this" because they don't want to upset anyone, so we had to learn to spot the signs. They really need people to recognise ways their body and behaviour are showing us they're overwhelmed, because often they can't verbally communicate that.

The relationship with parents and carers is really key and we usually meet them first. We spend a lot of time listening, making sure that we know them well. If a young person sees that their parents or carers trust us, they're more comfortable meeting

us. We really encourage families to let us know about any issues, and give us feedback, and we make changes based on that, knowing that they're the experts in their own experience. Lots of parents and carers feed back to us as the work progresses that they feel like they are getting their child back. That is how families experience the change they see in their children.

Some of our young people are non-speaking and we creatively adapt to that so that they can engage, but don't have to talk. There are no expectations that they will do anything they're not able to do. Often we start with card games or board games, it's low demand, shared social interaction. We try to get underneath the surface to find what motivates them and what interests them, and really communicate to them that we believe that they're interesting and worth being noticed as a person.

When the young person's ready, it's always at their pace. No session would look the same as another young person. The initial principle is always to re-establish the relationship since you last saw them, and monitor how they are. Are we good to go with what I planned, or do I need to adapt? You need to be observant and adapt to their needs in that moment. We try and gradually expand their world, whether that's their experiential world, their social world or their educational world – whatever is right for them with what they need and the level of provision they have with Citywall. I think that's what safety feels like. It's when young people know that we will go at their pace as we together create a set of personal development and academic targets that are entirely bespoke to them. If we get it wrong, we recognise that with them and we change. We celebrate the tiniest steps of progress because we've got time to see it and notice it. It's never straightforward progress, it's one big messy whirl of forward and backward steps but you stick in there.

These accounts tell of the very slow, gradual work which goes into forming a relationship with young people for whom things have gone wrong. "Going wrong" covers a wide range of possibilities. Some young people may be in the criminal justice system, while others may be stuck in their bedrooms due to high anxiety. Those who work with them start with establishing themselves as a safe relationship within which the young person's voice matters, usually by finding something which interests the young person and doing that together. Being able to connect with the young person is what makes the difference, rather than any specific training or qualifications. Over time they can introduce new opportunities and possibilities for learning, but this is always in the context of an ongoing relationship. These stories demonstrate the SOAR principles in action. All four areas continue to be important in their work with the young person.

Perhaps one of the most important ways in which these organisations make a difference is by offering hope to young people and their families, often at a point when it seemed like there was no hope left.

Working with Children Who Are Not Attending School

In this chapter, we've introduced the SOAR principles which we have derived from observing the work that professionals do with young people for whom things have gone wrong. These principles are based on self-determination theory and trauma-informed practice. They combine safety and relationships with opportunity and autonomy – and every part is equally important. Starting with safety and relationships is key, but not enough. More needs to be offered if young people are to grow and learn.

Summary

- School is not the only way to get an education.
- If a young person isn't able to attend school, then the adults around them need to find ways for them to learn anyway and there are many inspirational organisations trying to do just that.
- Young people for whom school has gone wrong often need an extensive period of recovery before they are able to engage in learning again. Professionals need to be aware of this and avoid "scaring them off" by going in with unrealistic expectations.
- The SOAR framework provides a way to think about this work and stands for Safety, Opportunities, Autonomy and Relationships.

- SOAR combines self-determination theory with trauma-informed practice. It can be helpful for young people in a range of contexts.
- In practice, people who work with young people out of school describes starting with safety and relationships, giving young people the autonomy to say no before they can offer opportunities.

References and Further Reading

Boles, B. (2010). *The Art of Self-Directed Learning*. Summertown, TN: Book Publishing Company.

Collins-Donnelly, K. (2015). *Starving the Stress Gremlin: A Cognitive Behavioural Therapy Workbook on Anxiety Management for Young People*. London: Jessica Kingsley Publishers.

Fisher, N. (2021). *Changing Our Minds: How Children Can Take Control of their Own Learning*. London: Robinson.

Fricker, E. (2021). *The Family Experience of PDA*. London: Jessica Kingsley Publishers.

Huebner, D. (2009). *What to Do When You Worry Too Much: A Kid's Guide to Overcoming Anxiety*. Washington, DC: Magination Press.

Kerbey, L. (2021). *The Educator's Experience of PDA*. London: Jessica Kingsley Publishers.

Llewellyn, G. (2001). *The Teenage Liberation Handbook: How to Quit School and Get a Real Life and Education*. New York: Holt Paperbacks.

Ryan, R. M. and Deci, E. L. (2000). *Self-Determination Theory: Basic Psychological Needs in Motivation, Development, and Wellness*. New York: Guilford Press.

Sedley, B. (2019). *Stuff That Sucks: A Teen's Guide to Accepting That Life is Tough and Finding Your Way Through It*. Melbourne: Allen & Unwin.

Thomas, A. and Pattison, H. (2007). *How Children Learn at Home*. London: Continuum.

9

One Step Removed
Indirect Work with Those Not Attending School

In this chapter you will find:

1. Implementing Change in Services and Schools

   Working to Shift the Narrative
   Multi-agency Pathways

2. Setting the Direction of Travel (Assessments and Reports)

   Bringing Hope
   How Do We Start?
   Writing a Plan
   Making Specific Recommendations

3. Funded Educational Packages Outside School (EOTAS or EOTIS)

Introduction

This chapter is particularly for professionals who are working indirectly with children with school distress – those who are doing assessments, writing reports, making recommendations and planning services. It assumes that you have read the rest of the book and so does not go over the same ground.

We'd first like to acknowledge that it is hard to be a professional working in this area. Many people told us that they felt torn between their different roles and competing priorities. Educational psychologists said that they did not feel able to criticise school policies, even when they could see that these were not working for children, because they did not want to alienate teachers and the education services who employed them. Clinical psychologists said that they felt that they received referrals where it was assumed that the problem was "mental health" or "neurodevelopmental", and they felt that their job was seen as diagnosing or "fixing" the child so they could return to school. Many professionals expressed their frustration that there was no space in the education system for reflection and how this might be contributing to a child's problems.

It's a theme of this book that children's behaviour and attendance is rarely seen as feedback on the system, but it's also the case that when other professionals give explicit feedback on the impact of the system, that feedback is not well-received. This means that it is not clear how the adverse effects which are seen in health and in services which support young people can be fed back into the education system.

One Step Removed: Indirect Work with Those Not Attending School

Many professionals say that they see that something needs to change, but that the constraints of their service do not allow them to work differently. If this is the case for you, one way to start is with looking at your service outcomes for those who do not return to school. What are they offered and how are they learning? If we accept that some young people do not thrive and learn at school, then the onus falls on adults to improve outcomes for this group, without assuming that school attendance will be the way to do it.

Many services focus explicitly on a return to school, thereby limiting how effective they can be when working with those for whom this is not realistic. This has the paradoxical result that a child attending school under duress and not learning would be counted as a positive outcome, while a happy child studying for (and obtaining) qualifications at home would be counted as a failure.

We suggest that as an alternative, the aim of a service should be to create opportunities for young people to learn and get an education, *whether or not* they can attend school. We see those who are not able to attend school as a disadvantaged group, and their needs are obscured when it is assumed that they can be understood as a group who are making poor choices.

Some services have recognised that having school attendance as the main outcome limits opportunities for those for whom this is not achievable. They have reorganised themselves to focus on outcomes which prioritise learning and wellbeing rather than attendance.

Implementing Change in Services and Schools

We discovered when doing the research for this book that many professionals are highly nervous about admitting to having any goal other than school attendance for young people. They feel that this is politically impossible in the current climate. We talked to psychologists who did not want their (very positive) story included in this book at all and even those who agreed to be quoted all wanted to be anonymous. They were worried about how their service would be perceived if they admitted that their priority wasn't always a return to school for every child.

This is a tension running through child services. Naomi recently talked with a group of child mental health professionals, and several of them expressed how hard they found it when a non-school attending child was referred to them for mental health treatment. They said that in some cases their assessment was that the child's mental health would be best served by not returning to school and accessing education in other ways. They found themselves at odds with the system, which assumed that a return to school could only be positive in terms of mental health and that this should be the primary goal of any therapy.

When we've talked to people who are working differently they told us how important it is that a team feels it has permission to focus on learning rather than school return. One specialist EBSA team told us that they had stopped collecting data about returning to school, as a concrete reminder that a return to school is not the only successful or positive outcome.

Nicola, an educational psychologist, spoke about her experience of implementing service level change.

Shifting the Narrative

In the services I work with we were noticing a significant number of young people who were really struggling in their school attendance and were presenting with high levels of distress. We decided to do a piece of project work, writing new guidance for schools and delivering training to schools and LA (local authority) colleagues as well. We invited health and social care along and opened it up to anyone else within the LA that wanted to come, and that was really successful, bringing different people together with schools to support them with this issue. What we found through that process was that the school refusal narrative was still strong within our schools, although schools welcomed the training and opportunity to shift towards a more compassionate and child-centred approach to school non-attendance. I've found that the school refusal narrative is still very dominant in areas where there hasn't been a significant effort to shift understandings.

My main experience was upskilling the workforce and leading on those systemic approaches to really change the landscape around school attendance difficulties. I found that even when schools were planning reintegration or return-to-school packages, they weren't matched to the child's needs, or what they wanted, and the packages moved quickly, and it would all fall apart. We spent a lot of time upskilling school staff and LA colleagues in person-centred approaches that enabled them to truly co-produce return-to-school plans with the young person, with the young person setting the pace and overarching goals.

I started thinking about the existing frameworks and models that we had, that had never quite felt totally right for the situation, particularly where the school non-attendance is chronic and persistent. The main literature that we have available is the school refusal literature and a legacy of reward/punishment-based approaches to school non-attendance. I tend to draw upon doctoral research from educational psychologists, who have reformulated school attendance difficulties through an ecological lens and I find this really helpful. What comes from the doctoral research was that young people with attendance difficulties were consistently saying, "I don't feel believed, I don't feel understood. I feel like people are conceptualising these difficulties as if I'm naughty, I'm lazy, they don't believe me." There is so much that we can learn from the literature around the child and young person's voice.

I use Bronfenbrenner's ecological systems theory, which takes it out much wider than the child. I talk a lot about experiences at the level of the child, the home, the school, and look at all three areas of what's happening for and around the child. Then we begin to look at school culture and ethos, what happens when schools take a punitive, academic-focused approach, with lots of targets and rewards around attendance, the type of culture that that creates and what young people say about that. There's some recent doctoral research that had some really interesting findings, about autistic children finding the current school systems quite rigid and inflexible, and it being very difficult for them to navigate, not just the social and sensory side of school, but actually the rigidity of the school systems, and the added layer of pressure that added. It looks at the school culture and climate and all the things we know of when schools promote relationships, connection, belonging... we see improvements in mental health, wellbeing and attendance.

I think schools have to go on a journey. It's a lot of psychological work and it can be invisible. If I'm training schools in this approach, I take them through the journey, reflecting on the school refusal narrative and the implication that children have choice and control over this, and using lots of case studies. We have videos of young people talking about their experiences, we have videos from parents/carers. Gently that builds to the point where you can discuss stereotypes and biases they may have and increases compassion for the child's lived experience.

When you work with families, they say that their child has been experiencing attendance difficulties for many, many years. We are most aware of the persistent non-attenders, but children can be attending school consistently and still be experiencing EBSA. We shouldn't be waiting until the child has stopped school, until that distress is escalated to such an extent that they can't come in. We need to be identifying these children earlier, and particularly at that transition point from primary to secondary schools as this is when we often see a spike in school attendance difficulties.

The most powerful thing is to keep returning to the young person's voice. We can come up with an action plan with the most well-intentioned ideas, but if it doesn't meet the child's needs or it isn't in line with their wishes, then it's going to be limited in its success. I manage some of the tensions between school and home by continuing to take it back to the child's voice and using those solution-orientated approaches.

Parent blaming is the legacy of school refusal and the punitive-based system that we have. It breaks down relationships, if we're always operating within that punitive system. Even though it feels like a rigid system for schools in terms of the coding of absence, actually there is more flexibility. Headteachers have a lot of discretion. Sometimes it's about having professional curiosity and feeling confident to question some of those approaches, and sometimes you need to do that quite directly. When I am in consultations with schools, they are really worried about attendance and they feel the pressure.

I really try and emphasise to schools that although they don't feel like they are the right place for these young people, and they feel like they're not meeting their needs, once these children are not attending school, if there isn't another plan in place, they fall off the radar of all professional input and support. And even if a child isn't attending your setting at all, there is still a role for you as a school in terms of supporting access to blended packages, online packages or even just offering a relationship, maybe keeping those connections with their peer groups, maybe attending a club or forest school provision.

Multi-agency Pathways

Philippa, a local authority educational psychologist, explained what they did in her service to respond to the challenges posed by the Covid-19 pandemic.

> After the pandemic, we anticipated there would be an increase in anxious children not wanting to come back to school. We wanted a process that brought families, children, schools and professionals together. We set up a multi-agency team and a team around the child/family approach. We used a model of free training for schools, drop-in problem-solving, a referral pathway process and some guidance that goes across health, education and social care.
>
> These are the children who don't fit with the typical referral pathways, routes, working practices of services. If this number of children are not able to access school, then it's not about the children, it's about the education system. It feels like the whole system is overwhelmed. We go with where the family is at, recognise that wellbeing is first and is the priority and that educational opportunity is what we're aiming for, for children. We want them to have a sense of belonging somewhere, some purpose, some meaningful connections, and some future opportunities in their life. The principles are being child-centred and understanding it's a mental health need, or it's anxiety-driven, and it's not a choice.
>
> We tell schools to trust parents, to listen to parents and to ask the families and the children what the problems are. We try to get people to be okay with sitting, with the fact that some young people might be at home for a period of time, not accessing education or doing learning in a different way and needing to trust parental instincts around that. Lots of children and lots of families that we've spoken to, when the pressure is taken off, when they're given the breathing space, they have the solutions, they have good answers. You can come up with ways forward. When there is this absolute pressure to be back in school and there's judgement and there's blame, that's when everyone shuts down. It feels very stuck and there will be no progress.

One Step Removed: Indirect Work with Those Not Attending School

We have a structured way of schools gathering information, coming together to hold an initial meeting, and coming up with a plan. For some children, we could hand that plan back to school, and they could work through it. For more cases than we envisaged, it was much more complicated. What it highlighted is that this was not a new issue for that family, that this had been going on for a long period of time. It captured lots of children who were autistic, who had social communication difficulties, who had been just coping within school, and having this time off probably highlighted to them that they didn't have to live a life that was about just coping, and also that the anxiety had become much bigger after this time of being outside of school.

We worked very closely with CAMHS to think about their triage and referral routes, and make sure that those children got picked up. Their standard anxiety screeners don't necessarily show a high amount of anxiety if the child has not been in school and there's no pressure to return to school.

In a number of the secondary schools we have developed specialist roles within Early Help. These practitioners are linked to the school and work using the Family Partnership Model and can go into the family home, where attendance is 50–80%. A detailed "Early Help Assessment" helps us to identify barriers to attendance and create plans based on the family's needs, goals and preferred outcomes. They're offering targeted support to think about what is going to help that young person's return to education. A third sector organisation is also working with families where attendance is under 50%. That's a one-to-one mentoring support intervention. They go into the family home, they work with the family to identify some goals, identify further support that's needed, and they work with them over a 20-week period. We also work with an alternative provision who do mentoring and tutoring. They're very good at relationship building, working on wellbeing, working on child-identified goals, then bringing in some academic tasks, then transitioning back into a school or college in a supported way, or an alternative provision college or an alternative provision.

For everybody else outside of that, we've got the multi-agency pathway co-ordinated by the EP service (this includes the Attendance Team, Early Help, School Improvement, Educational Psychology Service, Specialist Teachers and CAMHS). We have monthly triage meetings, and from that we identify a lead professional to work with the family and that school. We go in, do the information gathering, and then support through Assess, Plan, Do, Review cycles. For some children, that will be thinking about a return to school, and to support this, the LA has purchased AV1 robots which can be loaned to schools. For some other children, it might not be. For others, it might be way too soon to be having that conversation, and we just start off with them meeting someone on a weekly basis to have a conversation with someone outside of their immediate family. That's meant that for some children and young people, we've stayed involved over weeks and weeks and weeks, and we've advocated for them to access a more bespoke timetable, or alternative forms of education.

Setting the Direction of Travel: Assessment and Reports

Assessments and reports can be a key opportunity to redefine the goals away from attendance and towards wellbeing and relationships. However, there's often a problem here. Trust has often been broken, and families may assume that you're there to represent the school or the government. If their experiences to date have been punitive, then any professional going in is starting on the back foot.

Bringing Hope

Kendra (independent educational psychologist) explains how she ensures that it's clear that she is there for both the school and the family.

> When I work with families they really appreciate you just giving them a call before any meeting that you have with the school, just to let them know that actually you are an independent professional and that you're there to facilitate and support those conversations and that relationship. Often it does help to give them that little moment to voice their concerns separately to you before then bringing them together.
>
> I use a lot of goal setting at the beginning to try and bring schools and families together. This isn't a moment to hash out what we think, or blame each other. It's a time to think about what the barriers are in a more neutral way and to think about the ways forward. Setting a solution-orientated goal at the beginning of the meeting can help us to keep coming back to that when we are having moments of tension. I think we have a role as professionals to advocate for the parents as much as we're advocating for the children as well.
>
> There's this hopeless narrative that you get around school attendance difficulties, and we all get drawn into that. When children stop attending school, families sometimes think, "at least when they were attending school, they were getting up and dressed in the morning and showering". That hopeless narrative can be very paralysing. Ultimately what we need in these situations, is we need huge doses of creativity and flexibility and willingness from the school and family to work together to create something bespoke for the child.
>
> Psychologists can be very powerful here because we offer containment and the holding and validating of those feelings, and we support people to work through those emotions and then free up that creative space to think about the child's needs again. I have found that schools really want that support and they are open to thinking differently about it.

One Step Removed: Indirect Work with Those Not Attending School

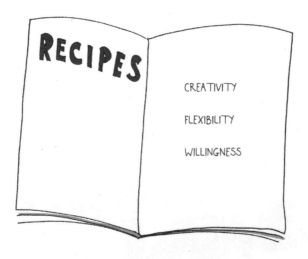

You have to be honest with schools that this is going to require dedicated one-to-one support if the child wants to return to school. You have to get the budget, commitment and resource in place. Without this, it will be difficult for staff to provide predictable, consistent support for a return to school in the way that the young people often need. It has to be a relational return at the beginning. You can't return a child to school if they still feel unsafe there or if they don't have safety in those relationships.

It's about negotiating expectations as well, often people imagine that the child will be in full time by the end of six weeks, and all the issues will have disappeared. In reality, it's a bumpy road, going back and forth. A full-time curriculum might not ever be possible. It's about working with them and their family and really celebrating that for some young people, coming into school for one hour a day is a humongous achievement.

A few years ago, services I work with had a huge flurry of assessment requests for children who had not attended school for several years. There were lots of discussions around what a statutory assessment would bring for this child, but what it brings is an educational psychology assessment. Often these children aren't accessing professionals. There isn't an understanding of their needs, so an assessment brings an in-depth psychological assessment and formulation of their needs in a holistic way, thinking about what the child's wants and wishes for the future.

As Kendra explains, there is no short cut or quick fix, and it can be hard to be the professional who brings that news. She thinks about how to make it easy as possible for this family to engage and how to make her meetings a positive experience for them.

How Do We Start?

That first meeting can be crucial – and the bottom line is, will they be happy to see you again? Getting it right could involve:

- Accepting when their parent says the child is too distressed to talk with you.
- Say explicitly that you aren't there to make them go back to school.
- Starting by talking to their parent and family, even if the child can't meet you.
- Believing what they say and not asking questions that could suggest you don't believe them.
- Starting by playing a video game together.
- Starting by asking about their interests, or learning about their interests.
- Being flexible about where you meet – not asking them to come to school, being prepared to meet remotely.
- Having very brief sessions and ending when they have had enough.
- Starting by sharing stories which might bring hope – children and young people learning in other ways, stories of progress.

Initial questions to ask yourself

Who does the child trust?
What is their behaviour communicating, even if they are not able to say it?
What relationships do they have outside the family?
What connections to the community do the family/child have?
What does the child like doing? What did they used to like doing?
What do they like doing that's good for their physical health/getting them into their body?
Are there any opportunities to do more of it?
How can this child learn?
How long has this problem been going on?
How long has this intervention been in use?
If they won't talk to professionals, then don't make that a deal breaker. Work with the parents instead.

Writing a Plan

If your involvement is to write a plan, or to conduct a one-off assessment, this can be highly influential in supporting the child and their family. Writing a plan is the chance to set the overall direction of travel. You might be the only person who really hears the whole story and just listening and validating how hard this has all been may be an intervention in itself.

When writing a plan for the child's future education while the child is in crisis, it can be hard to see the way forward or plan beyond the next few months. There can be a "hopeless" narrative which can feel overwhelming, because the family have been struggling for so long, and feel like they have made no progress, and no one can help them. It helps to identify that, so you can gain some distance from it, and hold the hope for the family and professionals working directly with the child.

As the professional writing the plan, you can make it clear that the priority should be emotional wellbeing and relationships rather than a quick return to school. You can include the SOAR tool, and explain the three phases of recovery (and in particular, the information that pressure is not helpful at any phase but particularly not in Phase 1).

Part of the work may be giving permission for other professionals to work this way as well by setting the tone. You can point out things that you see are unhelpful, or particularly helpful, for example recognising that tiny steps might be big steps of progress for this child, highlighting that any intervention should only happen with genuine consent from the child – and to make it clear that sometimes children will say yes but their behaviour, whether at the time or afterwards, will indicate it is actually too much for them.

It can also be valuable to be explicit about what doesn't work and what doesn't help. Sometimes you need to be very clear about which interventions you consider not to be appropriate, and to be explicit about what ways of working are needed. Parents tell us that each new person who comes in will often start with the same statement, which is some variation on "Let's see how we can get you back to school." They know immediately that this isn't going to work.

If things have been tried and have been unsuccessful, record this so that it isn't tried again. For example: "parenting programmes have already been tried and have not been helpful" or "professionals should not talk to X about returning to school as it has been agreed that this is not the priority right now".

Making Specific Recommendations

- Explain the role of Safety, Opportunities, Autonomy, Relationships, and how self-determination theory and trauma-informed practice interact.
- Describe the three phased progress model (Chapter 8) and where you think this child is right now.
- Make recommendations for professionals involved with this child as to what works best when trying to engage them.
- Give permission to other professionals to work indirectly with parents, or to work with them remotely, or spend time relationship building.
- Be explicit about what doesn't work for this child and what has been tried before and should not be tried again.
- Focus on building the child and family up and identify strengths.
- Identify a child's particular interests and make suggestions as to how those interests could be followed.
- Set wellbeing-focused outcomes rather than school attendance or academic achievement focused outcomes.

Funded Education Packages Outside School

Some psychologists are involved in supporting bespoke packages (called EOTAS or EOTIS in England) for children out of school through multi-disciplinary teams. A multi-disciplinary team works together, providing a package throughout the week, which could include therapies, specialist teaching, psychological support and respite provision. They provide an intensive period of support for several years. Although packages are usually statutory, it is easier to work flexibly when they are not, as then the team can be used more responsively to meet changing needs. These packages are usually not as expensive as a full-time specialist provision.

When a child has just come out of school or is in a state of withdrawal from the world, the work generally focuses on relationship building, both with the child and parent, and helping the parents understand a child's difficulties through psycho-education and education about trauma. School return is not the focus to reduce pressure. At this point the focus is on creating a therapeutic environment, giving the child experiences of joy and empowerment. The professionals look for ways to connect with the child, and this could include online interactions such as gaming, bringing food to share and doing activities alongside them, but not requiring them to engage. The aim is to form a connection, and this can require a lot of flexibility.

In many cases an educational psychologist has oversight of the team, and leads reflection sessions. An important part of this is that the professionals in the team need permission to feel confident in working differently, and changing their priorities away from attendance. This is often quite different to their previous work. Gaining the confidence to follow a child's lead and letting go of their own educational goals and expectations is a process. These services often use qualitative measures such as a wellbeing tracker to show impact, while others use the Engagement for Learning framework from the PDA Society to capture incidental learning. They don't use outcomes or adult intentions to plan the direction, but start from what's working for the child. This falls within a strengths-based model.

In this chapter we've talked about indirect work with children who are not attending school, and how services can reorientate themselves in order to prioritise learning, however that happens. This is controversial, because the

Table 9.1 The *SOAR Framework*

SOAR Framework – an example of what an EOTAS/EOTIS plan might look like. *This is just an example and isn't comprehensive.*	
Safety	- Creating an emotionally and physically safe environment - Listening to what parents are saying - Working indirectly with parents
Opportunities	- Looking for ways to increase opportunities for learning - Mentoring - Animal Therapy Farm – hour once a week - Driving round the local area – not insisting on getting out
Autonomy	- Allowing the child to make choices - Training in low demand approaches - Reflection sessions for professionals to support them in implementing autonomy-first approaches
Relationships	- Looking for ways to connect - Bringing food to share together - Dog Therapy, Equine Therapy - Playing online games together - Playing alongside the child
Measurement	- Wellbeing Tracker - Engagement for Learning framework - Child and solution-centred goals
Supporting the family	- Providing respite care - Helping them see the progress and see things positively - Supporting them so they can support their child

government agenda is clearly to prioritise school attendance and the prevailing culture is that a return to school should always be the priority, even when that is clearly damaging to a young person's mental health.

Writing and talking about the possibility of some young people not returning to school is transgressive. We discovered that some professionals did not want to be quoted at all out of fear as to how their work would be perceived, while others asked to be anonymous for fear of repercussions on their services. This is clearly a barrier to positive outcomes, as it means that there cannot be open professional discussion about what might help these young people. As one of the young people we talked to said, "All everyone ever talks about is getting back to school, but I can't learn at school."

Summary

- Many professionals report a tension between feeling that some children would be better learning out of school, but this being impossible to support in the current political climate.
- Professionals who talked to us about working with young people who were not returning to school wanted to stay anonymous, and some did not want their stories included at all for fear of professional repercussions.
- The narrative of "school refusal" is still strong in many schools, meaning that children are seen as "choosing" not to attend school.
- Indirect work is an opportunity to shift the narrative, both about school non-attenders and about individual young people.
- An important part of this is "giving permission" for those who work directly with the young person to focus on strengths and wellbeing before focusing on school attendance.
- The SOAR Framework can be used by services to establish priorities and set goals.

References and Further Reading

Fricker, E. (2023). *Can't Not Won't: A Story about a Child Who Couldn't Go to School*. London: Jessica Kingsley Publishers.

Morgan, F. and Costello, E. (2023). *Square Peg: Inclusivity, Compassion and Fitting In – A Guide for Schools*. Carmarthen: Crown House Publishing.

10

Stories of Hope After School Attendance Difficulties

In this chapter you will find:

1. Young People's Accounts
2. Parents' Accounts

Introduction

Including this chapter almost feels transgressive. There is a social taboo against talking about young people whose recovery hasn't necessarily meant a return to regular school attendance. There's a societal norm, backed up by recent government campaigns, which says that we must always emphasise the essential nature of school. It seems that some think that that just acknowledging the possibility of getting an education in other ways would immediately mean that thousands of young people would stop going to school. We are told that we just mustn't tell them that there might be another option.

We think differently. We think that this stance can lead to despair in some young people, and that we instead need to give them hope that their life can improve, no matter whether they are able to attend school or not. We think that fear isn't the best motivator for learning, and that we need to emphasise second chances and different opportunities to learn.

Some of the young people whose stories you will read here are home educated. Others have EOTAS packages and others have started college or university after years of not attending school. One young person has successfully changed schools to one which suits them better, and one has reintegrated to their original school.

These young people and their families are defining success in different ways. For some, this means taking exams either in or out of school. For others, that isn't their focus right now. For all of them, what matters most is their long-term future and wellbeing.

There is a chronic lack of narratives available of those for whom stopping attending school has not been a disaster. Parents often tell us that they have never known anyone who succeeded despite struggles with school attendance. This chapter is our attempt to redress the balance. Many young people tell us that they think they are the only person who has ever struggled in this way. We want to show them that this isn't the case.

We have found that sometimes, paradoxically, just knowing that it is possible to get an education outside school can make it easier for young people to attend school. When they feel like there is a choice, they become more able to attend and to learn. All of these stories are real, but identifying details have been changed.

Young People's Accounts

Hope Is Home Educated

Hope (10) had been out of school for a year when I talked to them. Hope now uses she/they pronouns. Hope wanted it to be clear that they felt lonely and an outsider at school because they felt like no one understood. They didn't feel safe in school.

> School doesn't come first. Friendship, family, self-care, and caring about others are more important. Caring about others is important, but so is doing things for yourself and what's right for you. Having adventures and treat days is important. School can be important if it helps you with everyday things. But Scouts helps me learn more. I learned Spanish at school, but I can only remember a little bit.
>
> Survival, life skills, nature, forest school, cooking, better strategies for chopping safely, helping me learn how to cook on my own, these are all things I'm learning in home education.
>
> When I did my first art thing at home, I cried because that was like the first time I had actually completed something that was art. I said to my mum that I had never finished anything at school [because I was never given enough time].
>
> I'm learning animal care skills, relationships with animals, confidence and helping my body regulate and balance. Dyslexia is not a condition, but how I am.

Rose Moved to a New School

Rose (8) has changed school and is much happier at her new school. She and her mum Rachel told me what it was like.

> Rachel: *When Rose stopped going to school completely, I said, "This isn't working. We need to think of something else." We went to look at this new school. I said, "It doesn't have to be this school, but let's think about another school." We talked about homeschool as well. At that point, she was begging me to be homeschooled. We chatted with a wellbeing coach for children. She said that the school that she's at now is really friendly for all varieties of children.*
>
> *She'd worked with a teacher who would be her class teacher. He has a lot of experience with neurodiversity and was quite accepting and supportive. I thought, if there's going to be a school that works, then it will be this one.*
>
> Rose: *At the new school, we started by going in for the morning and then leaving at lunchtime. I noticed that everyone was happy, and the headmistress is happy. The teachers are friendly and relaxed, and it's a lovely school.*
>
> *At my new school you still get house points, but they're called credits and rainbow points. They only get emptied at the end of the year, which is less stressful. At my new school, they don't empty the house points out each week, it's a lot more relaxed and there are prizes, but that's just if you get 75 and 25 and so on. All you got was*

What Can We Do When School's Not Working?

a little certificate, too. It wasn't anything big. When you get 100 points you get to choose a new book to keep which everyone is excited to do.

You don't have to do it all within a week, but you do have to do it within the year, because they empty it out at the end of each year.

Sam Who Makes Music Under the Name Avid Beats Got an EOTAS Package and Is Following His Passion for Music

When Sam was 15, he told me about how his life has changed since leaving school after Year 8.

> A turning point was when my EHCP was completed for EOTAS – although this was two years later. A WHOLE TWO YEARS of misunderstanding. Some people don't understand till this day.
>
> But NOW I am thriving. Why? Because I am doing my music. I am doing what makes me feel good. I am learning exponentially. Not how others would. But how I want to. And how I learn best is self-directing my learning. I still have some emotional difficulties, but I have learned about myself inside out, and am finding ways to manage my emotions, both through music and by noticing and listening to my feelings before situations become too overwhelming. CAMHS just made things worse, and so did school ... soooooo ... I AM UNSCHOOLED.

And for y'all who have been through/are going through something similar, I would just say, believe in yourself and your ideas. If the agencies or people who are meant to be "helping" aren't, then you will find a way out. Be patient and BELIEVE. As one of my songs says:

If you believe, your dreams become reality, and if you don't, they fall away like gravity, so keep it moving, and you'll find a sense of clarity, just keep improving what you're doing, then you'll find the key.–

(Believe, Avid Beats and Wavii)

This was two years ago and Sam is now 17. He wanted to add a paragraph talking about what life is like for him now:

I am continuing to thrive. Self-directing my learning, I feel that I have been able to progress hugely since leaving school – both regarding learning and my own understanding of my emotions. I have found that by reducing pressure and being able to take the time to understand myself and what I need, I have been able to heal myself through music, being closer to nature, and with emotional support from my parents and my amazing dog, Barney. This is my "therapy".

Alice (13) Is Home Educated and Is Taking Exams Out of School

When I first left school, we actually didn't intend on home-educating. We intended on waiting until I was fit enough to go back to a school because we didn't really know what home education was. Then, in those first months where I was really struggling, we were thinking, we've got to get you to a point where you can go back. Then once I was at that point I realised, absolutely not. I'm so much happier here. My parents were like, "Yeah, go for it. Just stay here."

It's been amazing, definitely. I think there's such a really lovely community of home educators. I've been able to choose my subjects way better. If I have bad days, then I can just do my work in the evening and have a relaxed day. I've got so many accommodations that I wouldn't have. I've got a swing. We've got a swing in the garden, which is probably my favourite thing about life in general. I spent three hours on that swing a day. I just do like 10 minutes on the swing in between lessons, and that just makes me way happier going to other lessons. We've got so many things. I can just sit with the cat while I do homework. It's been way, way better.

Also, I'm not actually a fan of being taught. I really like being self-led. I tend to be quite a very determined person. If I decide I'm going to do something, then I will do it. I will definitely do it. I decided I was going to be home educated, and then I joined the home education panels. I started leading groups for the children. I run things for children now. I've always been very "I'll do this" and then I'll do it full-on.

At the moment I'm doing A-levels. I am doing everything way earlier than I should be. I'm planning on going into speech and language therapy, so I've got a plan of how to do a degree in a Masters, and I've always had that. I saw a speech-language therapist when I was about seven. I went, "That's what I'm going to do." I'm still on that. I've picked all the GCSEs and the A-levels to get me there. I'm still going. Before that, I wanted to be a train, not a train driver, an actual train. I think they were very happy when I went from train to speech-language therapist.

I have tutors and that works well for me. I needed to self-study when I first left school because we weren't sure whether I would be alright with tutors. Later, I struggled a lot with picking the right subjects because I wasn't really sure. Because obviously, there are subjects you can pick outside of school which are very different to ones you can pick in school.

We picked this English tutor to tutor me because English was my favourite topic. They decided to do that first. It's been five years with Genevieve and for the first year I couldn't speak to her so we communicated through the online chat function. When I felt comfortable enough we moved to voice chat, then to cameras on and after three years we met in person (she lives two minutes from our house!). I've still got her. Because of the degrees I've chosen, I'm probably going to have her until I'm 18. I do three lessons a week with Genevieve because I know her so well; I'm probably going to just stay in touch with her for ever. I've always felt really comfortable having the same tutor for a while.

She met me where I was, and didn't ask why. The fact she didn't have any expectations for me to get better at speaking made me get better because she just accepted me. I always wanted to be able to speak but just couldn't back then. I've never learned more at any time than when I became comfortable with Genevieve. It's like I could learn now, with her.

I did GCSEs spread out. I'm doing mostly A-levels, but I've actually still got two GCSEs left to sit. I got my favourite subjects out of the way first.

Parents' Accounts

Wearing Clothes Again

Laura's son is now 11 and has been out of school since he was five. He is autistic and has sensory processing disorder. He was situationally mute at school and left after half a term of Reception.

> We have got to the point now where we consider him healed from the school experience. He could actually wear a set of clothes. That literally took us about five years. We never got past the point that it would only ever be the same set of clothes. It would be the same trousers and the same T-shirt every single day without fail. If something happened to them, it would be the end of the world and our lives would

go on hold until a substitute had been found. That's where we were at and that's how we've lived for most of his life, but we've accepted it.

He turned 11 during lockdown last May. It was a bit of a standout birthday, because you go, we're in this beautiful world I've created and that I am curator of and that everything within it works perfectly and it meets our needs. You suddenly look through the window and think, he's now Year 7. It does erode a little of your confidence because you go, "Those children are wearing blazers and ties."

More than anything, I felt thankful that we weren't doing that. At the same time, it highlighted to me that we just couldn't do it. Thank God we're not a part of that world, we're not trying to keep up appearances, because there is literally no way on Earth that my child could be a happy individual, and wear a blazer. There is no way that my child could be a happy individual and have ten different classes to get to during the day.

Stopping the Pressure Meant He Could Go Back to School

Emma told me how she stopped forcing her son to go back to school, and how he and she were then able to work out a less pressured way to reintegrate him together.

He started Year 7 well, but by late November and early December cracks started to show. He was getting increasingly distressed with homework expectations and the threat of a detention if it wasn't good enough. The different teaching and discipline styles were hard. All the changes in the timetable with Christmassy things going on.

The two-week Christmas holidays were lovely, but his school has assessments the first week back in January and this is where it all went downhill and my son started having panic attacks, self-harming and avoiding school.

We tried absolutely everything to get him back in . . . bribery, blackmail, begging, pleading, but nothing helped. Everything made it worse and the trauma was done. I have detailed diaries of it all. What changed for us was a Facebook post. It was about letting their No, actually mean No! Once I listened to him and stopped trying to force him in, he felt heard and ready to try again.

We were very lucky that the school listened, as I went in armed with legislation and researched beyond belief our rights.

My son had to start all over again in teeny tiny steps. First step was getting dressed and being in his uniform at home. Then getting dressed and walking most of the school run with me. Then walking into school to say hi to a teacher and going home. He then went in for one hour a day, but sat in his head of years office with her. We tried lots of different approaches to getting him back into class . . . Only doing first period and working up. That didn't work. Only doing form time. This worked for a while until they tried adding the class after.

I then sat down with my son and went through every tiny detail of his day and what was easy or difficult about it. We spoke about his socks, the walk to school, the size, smell and lighting in rooms, teachers, corridors. You name it, we went through it to try and figure out what could help him get back into lessons. Some great things came out of this and school made lots of reasonable adjustments for him like leaving lessons five minutes early to miss the crowds, always sitting in the back of class as he finds people sitting behind him stressful, no detentions for forgetting his pen and so on.

He still was struggling to get into classes as they were, so we broke the day up. He started by getting back into maths which was his favourite lesson. Then we added English. Then we added lunch, break and form time where they were connected to either English or maths. School weren't happy that he was in and out throughout the day, but it was this or nothing! I don't work, so I was able to make this work and take him to and from school throughout the day.

Slowly we have added Science, History, Geography, Computing and PE theory (not practical, that's next).

He is now in every day. If one of the lessons he doesn't attend is first period, he goes in late and if it is last period, he comes home early. Where classes fall in the middle of the day that he is not able to get into yet, he is able to go to their on-call room for the 50 mins (where they send children who are disrupting class).

It's not ideal, but it works.

Five Years of Not Attending School and She Went to University

Families and young people are often told that "every day missed counts" which can be a highly anxiety-provoking message when a child isn't attending school. This story is told by Ruth, whose daughter was unable to attend school for almost the entirety of her secondary school years and who sat her GCSEs at home thanks to a very supportive headteacher. She then attended sixth form college. She has now gone onto university and has successfully graduated.

> My daughter was challenging (read strong-willed, a force of nature) from a young age. She was the last to stop crying when she started in Reception and was eight years old when she first "school-refused" – perhaps the seeds of potential attendance difficulties were already sown.
>
> The first full-blown, desperate, impossible-to-even-countenance-it episode was preceded by three major events in her life. The first was the abduction of Madeleine McCann, the second was a burglary and the third was the attempted suicide of our next-door neighbour and her best friend's mum, who then subsequently disappeared to the other side of the country. When school started after the summer holidays my daughter managed just one day. Any professional worth their weight would probably investigate trauma as the trigger but instead, and because her sister was "fine" and we told professionals that she had always been quite challenging, trauma was not even considered. Instead a possible autism diagnosis was mooted, alongside her being a strong-willed child and me being a weak-willed and easily manipulated mother. The gaslighting began quite early ("she's fine it's you we're really worried about").

Looking back, I would do so many things differently.

First, I would listen – I would hold her in my arms and tell her she didn't have to talk to me, but that she was safe, and we would do whatever she needed us to do.

Second, I would ignore the "professional" voices that very quickly pipe up with "a day missed . . . " and "nip it in the bud". Those voices made me panic when I needed to stay calm and be my daughter's rock.

Third, I would challenge what can/can't be done. We were told by many individuals in the system that certain things were not possible, yet I later found out that simply wasn't true – some things might require effort (or just plain compassion), but they were entirely possible, and some didn't cost a penny either.

The first bout of attendance difficulties lasted a full half term, and it was probably a term and a half before she was back in school full time. Certain things like Brownies and saxophone lessons never really got back to where they were, and her sleep remained a huge issue for years. She learned very quickly that adults in authority were not to be trusted, that they came and went like buses, and that most had no idea how to help her. How scary must that be for an 8-year-old? Despite this, she made it through Years 5 & 6 (age 10–11) of primary school and was reasonably excited to start secondary school.

The secondary school she initially attended would probably be seen as the most desirable locally, although its reputation may well have changed since then. She managed it for almost a term, until an incident where she was caught on camera in the sixth form common room with a friend (I was late collecting her), pretending to be sixth formers and opening lockers. The following day she was hauled out of a lesson in front of everyone and made to sit in the SEND department and write a police-style report about what she had done wrong. She didn't even know her crime. When she came out of school that day she was shaking and couldn't speak. That was her last full day at that school, although we tried for months to persuade them to help her come back (in hindsight I have no idea why). Various initiatives helped to an extent, but were never enough and were always stressful for everyone involved, my daughter most of all. I can still hear the deputy head's words 15 years later: "Mrs G, who is the parent and who is the child in this relationship?"

When we realised there was no quick fix we were directed to a wonderful tutor by the SENDCO (who was subsequently advised not to speak to us). We paid for some interim tutoring at home, continued trying to work with the school in question, dragged my daughter to trial sessions at other schools, had numerous visits from Education Welfare Officers and eventually decided we might need a solicitor. I have no idea how much this all cost as we never dared add it up, but it was a lot, and we were just lucky that we were in a position to get legal advice and provide private tutoring while the system repeatedly blamed us and her, and desperately tried to pull her back in. Eventually we found a clinical psychologist who diagnosed several anxiety-related conditions, and, with the help of the solicitor, we managed to secure a Statement of Educational Needs based on this diagnosis and stipulating the skills of our very experienced tutor, which at least put some funding in place to continue this education of sorts.

I then visited the deputy head of another secondary school about a mile from the first, to see whether there was anything he could do. He took her on roll and told me (more words I will never forget for a very different reason): "If she never sets foot in this school, that's OK." It still gives me goosebumps.

There followed several years of tutoring at home, funded by the Statement and in liaison with this new secondary school, with work passing to and fro between tutor and teachers every fortnight, and with the tutor's invoices paid through the school to satisfy the local council. When it came to GCSEs, the school registered our home as an exam centre and sent invigilators so that my daughter could sit her exams. Without this, I don't know where we would be, as this was her ticket to sixth form college. Ironically, she would have got far higher results had the first school showed more compassion and facilitated her attendance, but it was enough to get into college.

Sixth form college was make or break time, and she knew it. She used her strength of character to propel herself through the doors at the beginning and it gradually got easier as she made friends. A key factor in my view was the very different attitude of a sixth form college. It's almost a stepping stone to university, with staff and students on first name terms and an assumption that students choose to be there and it's probably quite hard to force them.

With her A level/BTEC results she got a place at university (pushing herself to travel some distance away from home), obtained a degree and is now on her way to a successful career.

What else have I learned from our experience?

My daughter isn't a SEND child. Yes, she was anxious, and yes, she didn't feel safe at school, but she is bright and curious and the strength of character that protected her from a system that was harming her, will undoubtedly prove her greatest asset in whatever she chooses to do. We are creating too many SEND children by insisting on a label in order to access support, when actually some of these children probably just need a dose of compassion, flexibility and some control and choice, just as adults need in their own working lives.

As a parent I was too heavily influenced by "professionals". You are often told you are the expert in your child, and they are the expert in education, psychology, or some other specialism – but you are always outnumbered and your expertise in your own child simply doesn't stack up against specialist degrees and years of experience. One EWO insisted my daughter put her uniform on every morning, creating groundhog days of relived trauma. It also meant she refused to go out in case she was challenged about being out of school while in her uniform.

As adults, we look for problems so that we can find solutions. It took me far too long to accept that my daughter didn't know why she couldn't "do" school, she just couldn't. I kept wanting to find the problem so I could sort it, but that wasn't what she needed. In fact, she would probably have refused to tell us the problem, even if she had known, because that would have meant school being back on the agenda.

Every now and again we found a "champion" that gave us hope and the leg-up we needed to get through in the system – a Teaching Assistant, a SENDCO, a solicitor, a deputy head, and the amazing tutor who remains in contact. My advice would be (to professionals), be that champion, and (to parents) hold onto them as if your life depends on it.

The system CAN flex – but it needs those in authority to sanction it. Our old house (we've moved since) is perhaps still registered as an exam centre, although to this day I don't know what was required or how much it cost. Minor adjustments can be made so that children like my daughter can find their feet again within the system, whether that's healing time to recover, or some concessions around the practicalities of school life.

One day lost is NOT the end of the world. My daughter effectively "lost" about five years and, despite the system, she is now a university graduate with a promising career. And the list of successful celebrities who left school with no or minimal qualifications (Richard Branson, Jamie Oliver, Steve Bartlett to name a few) runs to several pages.

Last, and perhaps most importantly, we need to start questioning whether it's the system that's to blame, rather than our children or their parents? There are so many more effective education systems out there and a progressive government would be wise to remember that the increasing number of children we are forcing through an outdated system will soon be voters.

And Finally

We're going to give the last word to Tom, who started this book and who was fined for his daughter's non-attendance. He told me about what she is doing now.

> She's 16 now and she's just got a different attitude. She's got to find her own way to do things, but she seems very happy about her way of doing things.
>
> She said, "I don't have that pressure. I can just be me. Some days I can be little and some days I can be big." I think that really helped her. She didn't really feel a connection with her friends from school at first at all. It's weird. Some of her friends were going through anxiety, and one family was like, "We don't believe in anxiety," so this girl was just pushing herself through.
>
> She is going to college now. She still gets anxiety, so she does still miss days and things. But now I just go, "Well, whatever." I'm trying not to get into like, "Well, you need to get in school because the attendance person will ring us up."
>
> Luckily her college are very understanding and they try and put things in place, which is really good. They say, "Oh, poor you." Rather than going, "Well, will they be in tomorrow?" They actually say, "It must be really hard for your daughter," and that changes everything.

I asked Tom what he wished professionals knew about families like his.

> I think that we do really care. I think that doesn't always come across, maybe. We really care about our kids, and it's really hard. Luckily, I could move my job every day if I had to, but I had to lose a lot of well-paid work. And then that impacts on everything you do, so it's just really tough. It's not like you just go in your bedroom and chill out and do whatever, because you're worried about your kid's wellbeing. You can't.

As parents, I love my daughters, both of them. I want the best for them. And when they're falling to bits in front of you, you just want to try and help them. Maybe teachers don't know how it affects them, the kids at home, and it affects everything. It affects the house, it affects a lot. Their way of dealing with it is like, "Well, she's missed her maths." And, "She is behind, she'll never catch up in maths or whatever," and it's just like . . .

As a parent, you're going, "Well I want her to be in a life where she's happy. I'm scared of what happens." And maybe the enormity of it is not actually maybe so apparent to teachers because they're in this very close-up situation. They see kids in one environment. And kids are brilliant at hiding how they feel. Kids are so good at showing people. "I'm doing okay," even though internally, everything's going mad.

Index

Page numbers in **bold** refer to illustrations, page numbers in *italic* refer to tables

absenteeism 3–4
academic pressure 109–110
achievement 99–105
additional learning needs (ALN) 66–69, *see also* SEND
additional support needs (ASN) 66–69, *see also* SEND
ADHD 29, 56, 56–57, 151, 246
adolescence 38–39
adult concerns 161
adult learners 46
adult pressures 215–217, *217*
agency 16, 150
alternative provision 163, 186, 245–250
anger 238
anxiety 28, 51, 75–77, 120–122, 130–131, 133, 171–172, 173, 178, 246, 285; addressing 180–181; Cognitive Behavioural Cycle 134–135, **134**; and difference 53–55; and environment 181–182; exploring through conversation 248; exposure therapy 137–138, **138**; parents 61, 113; reduction strategies 14; teachers 50; treatments 134–136, **134**, 146
anxiety strategies 14
apprenticeship model 37
assessment and reports 262–267; aims 262–263; Early Help 261; first meeting 264–265; initial questions 265; recommendations 267; relationship building 267–268; statutory 263; writing a plan 265–267
Assess, Plan, Do, Review cycles 261
attachment and relationship-aware approach 93–96, 152
Attachment Aware Schools 94
attachments 96; focus on 93–96

attachment theory 152
attainment 88, 163
attention seeking 128
Australia 15
autism 29, 56, 56–57, 62–63, 151, 203–204, 246, 277–278, 280
autonomy 79, **79**, 80, 81–84, *89*, 91, 150, 157, 166, 167, 236–237, *239*
autumn-born girls 67
avoidance 132–135, 181–182, 209
Awoyelu, E. 86

background knowledge 44, 45
Bagley, C. 162–167
barriers to school attendance 25; removing 249
Barrowford Primary School, Lancashire 96–98
behaviour: and child development 48–51, **51**; choice lens 115–116, **116**; as communication 93–96, 103–104; conceptualisation 114–116, **116**; as feedback 51, 115, 116; media focus 7–8, **7**; politicised 114; and the problem 11; psychological lens 114–115; and school attendance difficulties 110–111
behavioural approach 205
behaviour and relationships policy 93–96
behaviour control 46–47
Behaviour Hubs project 115
behaviourism 116–119; model **119**; problem with 118; rewards 117, **119**, 120, 123–125; sanctions 118, **119**, 120–122, 125–126; school attendance difficulties recommendations 125–126, **126**, **127**; side effects 120–122; side

287

Index

effects at home 127–130; unintended effects of 123–125
behaviour management, time spent on 72
behaviour points 75, 76–77
behaviour tracking 120
behaviour tsars 114
Believe 275
belonging 84; culture of 150
belongingness 164, 165
Bennett, T. 115, 116, 125
blame 106, 285
body mapping 98
Brackett, M. 10
brains: amygdala 199–201; development 35, 38; maturation 37; pre-frontal cortex 37
Breaking the Silence project 162–167
bullying 73
burnout 190, 192–193, 193–194, 213–215; adult pressures 217, *217*; causes 214, 216, 217; conceptualisation 215–217; the final straw 214–215; recovery 218–223; symptoms 213–214, *216*; therapists 222

calm 95, 101
CAMHS 261, 274
can't/won't dichotomy 14–17
carers, relationship with 249–250
celebration 104
Centre for Self Managed Learning 157
certificates 79–80
champions 284
change, meaningful 136
changing schools 273–274
childcare 232
child development 35–39, 41, 73, 96, 118; and behaviour 48–51, **51**; diversity 51–55; neurological changes 35; relevance 48; and school attendance 48–51, **51**; stages 35, 40–41
child/family approach 260–261
childhood 15
children: diversity 51–55; experience of school 202–204, **203**; experiences of the world 202, **203**; individual characteristics 202, **203**; letting down 226–229; not the problem 146; place of safety 210, 218; responsibility on 116, **116**; threat perception 203, 205; voice 259; world response to 202, **203**
Children's Commissioner 114
child services, tension running through 255–256
choice 236–237, *239*, 272
chronic stress 214, 216
Citywall 245–250
class culture, collaborative 83–84
classrooms, low stimulus 98
clinical psychologists 254
coaxing 192–193
Cognitive Behavioural Cycle 126, **127**, 134–135, **134**
cognitive behavioural therapy 134–136, 137, 159
cognitive developmental psychology 47
cognitive load theory 42–45, 47; and motivation 46
cognitive profile, spiky 58, **58**, 160
cognitive science 42, 51
cognitive testing 58
collaboration 148, 164
Collaborative and Proactive Solutions™ 159–162
collaborative class culture 83–84
collaborative decision making (CDM) 82–84
collaborative problem solving 159–162
commitment 102
communication 243; behaviour as 93–96, 103–104
compassion 156, 167
competence 79, **79**, *90*, 91, 148, 149–151, 150, 163, 167
confidence 83, 157, 245
confidence building 248
connection 79, **79**, *89*, 91, 101, 148, 167, 250, 268
consent 137–138
consistency 55, 94, 96, 104
containment 262
control 119, 164, 230
coping mechanisms 179
co-production 162–167
counselling 171–172, 174–175
Covid-19 pandemic 3, 164, 195–196, 260–261
creativity: big C 45, 46; little C 45, *45*
crisis 187–188
cross-cultural research 41
Cunningham, I. 156, 157–159

Index

curiosity 49
curricula, generic 165

Davis, B. 99–105, **101**
Deci, E. 79
decision making 152, 236–237, *239*; sharing 81–84
deep learning 165
deep talk, culture of 84, 86–87
Define Fine 24
dehumanisation 85
demerits 75
Denmark 61
Department for Education 43
depression 28, 130, 135
deschooling 189
detention 77
developmental mismatch 195–196
developmental psychology 42, 117–118
developmental trauma 64, 152
diagnostic assessments 114
dialogic approaches 84
dignity 100
discovery learning 35, 37, 38, 48–49
disillusionment 10
disrupted relationships 238
distress 8–9
diversity 51–55; invisible *59–60*, 61; see also neurodiversity
dyscalculia 29, 56
dyslexia 29, 53, 56, 273
dyspraxia 29, 56

Early Help 261
Early Help Assessment 261
ecological systems theory 258–259
economic disparities 56
Edge Foundation 10
Education and Health Care Plan (EHCP) 67
educational opportunities 228
educational outcomes, and school attendance 226–229
educational psychologists 253–254, 268
education, devalued 180
education evaluation 164
education packages outside school 267–269, 272
education professionals, bias 11
education system, experience of 4
Education Welfare Officers 282, 284
emotional distress 23–24

emotional impact 192–193
emotionally based school avoidance (EBSA) 16, 23–24, 25, 26–29, 130, 259
emotional reactions 14; 131–133, 236
emotional regulation 58
emotional safety 56, 232
emotional understanding 275
emotional wellbeing 12, 125
emotion coaching 95
emotions, talking about 210–211
empathy 161
empowerment 148, 149–151, 156–159
engagement 247
Engagement for Learning framework 268
environment: and anxiety 181–182; hostile 27; influences 14
EOTAS (Education Otherwise Than At School) 184, 188, 241, 242–244, 267–269, 274–275
exams 198, 276, 282
exclusions 65–66, 97, 101–102
executive functioning 37
expectations 55–56, 61, 96, 160, 243, 263
experience, and trauma 198
exposure therapy 137–138, **138**
external facilitators 155
extrinsic motivation 80, 97, 124

family 184–185, 259, 285; rebuilding relationships 238; trauma 207–209
Family Partnership Model 261
fears, irrational 18–19
feedback, behaviour as 115, 116
feelings: hiding 286; talking about 210–211
fidgets 179
Finding My Voice whole school approach 84–88, 149–151
fine at school narrative 127
fines 13
Finland 61, 115–116
fitting in 27
foetal alcohol spectrum disorder (FASD) 64, 195
Foley, C. 86
Football Beyond Borders (FBB) 151–155
Foundation for Education Development 43
frustration 244

Index

functional approach 18
future 212–213

games 247
Garfi, J. 134, 173, 180–181
gaslighting 280
genetic differences 66
Getting Your Child Back to School (Kearney) 18
goal setting 262
goals, redefining 262
Golann, J. 47, 73
good schools, definition 48
Gopnik, A. 35, 37, 42, 50
government agenda 269
Greene, R. 160
group behaviour policies 120–122
groupings 98
guilt 207–208

happiness 186, 276
headteachers, discretion 259
healthcare, side effects 74
helplessness 244
hidden curriculum 72, 73, 91
Higginson, R. 84–88, 149–151
high control environments 119
high control techniques 80–81
home, making less pleasant 125–126, 127–130, 136–137, **137**
home education 53, 184–185, 188–189, 229, 272–273, 275–277, 282
hope, offering 250
humanistic theory 152, 153

improvement, acknowledging 104
incentives 79–80
incidental learning 268
inclusion 93
inclusion strategies 102
incompetence, feeling of 150
independence 210
infant schools, attachment and relationship-aware approach 93–96
information gathering 261
information sharing 102
injustice 73
inquiry learning 49
intelligent inconsistency 99–105, **101**
intensive support 151–155
interests 235
intrinsic motivation 80, 97, 124–125

invisible power 113–114
invitation 161
irrational fears 18–19
isolation 77

Kearney, C. 18
Kerbey, L. 242–245
key adults 93–96
key workers 97
KITE (tutoring agency) 242–245
knowledge creation 165
Kohn, A. 79, 124
Kurtz, A. 153

labels 65, 150
lagging skills 160, 161
language use 88
large school environments 53
leadership dynamic 155
learner first approach 88
learning 118, 167; academic focus 49–50; apprenticeship model 37; capacity for 235; cognitive load theory 42–45, 46, 47; creative exploration 45; and creativity 44, 45–46; direct instruction 43–44; discovery 35, 37, 38, 48–49; eclectic 190; evidence based 45; evolutionary necessity 47; facilitating 243; guiding 243; home education 189; incidental 268; inquiry 49; mastery 37–38, 41, 48–49; motivation 46–47; multi-sensory 50; quality 91; real 72; re-engaging with 240; science of 42–47; self-directed 274–275, 276; self-managed 156–159; through play 35–36, 69; and view of children 42
learning communities 232
learning environment, structured 43
learning model 48
learning opportunities 176–177, 228; SOAR *234*, 235–236, *239*
legal advice 282
lens changing 146–147
life; differences in experiences 55–56; re-engaging with 240
life skills curriculum 152
listening 128, 281
literature 5, 21, 257
London School of Economics 67
long-term outcomes 184

Lovell, O. 42
low demand approach 232–233, *233*

mastery learning 37–38, 41, 48–49
maturity 115
media focus 7–8, **7**
medical model, the 56, 131–132
memories 199–200, 209, 211
mental health 23–24, 166, 255–256, 260, 269
mental health lens 130–136
mental health services 24
mentors 245–250, 261
messages, reinforcing 102
metacognition 71, 88, 157–159
Michaela School, West London 46–47
misbehaviour, choice lens 115
mission 100–101, **101**
mitching 22–23
mixed ability classes 163
Morgan, F. 24–25
motivation 39, 80–81, 83–84, 91, 150, 229, 271; extrinsic 80, 97, 124; intrinsic 80, 97, 124–125; learning 46–47; and rewards 123–125; self-determination theory 78–79
multi-agency pathways 260–261
multi-disciplinary teams 267
Multiplication table check 48
multi-sensory learning 50
music 274–275

narrative change 149–151, 257–259
national attendance targets 114
natural variation 51–55
needs, unmet 25, 28–29
neuro-affirmative practice 61–66
neurodevelopmental diagnosis 61–66; relationship with 64–66; and school distress 63
neurodiversity 29–30, **57**, *59–60*, 61, 151, 242–245, 273; definition 56; diagnosis 56–57, 61–66; and exclusion 65–66; late-diagnosed adults 64; and lived experience 62; neuro-affirmative practice 61–66; post-diagnostic support 64; relationship with diagnosis 64–66; spiky cognitive profile 58, **58**
neurological changes 35
neuroscience 152
no excuses approach 46–47, 73, 75, 90

Not Fine in School 24
nurture groups 96

Ofsted 11, 166
Open College Network 244
opportunities *239*
oppositional defiant disorder 160
oracy 84, 87
outcome measures 74
outcomes 74–75
outside relationships 238
outsiders 149–151

parent advocacy groups 24–25
parent blaming 259, 280
parents: accounts 277–285; anxiety 61, 113; complaints 5; goals 286; relationships with schools 113–114; relationship with 249–250; school attendance difficulties and 108–109, 110–111, 112–113; school trauma symptoms 208; and self-managed learning 158; shift in attitudes 3; threats towards 205; trust in 260
parent-school contract 8–9, **8,** 113–114
parent-school struggle, polarised 15
parent support organisations 15
pastoral support 94
patience 275
PDA Society 268
peer problems 106, 110, 131
personal development 84–88
person-centred approaches 257
phobia 18–19
Phonics Screening Check 61, 67
physical safety 231–232
Pink, D. 79
place of safety 210, 218
plans, writing 265–267
play, learning through 35–36, 69
playtime 98
point system 78
politicians 22
positive feedback 195
positive outcomes, barrier to 269
positive reinforcement 79–80, 119
positive relationships 56
post-traumatic reactions 193–194
post-traumatic stress disorder (PTSD) 198
potty training 119

291

Index

pressure 48, 236, 245, 258–259, 260, 268, 273–274, 278–279, 285
primary schools 196; Finnish 115–116; relational approaches 96–98
problem, the: alerts 12; defining 11–14, **14**; location 16, 18, 19, 25, 29–31, 34; perspectives on 12–13, **14**; school environment 147
problem areas, assessment 161
problem solving 44, 83, 159–162
professionals: bias 11; frustration 253–255; invisible power 113–114
psychological distress 25
psychological flourishing 81, 81–88
psychological health 100, 105
psychological needs 78–81; autonomy 79, **79**, 80, 81–84, *89*, 91; competence 79, **79**, *90*, 91; connection 79, **79**, *89*, 91; meeting 72; meeting in the classroom 88, *89–90*, 90–91; prioritising 81–88; pupil voice 84–89
psychological safety 102, 103
psychological trauma: adult response 204–205, **204**; children's experience 202–203, **203**; conceptualisation 198; survival system 199–201; vulnerability 201–202; *see also* school trauma
psychosocial interventions: break clause 138–139; exposure therapy 137–138, **138**; risk assessment 136, 139; side effects 136–137; unintended consequences 139, *139–141*, 141
puberty 38–39
pull factors 126
punishment-free 97
punitive interventions 13
pupils, shift in attitudes 3
pupil strategic meetings 98
pupil voice 84–89, 156, 259
purpose, sense of 157
pushback 154
push factors 126

quality learning 91
questions 158; asking 86
quick fixes 168

Rae, T. 23, 28
reading 52–3, 55, 61
real learning 72
recognition 104

referral pathways 260
reflective practice groups 153–155
registration 97
regulation plans 98
relatedness 84, 84–85
relational approaches 96–98
relational culture 84–85
relationship policy 96–98
relationships 73, 93, 150, 152, 153, *239*, 267–268; building 248; disrupted 238; focus on 93–96, 99–105, **101**; rebuilding family 238; supportive 237–238
reparative experiences 56
resilience 122
resourcing, prioritising 102–103
responsibility 150; on children 116, **116**
responsible adults 231
restorative practice 95
return-to-school: approaches 279; expectation of 172–174, 256–257; less pressured 278–279; negotiating 263; support 263
return-to-school plans 257
reward-free 97
rewards 79–80, 117, **119**, 120, 235–236; and motivation 123–125
risk assessment 136, 139
risk-taking 39
Rogoff, B. 41
routines 101
Rowe, G. 82–84
rules 101
Ryan, R. 79

safe persons 232
safe spaces 103
safety 99–105, 229–230, 231–233, *233*, *239*, 273
St. Ambrose Barlow RC High School 99–105, **101**
sanctions 8, 12, 75, 118, **119**, 120–122, 125–126, 188
school attendance: barriers to 24–25; and child development 48–51, **51**; and educational outcomes 226–229; focus on 183–184, 187, 255; media focus 7–8, **7**; perspectives on 4–6; politicised 114; and school environment 78
school attendance difficulties: barriers to school attendance 24–25; and

Index

behaviour 110–111; behavioural lens 125–126, **126**, **127**; can't/won't dichotomy 14–17; choice framing 14–17; cognitive behavioural therapy 134–136, **134**; contributing factors 109–110; diagnostic assessments 114; ecological lens 258–259; emotionally based school avoidance (EBSA) 16, 23–24, 26–29; exposure therapy 137–138, **138**; illness analogy 231; journey to 106–107, 108–111, **109**, **110**; language of 14–29; location 16, 18, 19, 25, 29–31, 34; mental health lens 130–136; narrative 262; narrative change 257–259; and neurodiversity 29–30; parents and 108–109, 110–111, 112–113; and the problem 11; professional responses 111–113; professional stance 172–174; psychosocial interventions 136–137; recovery 271; school distress 19–20; school refusal 17–18, 26–29; sense-making 111–114, **112**; slow deterioration 110–111; support policies 113; as system feedback 51; truancy 20–22; variety of causes 29–31; wilful decision 14–17

School Can't 15
School Councils 97
school culture 258–259
school distress 19–20, 63, 238
school environment 28–29; and attendance 78; primary school 77–78; problem, the 147; psychologically healthy 72; safe and secure 93–96; secondary school 75–77; side effects of 75–78
school ethos 258
school evaluation 166
school phobia 18–19
school-readiness 56
school refusal 17–18, 25, 26–29; adult decision 187; alternatives to school 183–184; causes 171–172; crisis 187–188; decision 184–188, 190; expectation of return to school 172–174, 174; negative impacts 177–183; post decision 188–190; professional stance 172–174; reintegration efforts 172–183; relief 185–186; school phobia 18–19; stigmatisation 180–183; stress 178;
struggle 178–180; unanticipated consequences 174; work provision 176–177, 178; worries 176; young person's decision 185–187
school-related distress 8–11, **9**, **10**, 19–20; contributing factors 109–110; manifestation 9–11, **10**; slow deterioration 110–111; symptoms 31
schools: academic focus 49–50; alternative to 183–184; as beneficial places 34; changing 26–27, 28–29, 147; contract 8–9, **8**; experience of 4, 53–55; expectation of return to 172–174, 174; goals 52; hostile environment 27; invisible power 113–114; learning model 48; reintegration efforts 174–183; relationships with parents 113–114; short-comings from a developmental perspective 50; side effects of 74–75, 75–78
school successes 194–195
school trauma 192–194, 194–198, 202; adult response 204–205, **204**; avoidance 209; children's experience 202–203, **203**; family impacts 207–209; and the future 212–213; parents symptoms 208; and place of safety 210; recovery 208–213; sense making 211–212; symptoms 205–207; talking about 210–211
school uniform 56, 95, 104
Scotland 66–67
secondary school 197–198, 261, 281–282; intelligent inconsistency 99–105, **101**
secure attachments, at home 93, 94, 95
self-control 40
self-determination 150
self-determination theory 78–79, 80–81, 84–88, 107, 123–125, 147, 148, 150, 163, 165, 229
self-directed learning 274–275, 276
self-discipline 40
self-esteem 120–122, 125, 245
self-managed learning 156–159
Self Managed Learning College (SMLC) 156
Self-Managed Learning in Action, YouTube 159
self-management 39–40, 58
self-regulation 71, 88, 152
self-worth, co-production 162–167

293

Index

SENDCO 282
sense making 211–212
sensory processing differences 203–204
sensory processing disorder 277–278
service constraints 255
service level change 257–259
setting 163
shame 55, 100, 205, 206
shouting 94
single parents 184–185
situational mutism 277–278
sixth form college 282–283, 285
skiving/mitching/wagging 22–23
Sky News 22
sleep 281
SOAR (Safety, Opportunities, Autonomy and Relationships) 265; autonomy 236–237, *239*; framework 229–231, *239, 269*; low demand approach 232–233, *233*; opportunities *234*, 235–236, *239*; in practice 240–251; recovery phases 240, *241–242*; relationships 237–238, *239*; safety 229–230, 231–233, *233, 239*
social awareness 152
social interaction 192
social media 97, 131
social norms 85
social rewards 39
socio-emotional learning 152
special educational needs and disability (SEND) 28, 50, 56, 66–69, 103, *see also* ALN, ASN
Spielman, A. 3–4, 4, 11, 12, 28, 166
spiky cognitive profile 58, **58**, 160
Square Peg 24, 25
stability 55
staff 93, 104–105; quality 102; recruitment and retention 105; reflective practice groups 153–155
staff meetings 86–87
staff training 93–94
Star of the Week certificates 79–80, 97
Statement of Educational Needs 282
States of Mind 162–167
Steiner Kindergarten 61
storytelling 211–212
strengths-based model 268
stress 178
student voice 84–89, 156, 259
substance abuse 103
suicide 135
summer-born boys 67

supportive relationships 237–238
support policies 113
support staff 104–105
Sussex, University of 159
Sweller, J. 42
symptoms 27, 27–28; burnout 213–214, *216*; parents 208; school related distress 31; school trauma 205–207, 208
system, challenging 281
system feedback 51

table points 121
teacher-first approach 88
teachers 5; anxiety levels 50; belief system 10; focus 56; resentment towards 107; role 72–73
teaching assistants 98
teaching quality 88
terminology 14–29; emotionally based school avoidance (EBSA) 16, 23–24; school distress 19–20; school phobia 18–19; school refusal 17–18; truancy 20–22; wilful decision 14–17
testing, increase in 48–49
Thambirajah, M. 21, 28–29, 125, 172–173
thinking skills 44
threat perception 203, 205
Tomlinson, R. 96–98
tough love 188
Tower of Right Knowledge 165
trade-offs 101–102
transitions 109, 197–198, 242, 243
trauma 95–96, 96, 181–182, 190, 280; conceptualisation 198; and experience 198; family 207–209; psychological 198–205; survival system 199–201; vulnerability 201–202; *see also* school trauma
trauma-informed practice 93–96, 229–230
trauma therapy 209
Treisman, K. 98
triage meetings 261
truancy 20–22
trust 83, 209–210, 243, 244, 246, 248, 249–250, 260, 281
Trust Test, the 142, *142–143*
tutors 243–244, 245, 276–277, 282

uncertainty 184
undesirable behaviour, definition 129–130

unexpected things 248
unhappiness 11–12; leveraging 137
United States of America 10, 47
university 280, 283
unmet needs 25, 28–29
unwritten agreement, the, breakdown in 3–4

violence 158
Virtual Schools Derbyshire 94
vision 100–101, **101**, 245
vulnerability points 109–110

wagging 22–23, *see also* skiving/mitching/wagging
Wales 66–67

warm-strict approach 46–47, 75
what works 74–75
wilful decision 14–17
Williamson, G. 43
workforce, upskilling 257
workplace, the 180–181
World Health Organization 215–217
www.livesinthebalance.org 160
www.thinkkids.org/research 160

young offenders 245
YouTube 24–25; Self-Managed Learning in Action 159

Zhao, Y. 74